CW00585012

THE POLICE
AND CRIMINAL
EVIDENCE ACT 1984

A GUIDE FOR THE
PRACTITIONER

Alan E Greaves
David Pickover

1st edition 1986
2nd edition 1990
3rd edition 1991
4th edition 1996
Reprinted (revised 4th ed) 1997

ISBN 0 85164 074 5

**Police Review
Publishing Co**

Celcon House
289-293, High Holborn
London WC1V 7HU

Printed and bound in Great Britain by
The Cromwell Press Ltd
Melksham, Wiltshire

THE AUTHORS

Alan Greaves LLB (Hons), LLM, Solicitor of the Supreme Court, and David Pickover

Alan Greaves and David Pickover are former police officers who served in the South Yorkshire and West Yorkshire Police Forces respectively. For a number of years they have been regular contributors to the *Police Review* and occasionally to other legal periodicals on the criminal law.

Their previous books comprise a *Criminal Law* series on Offences Against Property, Offences Against the Person, General Principles and Public Offences and Evidence and Procedure.

Alan Greaves retired in 1992 as a superintendent and is presently a practising solicitor in the Barnsley area. David Pickover was until recent times the Commandant of the prestigious West Yorkshire Police Training School at Wakefield, which trains police officers from Forces throughout England and Wales. He was previously head of the renowned Detective Training School and was recently seconded to the Namibian Government as police advisor. He retired from West Yorkshire in 1994 as an assistant chief constable.

FOREWORD TO THE FIRST EDITION

Police officers joining the service today face a world which is infinitely more complex and difficult than it was when I first put on police uniform. Criminals and the crimes they commit reflect the sophistication of today's society in addition to which, modern systems of communication ensure that any incident involving police action is quickly and widely reported and subsequently exposed to the spotlight of public debate.

Some years ago, when the validity of a police officer's actions were being tested in the courts, it was often sufficient to demonstrate that the officer was taking bona fide action which appeared to him at the time to be in the best interests of the community. That sort of test was often applied during the legal challenges to the application of either the statute or common law and this generated a body of `best practice' to which police officers who were unsure of their powers and responsibilities could refer. The results of some of these tests were of course incorporated in specific codes such as the `Judges' Rules' for the interrogation of suspects and the detention of offenders.

Because of the complexities of life to which I have referred earlier, it has now become necessary to express the powers and responsibilities of police officers investigating crime in a much more precise way and the Police and Criminal Evidence Act sets out to answer many of the difficult questions surrounding the practical implementation of the criminal law.

The Act is complicated enough to pose difficulties for lawyers and it is not surprising that it has cost something of the order of £50m to train the country's 120,000 policemen in its basic requirements. The two to five day training programmes which chief constables have provided will undoubtedly have given all officers a reasonable insight into the main provisions of the Act. There is, however, an urgent need for some authoritative work of reference to be available in police stations until its practical operation has been fully absorbed into the working practices of the service.

The Practitioner's Guide to the Police and Criminal Evidence Act 1984, by Alan Greaves and David Pickover meets this requirement. It follows the pattern laid down in their earlier works and is notable for the clarity of its layout and text and the way in which it deals with practical as well as theoretical considerations. A clear table of contents coupled with the question and answer format means that an authoritative statement of the law can be found with a minimum of delay. Although it is inevitable that the interpretation of some of the Act's many provisions will be tested in the courts in due course, this edition is an excellent point of reference and I am pleased to commend it to police officers and others to whom the implementation of the Police and Criminal Evidence Act is of professional interest.

Sir Lawence Byford, CBE, QPM LLB
HM Chief Inspector of Constabulary

PREFACE

There can be few Acts of Parliament which have provoked as much controversy as the Police and Criminal Evidence Act 1984.

During the parliamentary stages of the Act its provisions were described as being 'profoundly obnoxious' and representing a 'Stalinistic' attempt to re-write history'. Some commentators were less emotive and viewed the provisions as being necessary to arm the police with sufficient powers to investigate and detect crime without detriment to the rights of the individual to be free from unnecessary interference.

This work is presented not as an academic treatise but as a guide to the practitioner in his everyday duties. The authors make no apology for simplifying this controversial piece of legislation to the form of questions and answers for, it is submitted, such an approach strikes at the very roots of the contentious issues of policing methods and the rights of the individual; be he suspect or otherwise.

The work incorporates substantial reference to the new Codes of Practice which are Crown-Copyright, a matter which the authors are pleased to acknowledge.

Since the work was originally published the Courts have offered interpretation on some aspects of the Act which has also been amended by a variety of statutory provisions. This revised edition pays due regard to these matters and also incorporates detailed reference to the revised Codes of Practice and the Criminal Justice and Public Order Act 1994.

Alan E Greaves
David Pickover
January 1996

CONTENTS

Seizure

Code of practice for the searching of premises and seizure of property

Chapter 3
ARREST

Arrest

Search upon arrest

Chapter 4
DETENTION

Detention

Chapter 5
DETENTION TREATMENT AND QUESTIONING OF PERSONS BY POLICE OFFICERS

Intimate and non-intimate samples

Destruction of samples

Charging of detained persons

Chapter 6
CODES OF PRACTICE

Chapter 7
EVIDENCE

Chapter 8
A MISCELLANY

Chapter 9

CODE OF PRACTICE FOR IDENTIFICATION OF PERSONS

Chapter 10

CODE OF PRACTICE ON TAPE RECORDING

CHAPTER 1

POWERS TO STOP AND SEARCH

Section 1 of the Police and Criminal Evidence Act 1984 provides constables with a power to stop and search persons and vehicles.

Section 2 of the Act details general provisions concerning searches made not only under section 1 of the Act but also those under any other statute which authorises a constable to search a person without first arresting him: for example section 23, Misuse of Drugs Act 1971; section 47, Firearms Act 1968; and section 7, Sporting Events (Control of Alcohol etc) Act 1985.

Section 3 of the Act imposes on officers effecting searches (whether under the Police and Criminal Evidence Act 1984 or any other enactment), a duty to make records concerning them.

Section 4 of the Act makes provision for the authorisation of road checks.

Stop and search

Q: For what purposes may a constable stop and search a person?
A: The power provided in section 1 of the Act authorises a constable to search any person or vehicle, or anything which is in or on a vehicle, for stolen or prohibited articles or any article in relation to which a person has committed or is committing or is going to commit an offence under section 139, Criminal Justice Act 1988, and detain the person or vehicle for the purpose of effecting the search. The power cannot be exercised unless the constable has reasonable grounds for suspecting that he will find stolen articles or prohibited articles (section 1(2) and (3)). The expression 'vehicle' includes vessels, aircraft and hovercraft (section 2(10)).

1

Q: Where may the power be exercised?

A: Generally speaking in a public place or in a place to which people have ready access. In respect of places falling into the latter category, restrictions exist to prevent police officers unnecessarily intruding into dwelling-houses and land within the curtilage thereof. More precisely, the Act provides that a constable may exercise the power conferred by section 1:

(a) in any place to which at the time when he proposes to exercise the power, the public or any section of the public has access, on payment or otherwise, as of right or by virtue of express or implied permission; or

(b) in any other place to which people have ready access at the time when he proposes to exercise the power, but which is not a dwelling (section 1(1)).

Falling into (a) above will be parks, beaches, streets, roads, public car parks, thoroughfares etc and, while they are open to the public, such premises as supermarkets, dance halls, licensed premises and sports grounds. Paragraph (b) embraces such places as school yards, hospital grounds, and the gardens/yards of dwellings, provided people have ready access to them.

If the person or vehicle to be searched is in a garden or yard or other land used for the purpose of a dwelling, a constable may not carry out a search unless he also reasonably believes that the person, or person in charge of the vehicle, does not reside in the dwelling and is not in the garden, yard etc with the express or implied permission of the person who resides there (section 1(4) and 1(5)). Effectively, section 1(4) and (5) prevents people or vehicles being searched on their own property but this does not prevent a person from being arrested on suspicion of the relevant offence, provided the circumstances exist to justify it. The same considerations apply in respect of invitees on the owner's/occupier's property or land. The expression 'land occupied and used with a dwelling' will include basement areas and land adjacent to a dwelling, of the kind used as a caravan/boat/car standing.

Q: What does the expression 'stolen articles' mean?

A: Surprisingly the expression is not defined in the Act. On the face of it, it means articles obtained in circumstances amounting to theft but there is scope for argument that the term extends beyond the pure definition of the offence of theft. It is submitted that 'stolen articles' includes not only goods acquired in circumstances offending against sections 1-7, Theft Act 1968, but also those obtained or acquired contrary to section 15, Theft Act 1968 (obtaining property by criminal deception) and section 22, Theft Act 1968 (handling stolen goods). So far as the former offence is concerned, the cases of *Lawrence v Metropolitan Police Commissioner* (1972); and *R v Morris* (1982) indicate that the offence of theft and that of obtaining goods contrary to section 15, Theft Act 1968 are not mutually exclusive. It might also be argued that property obtained in circumstances amounting to blackmail could be construed as 'stolen articles'.

Q: What are 'prohibited articles'?

A: Effectively section 1 of the Act remedies deficiencies in previous legislation. Section 1, Prevention of Crime Act 1953 creates an offence in respect of a person having with him, without lawful authority or reasonable excuse (proof of which lies on the accused) in a public place an offensive weapon. Section 4, Vagrancy Act 1824 also creates an offence in respect of the possession of offensive weapons yet neither of the Acts provide any machinery for discovering evidence of the offences.

Similarly, section 25, Theft Act 1968 contains another preventive measure. It provides it is an offence for a person, when not at his place of abode to have with him any article for use in the course of, or in connection with, burglary, theft, or cheat (ie an offence contrary to section 15, Theft Act 1968) or of taking a conveyance without lawful authority etc but, yet again, provides no powers to aid detection of the offence. Section 1 of the Police and Criminal Evidence Act 1984 remedies the flaw.

For the purposes of the Act an article is prohibited if it is an offensive weapon, ie an article made or adapted for use for causing injury to the person of another or intended by the person having it with him for such use by him or some other person (section 1(9)); or any article made, adapted or intended to be used by the person having it with him or by some other person, in the course of, or in connection with, an offence of burglary, theft, taking a conveyance without authority or obtaining property by criminal deception (section 1(7) and 1(8)).

By virtue of section 139, Criminal Justice Act, the power of search is extended to include searches for any article which has a blade or is sharply pointed, except a folding pocket knife. Pocket knives fall within the purview of section 139 and thus the power to stop and search if the cutting edge to the blade exceeds 3in.

In a nutshell the Act provides a power to search a person or vehicle for stolen articles, offensive weapons or articles with which a person may go 'equipped for stealing', and 'articles possessed' in contravention of section 139 Criminal Justice Act 1988.

Q: What will constitute the reasonable grounds for suspicion necessary to justify use of the coercive power?

A: The Code of Practice for the Exercise by Police Officers of Statutory Powers of Stop and Search applies to stops and searches under powers:

(a) requiring reasonable grounds for suspicion that articles unlawfully obtained or possessed are being carried;

(b) authorised under section 60 of the Criminal Justice and Public Order Act 1994 based upon a reasonable belief that incidents involving serious violence may take place within a locality;

(c) authorised under section 13A of the Prevention of Terrorism (Temporary Provisions) Act 1989 as amended by section 81 of the Criminal Justice and Public Order Act 1994;

(d) exercised under paragraph 4(2) of Schedule 5 to the Prevention of Terrorism (Temporary Provisions) Act 1989.

The code dictates that the exercise of the powers requires reasonable grounds for suspicion that articles unlawfully obtained or possessed are being carried. Where there are reasonable grounds to suspect that a person may be in innocent possession of stolen or prohibited articles, the power to stop and search may be utilised even though there is no power to arrest. Nevertheless powers of persuasion should be attempted before resorting to force.

There can be no hard and fast rule measuring when reasonable grounds for suspicion arise. The code offers some guidance which is based on the notion of common sense rather than any specific evaluation.

Information about a specific offender may warrant a search of that person as may the carrying by a person of housebreaking implements in a high burglary-rate area. In short, the power cannot be carried out on a whim or a fancy. There must be some objective basis for it, bearing in mind, of course, that that basis may be subject to considerable scrutiny subsequently.

Reasonable suspicion cannot be based purely on personal factors (hair, colour, relevant previous conviction) nor on a perception that certain people are more likely to commit offences. There must be some objective basis for the grounds for suspicion.

The importance of police officers using their powers only in appropriate circumstances and in a professional and courteous manner is emphasised in a note of guidance. It should always be to the fore of an officer's thoughts that the consequence of his actions could be far-reaching and may result in police/public relations being severely damaged.

Q: What specific powers and requirements are contained in the power provided by section 60 of the Criminal Justice and Public Order Act 1994?

A: A superintendent (or above) who reasonably believes that incidents involving serious violence may take place in any locality in his area may authorise in writing stopping and searching of people and vehicles at any place within that locality for a reasonable period not exceeding 24 hours.

The authorisation may be extended for a further six hours by the original authorisor or a superintendent and the power of authorisation may be exercised by an inspector or chief inspector if he reasonably believes that incidents involving serious violence are imminent and no superintendent is available.

The authorisation must specify the locality in which the powers are to be exercised. Section 60 confers upon a constable in uniform power to stop any pedestrian and search him or anything carried by him or any vehicle, its driver and passengers, for offensive weapons or dangerous instruments and he may stop any person or vehicle and make any search he thinks fit, whether or not he has any grounds for suspecting that the person or vehicle is carrying weapons or articles of that kind.

Q: What are the requirements in relation to the powers of stop and search under section 13A of the Prevention of Terrorism (Temporary Provisions) Act 1989?

A: Authority to exercise the powers may be given by an officer of the rank of assistant chief constable (or equivalent) or above, in writing, where it appears expedient to do so to prevent acts of terrorism. The authorisation must specify where the powers may be exercised and the period of time, not exceeding 28 days, for which they are to remain in force. A further period may be authorised of up to 28 days. The power allows a constable in uniform to stop and search for articles of a kind which could be used for a purpose connected with the commission, preparation or instigation of acts of terrorism.

In relation to the powers conferred by the Criminal Justice and Public Order Act 1994 and the Prevention of Terrorism (Temporary Provisions) Act 1989, additional notes of guidance to the code of practice advise that the responsibility for determining the time scale of the powers being authorised is placed upon the authorising officer who should base this decision on necessity in respect of the prevailing risk of violence or terrorism. He can only give a direction once and further use of the powers requires a further authorisation.

In addition, he must nominate the area where the powers are to be used. The note of guidance gives examples of factors which an authorising officer may take into account including matters such as the expected level of violence, the place and the form of the expected trouble, where it is expected and the numbers involved. He should be careful not to cast the net of the area set too wide.

Above all, the powers of stop and search must be exercised responsibly and upon objective grounds.

Q: Pre-supposing that an officer does have 'reasonable suspicion' of possession of stolen or prohibited articles or of some other article which will entitle him to exercise a power of search, can a police officer conduct the search without any explanation?
A: No. The Act is designed to ensure that persons are dealt with courteously and considerately and that the powers of search are used responsibly and sparingly. To achieve these ends the Act demands that if an officer contemplates a search, whether under the provisions of the Police and Criminal Evidence Act 1984 or any other statute (except one under the Aviation Security Act 1982 or section 6 of the Police and Criminal Evidence Act 1984 – searches conducted in goods areas by constables employed by statutory undertakers, ie transport undertakings) the constable, before commencing the search shall:

- if he is not in uniform, produce documentary evidence that he is a constable;
- give his name and the name of the police station to which he is attached;
- give the object of the proposed search;
- give the grounds for making it; and
- notify the person to be searched or the person in charge of the vehicle to be searched of their entitlement to a copy of any record made of the search within 12 months from the date of the search (sections 2(2)-(3) and 3(7)-(9)). These requirements are repeated in the relevant code of practice, with the amendment that if not in uniform, the officer must show his warrant card. In cases of inquiries linked to the investigation of terrorism, an officer need not give his name.

In addition to the foregoing, the codes of practice direct that powers under section 60 of the Criminal Justice and Public Order Act 1994 and section 13A of the Prevention of Terrorism (Temporary Provisions) Act 1989 may be exercised only by a constable in uniform.

1: Stop and search

Q: What provision exists to cater for the person who does not understand what is being said to him about his rights in respect of stop and search?
A: The code of practice dictates that if the person to be searched, or in charge of a vehicle to be searched, does not understand what is being said, the officer must take reasonable steps to bring to his attention his name, station, the object and grounds of the search; produce his warrant card if not in uniform and explain that a record of search can be obtained. If the person has someone with him then the officer must try to establish whether that person can interpret, or otherwise help him to give the required information.

Q: If a search of a vehicle is effected must the owner be present?
A: No, but the officer conducting the search must leave a written notice:

- stating that he has searched it;
- giving the name of the police station to which he is attached;
- stating that an application for compensation for any damage caused by the search may be made to that police station, and
- detailing his entitlement, within 12 months, to a copy of the search record made.

The notice must be left inside the vehicle unless it is not practicable to do so without damaging the vehicle (section 2(6) and (7)). These requirements are also demanded by the code of practice, which adds that the vehicle must, if practicable, be left secure.

Q: For how long may a person or vehicle be detained in order that a search may be effected?
A: For such time as is reasonably required to permit a search to be carried out either at the place where the person or vehicle was first detained or nearby (section 2(8)), a restriction reiterated in the code of practice.

The length of time will thus depend on the circumstances and could be a matter of seconds – as in the case of a quick 'frisk' for an article of some substance – to a much longer period for a smaller or a minute article, such as an LSD micro-dot.

What amounts to 'nearby' is a matter of fact to be decided in each particular case. In *Arnold v Chief Constable of Hull* (1969) – a case under the breathalyser legislation – the High Court declined to interfere with a decision of magistrates that a police station situated one and a half miles from a traffic incident was not 'there or nearby'.

In *Donegani v Ward* (1969) the Divisional Court again chose not to interfere with a finding by magistrates that 160 yards was not 'there or nearby'. It should not be presumed that these cases provide conclusive argument that a narrow interpretation be placed on the word 'nearby' in section 2(8).

In *Farrow v Tunnicliffe* (1976), a case of obstructing a police officer in the exercise of his power of search under section 23 of the Misuse of Drugs Act 1971, it was held that a constable had the power to take a person away to be searched and it was lawful to make such a requirement of a person without first arresting him.

Farrow v Tunnicliffe can be distinguished from the road traffic cases cited on the ground that it was practicable to carry out a breath test at the place of the incident giving rise to the exercise of the power to demand a specimen of breath for a test, whereas it is not usually practicable to effect a search for controlled drugs in public.

It is submitted that 'reasonableness' is the criterion for the application of section 2(8) and, whether a constable may take a person to a police station to be searched will be determined by the thoroughness and extent of the search necessary; a matter determined by the article sought in the proposed search. Obviously, the majority of searches will be effected within yards of where the person is stopped but in some instances it will only be possible to effect a search in a police station.

Q: How does the code of practice treat the question of the amount of time for which a person may be detained to allow a search to be conducted?
A: The code of practice develops the tone of the statute and does not attempt to lay down hard and fast timing restrictions. In practice, common sense will determine the issue. Each particular search depends upon its own merits but there should be no delay in carrying out the powers provided. Much will depend upon the nature of the search and the article which a person is suspected of carrying. If, for example, a person is suspected of being in possession of a 'qualifying' knife which he has been seen to place in his right trouser pocket, the search will be quickly carried out. A person suspected of street corner drug dealing will invariably require more detailed attention.

In the case of articles to which section 60 of the Criminal Justice and Public Order Act 1994 and those under section 13A of or paragraph 4(2) of Schedule 5 to the Prevention of Terrorism (Temporary Provisions) Act 1989 apply, which do not require reasonable grounds for suspicion, a police officer is entitled to carry out any reasonable search in order to discover the article that he is entitled to search for. Searches which are carried out in public and which, according to an accompanying note of guidance, should only amount to a superficial examination of outer clothing, should be completed with alacrity.

In the event of a pedestrian being stopped under the provisions of section 13A of the Prevention of Terrorism (Temporary Provisions) Act 1989, anything which he is carrying may be searched but the power does not extend to searching the person. This would not, however, prevent the use by a police officer of another power if this was considered appropriate.

Q: In exercising a lawful power of search what restrictions are imposed on a constable?

A: Neither the power to stop and search conferred by section 1, Police and the Criminal Evidence Act 1984 nor any other power to detain and search a person without first arresting him shall be construed as authorising a constable to require a person to remove any of his clothing in public other than an outer coat, jacket or gloves (section 2(9)). This restriction is reaffirmed in the code of practice, which also dictates that every reasonable effort must be made to reduce to a minimum the embarrassment that a person being searched may experience.

This does not, of course, prevent a person from removing additional items voluntarily or being required to do so elsewhere than in public; for example in a police van; a nearby police station or in the privacy of say, the manager's office in a supermarket in the case of a suspected shoplifter.

Any search involving the removal of more than an outer coat, jacket, gloves, headgear or footwear may only be made by an officer of the same sex as the person searched and may not be made in the presence of anyone of the opposite sex unless the person being searched specifically requests it.

A note of guidance in the code of practice adds that a search in the street itself should be regarded as being in public even though it may be empty at the time a search begins. Although there is no power to require a person to do so, there is nothing to prevent an officer from asking a person to voluntarily remove more than an outer coat, jacket or gloves in public. The object of section 2(9) is to prevent public embarrassment and humiliation and to lay down the extent of the coercive power in a public place.

A further restriction is that the powers to stop and search persons and vehicles do not empower a constable, not in uniform, to stop a vehicle (section 2(9)).

9

Q: In the event of a person objecting to being searched, can a police officer use force?

A: Yes. In the exercise of the power under section 1 of the Act an officer may use reasonable force, if necessary (section 117). Any force used, however, must not be excessive or disproportionate to the resistance offered. Reasonable force may also be used against a vehicle to gain entry.

Where a power of search is being lawfully exercised, any wilful obstruction of the officer will constitute an offence contrary to section 51, Police Act 1964.

The code of practice spells out graphically the need for a judicious approach to the stop and search powers. Every effort should be made to secure a person's consent to a search before a decision is made to exercise the power. Force may only be used when the person refuses to co-operate or offers resistance.

Q: If stolen or prohibited articles are found in the course of a search what action may be taken?

A: The constable may seize any article he has reasonable grounds for suspecting to be stolen or prohibited (section 1(6)). Obviously the discovery of such property could also lead to arrest in some circumstances.

Q: Can the power of search for stolen or prohibited articles be used against a person in innocent possession of the articles?

A: Yes – but every effort should be made to secure the voluntary production of the article before the coercive power is used.

Q: Having exercised a power to search under the Police and Criminal Evidence Act 1984 or any other Act when must a record of search be made and what must it contain?

A: A record of a search shall be made in writing, unless this is not practicable (section 3(1)). The code of practice envisages that in some cases it may not be possible to do so, for example, in public disorder situations. Where a record is made and it is not practicable to make it on the spot, the record shall be made as soon as practicable after completion of the search (section 3(2)).

The code quotes other immediate duties or very bad weather as examples of circumstances where immediate recording may be impracticable. No records are required in respect of searches effected under the Aviation Security Act 1982 or by a statutory undertaker, as defined in section 6 of the Police and Criminal Evidence Act 1984.

The Act seeks to ensure that the powers of stop and search are not used at random and indiscriminately and are not misused or over-used. To achieve these aims; prevent harm to police/public relations and, above all else, to facilitate accountability, the Act requires that a record of a search of a person or vehicle:

    (a) shall state:
        (i) the object of the search;
        (ii) the grounds for making it;
        (iii) the date and time when it was made;
        (iv) the place where it was made;
        (v) whether anything, and if so what, was found;
        (vi) whether any, if so what, injury to a person or damage to property appears to the constable to have resulted from the search; and
    (b) shall identify the constable making it (section 3(6)).

The record of a search of a person shall include a note of his name if the constable knows it, but the officer may not detain a person to find out his name (section 3(3)).

If the constable does not know the name of the person searched, the record shall include a note otherwise describing him (section 3(4)).

There is no obligation on the part of a person to provide details of his identity if he is unwilling to do so. Despite a person's unwilling-ness in this respect the matters mentioned in section 3(6) itemised above must always be recorded. It is usual practice for the police to obtain the name, address and date of birth of the person to be searched but he is not under any obligation to provide them. He can-not be detained merely if he refuses to co-operate. Even though a person may refuse to provide his details, a searching officer should include the following in the search record:

    (i) the person's name and/or his description;
    (ii) his ethnic origin;
    (iii) if a vehicle is searched, a note of its description and registra-tion number;
    (iv) the object of carrying out the search and the basis upon which it was conducted;
    (v) the time and place;
    (vi) the result;
    (vii) details of injuries or damage;
    (viii) details of the officers involved (except for searches conducted under the anti-terrorism legislation where the officer's warrant or other identification number will suffice).

Search records must be completed in respect of every person and every vehicle searched except where a person is in a vehicle and both are searched.

In addition, the record must briefly show the reasons why the search was carried out whether that was because of the person's conduct or the circumstances.

In the case of searches carried out under section 60 of the Criminal Justice and Public Order Act 1994 or section 13A of or paragraph 4(2) of Schedule 5 to the Prevention of Terrorism (Temporary Provisions) Act 1989, the authority provided to carry out the search must also be recorded. The identity of all the officers engaged on the search must also be recorded.

The code of practice reaffirms the restrictions, requirements and procedures outlined in section 3 of the Act.

Q: Can a police officer detain a person in order to establish if the person is liable to search?

A: He cannot be compulsorily detained. The code dictates that the power may only be exercised where reasonable grounds exist to stop and search him. It is not a power to needlessly interfere with a person's liberty by stopping him to find out if there is anything upon which a search may be based. In other words it is not a blanket power to be conducted by whim or by fancy in order to find out if there is a foundation for a search.

It is perfectly proper, however, for a police officer to ask a person questions about his conduct or in relation to the grounds upon which a suspicion may be based. After all, the conduct appearing to be suspicious and which might lead to a search may be explained away quite satisfactorily. Naturally, if the conversation has the effect of removing the element of suspicion, grounds for a search are automatically removed and a search may not take place.

A helpful note of guidance points out that there will always be circumstances where such questioning will not be necessary. However, according to the guidance, a short exchange between the officer and the person concerned is recommended if only to assist in lessening the number of instances where a search might otherwise be unsuccessful. Furthermore, according to the note, a lawful detention for the purposes of a search is not rendered unlawful if a search does not follow.

The code of practice adds that questioning a person may provide answers which confirm the grounds of the intended search or may, in fact, remove those grounds. It may even provide grounds for search which are different to those which were in the mind of the conducting officer. Rather obviously, the code points out that there can be no retrospective suspicion provided by later questioning or by the person who may be unwilling to answer questions.

A note of guidance endorses the right of police officers to speak with or question anyone when carrying out their ordinary duties even when there is no suspicion about a person or his conduct. To restrict that right would create an impassable barrier in the investigation of crime or any other matter. The note highlights the fact that such relationships between police officer and member of the public are not restricted by the code and that the principle enunciated in the old 'Judges' Rules that all citizens have a duty to assist the police in their effort to prevent crime and to identify offenders remains.

Q: What provision exists to provide records of searches carried out under section 60 of the Criminal Justice and Public Order Act 1994 and section 13A of the Prevention of Terrorism (Temporary Provisions) Act 1989

A: A driver of a vehicle which is subjected to a stop and search under these provisions is entitled to a written statement of that fact within 12 months of the day of the search. The written statement is, quite simply, a record of the search.

The right does not extend to a passenger in a vehicle but there is provision for a pedestrian stopped and searched to be supplied with a written statement.

Q: If a police officer contemplates a search and then abandons his intention because the person voluntarily surrenders the article must a record be made?

A: No.

Q: If the exercise of a coercive power of search results in the finding of stolen or prohibited articles or other articles unlawfully obtained or possessed and the person is then arrested need a record be made?

A: Yes – particularly since searches recorded under section 3 must be referred to in the Annual Reports of Chief Constables and that made by the Commissioner of Police of the Metropolis.

While the reports shall not include details of specific searches, they shall include the total number of searches in each month for stolen articles; offensive weapons and other prohibited articles, and the number of persons arrested in each month in consequence of such searches (section 5(1) and (2)). For this purpose the expression 'other prohibited articles' includes not only those for use in the course of or in connection with a burglary, theft etc but articles searched for in exercise of the powers conferred on a constable by, for example, the Firearms Act 1968 and the Misuse of Drugs Act 1971.

Q: Are all searches governed by the Police and Criminal Evidence Act 1984 and the code of practice?
A: No. In addition to the exceptions of searches under the Aviation Security Act 1982, excepted from the provisions are those routine searches of persons entering sports grounds or other premises with their consent or as a condition of entry.

Neither does the code affect the ability of an officer to search a person in the street on a voluntary basis. In these circumstances, an officer should always make it clear that he is seeking the co-operation of the person concerned to the search being carried out by telling the person that he need not consent and that without his consent there will be no search.

Accordingly, while use of a coercive power demands the acceptance of 'reasonable suspicion' a search founded on 'mere suspicion' will not be unlawful provided the person consents to it being effected. The code of practice specifically declares that it does not affect the ability of an officer to speak to or question a person in the course of his duties (and in the absence of reasonable suspicion) without detaining him or exercising any element of compulsion. Quite clearly, if in the course of such activity a person volunteers to be searched, perhaps to display his innocence, there is no reason why a search should not be conducted.

A rider is, however, added to the notes of guidance indicating that if an officer acts in an improper manner this will invalidate a voluntary search. In addition juveniles, persons suffering from a mental handicap or mental disorder and others who appear not to be capable of giving an informed consent should not be subject to a voluntary search.

Q: If a constable embarks upon a search must he complete it?
A: A constable who detains a person or vehicle in the exercise of any power of search which may be exercised without first arresting him need not conduct a search if it appears to him subsequently:

(i) that no search is required; or
(ii) that a search is impracticable (section 2(1)).

This provision is reinforced in the code of practice.

Q: Once a police officer decides to exercise a power of search does that entitle him to conduct a full search?
A: The short answer is no. The code of practice is quite unambiguous in directing police officers that where they merely suspect that a specific article is carried by a person in, for example, an inside jacket pocket, any search carried out is restricted to that pocket unless, of course, the officer suspects it may have been transferred elsewhere.

Q: What redress does a person have in the event of a constable unlawfully searching him or his vehicle without his consent?
A: He may institute civil proceedings. In doing so a failure to comply with any aspect of the code of practice shall be admissible in evidence to any question arising in those proceedings but failure on the part of a constable to comply with any aspect of the code of practice shall not in itself render him liable to civil proceedings (section 67). Abuse of authority constitutes a police discipline offence and any non-compliance with the code of practice may render an officer liable to disciplinary proceedings.

Road checks

Section 4 of the Police and Criminal Evidence Act 1984 restricts and regulates the law as it stood prior to the Act coming into force and, in particular, demands that road checks are authorised in writing by an officer not below the rank of superintendent.

Q: What constitutes a road check for the purpose of the section?
A: The use in a particular locality of the power conferred upon a constable in uniform by section 163, Road Traffic Act 1988 to stop a person driving a motor vehicle or riding a cycle, in such a way as to stop all vehicles or vehicles selected by any criterion (section 4(2)).

Q: Is the authority of a superintendent required for every road check?
A: No. The provisions do not extend to road checks to establish whether a road traffic or vehicle excise offence is being committed (section 4(1)(a)). Additionally, not every exercise of the power under section 163 Road Traffic Act 1988 will constitute a road check. The spirit of the section – to prevent unnecessary intrusion and ensure accountability – is aimed at those checks where large numbers are

stopped by virtue of all vehicles being selected or vehicles selected by any criterion; for example all motor cars; all Datsuns; all red vehicles etc.

Authorisation is not required for checks carried out independently of each other at various locations, as in the case of a patrolling police officer stopping at random one motor vehicle here and another there; or a mobile patrol stopping vehicles at various locations on an estate during a tour of duty. Additionally, in cases of urgency, an officer below the rank of superintendent may authorise a check provided the grounds exist whereby a superintendent may authorise a road check to be conducted.

Q: When will a superintendent's authority be required?

A: Generally speaking those checks set up in connection with the investigation of crime or to trace a person unlawfully at large require authorisation. But the Act is couched in such terms so as to ensure that crime checks are restricted to those in connection with serious crime only. More precisely, a superintendent may only authorise a road check for the purpose of ascertaining whether a vehicle is carrying:

(a) a person who has committed an offence other than a road traffic or excise offence – but only if he has reasonable grounds for believing that the offence is a serious arrestable offence and for suspecting that the person is or is about to be in the locality in which vehicles would be stopped;

(b) a person who is a witness to such an offence, but only if reasonable grounds exist for believing that the offence is a serious arrestable offence;

(c) a person intending to commit such an offence, but only if he has reasonable grounds for believing that the offence would be a serious arrestable offence and for suspecting that the person is, or is about to be, in the locality in which vehicles would be stopped;

(d) a person who is unlawfully at large, but only if he has reasonable grounds for suspecting that the person is or is about to be in that locality (section 4(1) and (4)).

Q: What action must be taken in the event of a road check being authorised by an officer below the rank of superintendent?

A: He must make a written record of the time he gives permission and must cause an officer of the rank of superintendent or above to be informed of his action as soon as practicable (section 4(6)).

Q: On receiving a report of a road check within the Act's purview being set up as a matter of urgency by an officer below his rank what action may the superintendent take?

A: He may authorise in writing the road check to continue. If he does not authorise its continuance he must record in writing the fact that the road check took place and the purpose of it (section 4(8) and (9)).

Q: In authorising a road check, what procedural steps, if any, must an authorising superintendent adhere to?

A: He must:

(a) specify a period not exceeding seven days during which the road check may continue; and
(b) may direct that the road check:
    (i)   shall be continuous; or
    (ii) shall be conducted at specified times during that period.

If it appears to a superintendent, or above, that a road check ought to be extended, he may from time to time specify in writing further periods of seven days during which it may continue (section 4(11) and (12)).

Additionally, the written authorisation should include the name of the authorising officer; the purpose of the road check and the locality in which vehicles are to be stopped and details of any relevant serious arrestable offence (section 4(13)).

Q: What rights does the Act give to a person stopped in a road check?

A: The person in charge of the vehicle in a road check at the time it is stopped, shall be entitled to obtain a written statement of the purpose of the road check if he applies for such a statement. Application must be made within 12 months from the day on which the vehicle was stopped (section 4(15)).

Q: What measures exist to satisfy the public at large that the power to hold road checks is not abused?

A: In every Chief Constable's Annual Report made under the Police Act 1964 or by the Commissioner of Police of the Metropolis, reference shall be made to road checks authorised under section 4 of the Act and the information provided must include information about the reasons for authorising each check and the result of each of them (section 5(1) and (3)).

Q: Is a power of search for offenders implicit in the power to conduct a road check?

A: No. In appropriate circumstances, however, the power to search under section 1 of the Police and Criminal Evidence Act 1984 (ie for stolen or prohibited articles) may be utilised. Similarly, if it is reasonably suspected by the constable that the vehicle stopped in the check is carrying a person who has committed a serious arrestable offence or a person unlawfully at large, he may enter the vehicle, by force, if necessary, for the purpose of arresting him.

CHAPTER 2

POWERS OF ENTRY, SEARCH AND SEIZURE

Search warrants

Prior to the Police and Criminal Evidence Act 1984 coming into operation, while a number of enactments empowered magistrates to issue warrants authorising police officers to search for specific articles, for example explosives, firearms, stolen goods, controlled drugs, there was no general statutory provision by which a police officer could obtain an authority to search for evidence of offences having been committed. Section 8 of the Act seeks to remedy this deficiency but in doing so imposes restrictions designed to prevent 'fishing expeditions'.

Sections 15 and 16 of the Act detail safeguards and procedural considerations applicable to all search warrants irrespective of which statute they are issued under.

Q: What conditions must exist before a justice of the peace may issue a warrant under section 8 of the Act to search for evidence?
A: There must be reasonable grounds for believing that:

- a serious arrestable offence has been committed;
- there is material on the premises likely to be of substantial value (whether by itself or together with other material) to the investigation of the offence;
- the matter is likely to be admissible evidence;
- the material is not 'excluded' or 'special procedure material' or subject to legal privilege;

19

- and any of four conditions concerning access to the premises and availability of the evidence apply (section 8(1)).

Before issuing a warrant the justice of the peace must be additionally satisfied that one or more of the following four conditions apply:

(1) that it is not practicable to communicate with any person who is entitled to grant entry to the premises;
(2) although (1) above is practicable, it is not practicable to communicate with any person entitled to grant access to the evidence;
(3) that entry to the premises will not be granted unless a warrant is produced; or
(4) that the purpose of a search may be frustrated or seriously prejudiced unless a constable arriving at the premises can secure immediate entry to them (section 8(2)).

Effectively, section 8 of the Act creates a presumption that before applying for a warrant under the section, the police should endeavour to secure the evidence with consent unless the interests of justice would be defeated by pursuing such a course of action.

Q: What material constitutes 'excluded' or 'special procedure' material and items subject of 'legal privilege' and how can such items be obtained?

A: The term 'excluded material' means:

(a) personal records which a person has acquired or created in the course of any trade, business, profession or other occupation or for the purposes of any paid or unpaid office and which he holds in confidence;
(b) human tissue or tissue fluid which has been taken for the purposes of diagnosis or medical treatment and which a person holds in confidence;
(c) journalistic material which a person holds in confidence and which consists – (i) of documents; or (ii) of records other than documents (section 11(1)).

By virtue of section 12(1) the term personal records includes medical records and other personal records as to a person's mental or physical health, assistance or counselling given to a person on spiritual or welfare grounds and the personal records kept by caring agencies such as social services, the probation service and their voluntary counterparts such as the Samaritans, Citizen's Advice Bureaux and Marriage Guidance Counsellors.

'Excluded material' is not obtainable by a warrant under section 8 of the Act. However, if the excluded material is liable to be searched for and seized by virtue of a warrant issued under another enactment, for example, stolen goods under a warrant granted under section 26 of the Theft Act 1968; such a warrant must be obtained by utilising the procedure laid down in Schedule 1 to the Police and Criminal Evidence Act 1984 which necessitates an application for the warrant being made to a circuit judge (sections 9 and 11 and Schedule 1).

'Special procedure' material comprises of material acquired or created in the course of any trade or business, profession or occupation and held on a confidential basis by a third party, for example documents and papers in the possession of an auditor or accountant or bank records. The term also includes material acquired or created for journalism which is not 'excluded material', ie not held on a basis of confidentiality or subject to legal privilege. Such material will only be obtainable in accordance with the special procedure detailed in Schedule 1 to the Act which entails application being made to a circuit judge. The person in possession of the evidence has the right to make representations as to why the matter subject of the application should not be disclosed. Provided the circuit judge is satisfied that the evidence relates to a 'serious arrestable offence', that the evidence would be admissible at a trial and would be of substantial value to the investigation; that other methods of obtaining it had been tried without success or had not been tried because failure seemed inevitable and that disclosure would be in the public interest; he may issue an order requiring the person to produce the material. In the event of that person failing to comply with the circuit judge's order the non-cooperation could be punishable as contempt of court. In the event of the order being ignored a circuit judge then has the power to issue a warrant in respect of the material.

In circumstances where it is impracticable to gain entry to the premises or to communicate with the person who may grant access to the material, or the investigation may be prejudiced by trying to secure the evidence by means of an order of disclosure; a circuit judge may issue a warrant in the first instance as he would also be empowered to do if the material were held subject to a restriction on disclosure or obligation of secrecy and a likelihood of disclosure exists (sections 9 and 11 and Schedule 1).

The expression 'items of legal privilege' means:

(a) communications between a professional legal adviser and his client or any person representing his client made in connection with the giving of legal advice to the client;

(b) communications between a professional legal adviser and his client or any person representing his client or between such an adviser or his client or any such representative and any other person made in connection with or in contemplation of legal proceedings and for the purposes of such proceedings; and

(c) items enclosed with or referred to in such communications and made –
   (i) in connection with the giving of legal advice; or
   (ii) in connection with or in contemplation of legal proceedings and for the purposes of such proceedings, when they are in the possession of a person who is entitled to possession of them (section 10(2)).

Such items may never be obtained without consent of the person in possession of the material.

Q: In applying for a search warrant under section 8 of the Act (to enter and search premises for evidence) or under any other enactment, what safeguards exist for the protection of the public?
A: The Act prescribes requirements which must be rigidly adhered to when constables make application for such warrants and when executing them. Any entry to or search of premises in non-compliance with the provisions will be unlawful; with all the attendant consequences that that would entail. In applying for a warrant a constable must state the ground upon which he makes the application; the relevant statute; the identity of the premises and so far as practicable the articles or persons sought.

The application must be made in writing and on oath and the constable must answer any questions put to him (section 15(2) and (3)).

The Code of Practice reiterates the Act's provisions by directing that an application for a search warrant must be supported by an information in writing, specifying:-

(i) the enactment under which the application is made;
(ii) the premises to be searched and the object of the search; and
(iii) the grounds on which the application is made (including, where the purpose of the proposed search is to find evidence of an alleged offence, an indication of how the evidence relates to the investigation).

In addition, an application for a search warrant under paragraph 12 (a) of Schedule 1 to the Police and Criminal Evidence Act 1984 or under Schedule 7 to the Prevention of Terrorism (Temporary Provisions) Act 1989, shall also where appropriate, indicate why it is believed that service of notice of an application for a production order may seriously prejudice the investigation.

The provisions are thus designed to prevent warrants being applied for or granted without ample justification.

Q: What details will be included in a search warrant?
A: A warrant must specify –

- (a) (i) the name of the person who applies for it;
    - (ii) the date on which it is issued;
    - (iii) the enactment under which it is issued; and
    - (iv) the premises to be searched; and
- (b) shall identify, so far as is practicable, the articles or persons to be sought (section 15(6)).

The warrant need not be executed by the person who applies for it; it may be executed by any constable and may authorise other persons to accompany the constable who executes it (section 16(1) and (2)).

Q: How long will a search warrant last?
A: All search warrants are restricted to one month from the date of issue and may only be executed once (sections 16(3), 15(5)) and Code B.

Q: Is any further protection afforded to the occupier of the premises searched under a warrant issued under the Police and Criminal Evidence Act 1984 or any other statute?
A: Yes. The Act dictates that in the execution of all search warrants the entry and search must be effected at a reasonable hour unless it appears to the constable executing it that the purpose of the search may be frustrated on an entry at a reasonable hour. Where the occupier of the premises is present at the time the warrant is executed the constable shall identify himself and, if not in uniform, produce evidence of his identity, shall produce the warrant and supply the person with a copy of it (section 16(4)-(5)).

Q: Can a police officer execute a search warrant in the absence of the occupier of the premises?
A: Yes. In the event of the occupier of the premises not being present but some other person being present who appears to be in charge of the premises; that person shall be treated as though he were the occupier. If there is no person present who appears to be in charge of the premises then the constable must leave a copy of the warrant in a prominent place in the premises (section 16(6) and (7) and relevant code of practice).

Q: Once in the premises under the authority of a search warrant to what extent may a search be effected?

A: Only to the extent required for the purpose for which the warrant was issued (section 16(8)). It follows that while searching for a stolen video recorder an officer may look into a broom cupboard but not the biscuit barrel. A search warrant does not authorise a police officer to embark upon a general fishing expedition. The limitation in this respect is outlined quite clearly in Code B.

Q: Do any other safeguards exist to ensure that the issuing of warrants is tightly controlled?

A: The Act recognises that the execution of a search warrant can cause annoyance and distress in consequence of privacy being invaded. As a further means of exercising control in respect of the issue of warrants and making the police more accountable, the Act requires that once the warrant has been executed the officer must endorse it as to whether the articles or persons sought were found and whether any articles, not sought, were seized. Code B extends the obligation to show also the date and time at which it was executed; the names of the officers who executed it (except in the case of inquiries linked to the investigation of terrorism, in which case the warrant or other identification number and any duty station of each officer concerned shall be shown), and whether a copy, together with a copy of the Notice of Powers and Rights was handed to the occupier; or whether it was endorsed as required by paragraph 5.8 of the Code, and left on the premises together with the copy notice and, if so, where.

The warrant must be returned to the clerk to the justices or, if issued by a judge, to the appropriate officer of the court (section 16(9) and (10)), a requirement reiterated and developed in the code of practice.

Q: May a constable use force to gain entry to premises to effect a search under a warrant?

A: Yes. In respect of a warrant issued under section 8 of the Police and Criminal Evidence Act 1984 (to search for material evidence) the authority is found in section 117 of the Act which stipulates that in the exercise of any power conferred on a constable by the Act, which does not provide that the power may only be exercised with the consent of some person, other than a constable; the constable may use reasonable force, if necessary, in the exercise of the power. In respect of other search warrants the authorising statute expressly or implicitly provides authority for entry being effected 'by force if need be'. The use of force is also referred to in Code B.

Q: Can a search warrant under section 8 of the Police and Criminal Evidence Act 1984 or any other statute which empowers a justice to issue a warrant to search for specific items, be executed at the premises of a person in innocent possession of the item(s)?
A: Yes but a warrant under section 8 may only be granted if any one of four conditions concerning access and availability, referred to previously, apply.

Q: What is there to prevent an officer seeking to obtain a search warrant on an anonymous telephone call or the most tenuous of grounds?
A: Apart from having to support his application for a search warrant by giving evidence on oath, the Code of Practice for the Searching of Premises by Police Officers describes the action which must be taken before an application is made.

The code requires that where an officer receives information which may lead to an application being made for the issue of a warrant, he must first of all make efforts to verify the information. He should attempt to establish that the information has not been provided irresponsibly or with malicious intentions.

The code forbids the making of an application based on anonymous information where there has been no efforts made to establish some degree of corroboration. Of course, there might be nothing further obtained which bolsters the application but the point of the code is to ensure that there should be an attempt made before the application is formally submitted.

In laying down guidelines relating to background measures, Code B perhaps overstates the obvious but in doing so leaves little doubt as to the detail required before an application for a warrant is made. What kind of property is involved and where it is suspected to be seems elementary as does the requirement regarding background information about the occupier and the premises to be searched, including information about any recent searches conducted there.

The mandatory requirement that any application for a search warrant must be sanctioned by an inspector is softened in urgent cases where the senior officer on duty – perhaps a constable – may give authorisation. This requirement is slightly different in cases of applications under Schedule 7 to the Prevention of Terrorism (Temporary Provisions) Act 1989 where a superintendent's authorisation is required.

Q: Instances have occurred in the past where the execution of search warrants has allegedly caused serious public disorder. What measures exist to prevent this?

A: It is sometimes the case that the carrying out of a lawful activity by the police results in some sort of backlash in the community. While the Rule of Law must prevail in any community, due regard must be paid to the possibility of subsequent reactions. With this in mind, the code of practice gives directions regarding such circumstances by providing that unless there is some urgency involved, the local police/community liaison officer must be consulted before a search is carried out if there are grounds to suspect that the police/community relationship might be damaged. Where the search must be carried out urgently, the local police/community liaison officer must be advised of the search as soon as is practicable afterwards.

In addition to the foregoing a note of guidance provides that where the police have grounds to believe that police and community relations might be damaged, the local police/community consultative group should also be informed that a search has been carried out.

Q: Can a warrant be obtained on the information provided to the police by an informant?

A: Yes. This matter is touched upon in Code B. Where an application for a warrant is made on the information supplied by an informant, his identity may be withheld but the officer making the application must be in a position to answer questions from the judge or the magistrate about any previous information provided by the same person and whether it was accurate.

Q: An application for a warrant having been refused, what is there to prevent the police making a further application?

A: If an application is refused, no further application may be made for a warrant to search those premises unless supported by additional grounds. (Code of Practice)

Q: What effect does the Act have on those statutes which authorise a superintendent to issue a written order to enter and search premises?

A: The Act repeals section 26(2) of the Theft Act 1968 (superintendent's written authority to search for stolen goods). The power of a superintendent to issue written orders of search under section 73 of the Explosives Act 1875 (to search for explosives in cases of emergency) and section 9(2) of the Official Secrets Act 1911 (to search for evidence in case of great emergency that in interests of State immediate action is necessary) are preserved.

Entry and search without warrant

Section 17 of the Police and Criminal Evidence Act 1984 empowers a constable to enter premises for the purpose of arresting a person for various reasons, for recapturing persons unlawfully at large and for the purpose of saving life or limb. Section 18 of the Act on the other hand authorises a constable in some circumstances to enter and search premises for evidence following a person's arrest. Section 32 of the Act also incorporates provisions relating to the searching of premises immediately upon a person's arrest. This section is examined in Chapter 3.

Entry for the purpose of arrest etc

Q: In what circumstances may a police officer enter premises without a warrant for the purpose of arresting a person?

A: The Act stipulates that a constable may enter and search any premises for the purpose of arresting a person:

- on a warrant issued in connection with or arising out of criminal proceedings;
- on a commitment warrant;
- for an arrestable offence;
- for an offence under section 1 of the Public Order Act 1936 (which relates to political uniforms);
- for offences contained in sections 6-8 and 10 of the Criminal Law Act 1977 (offences concerning entering and remaining on property);
- for an offence under section 4 Public Order Act 1986 (fear or provocation of violence);
- for an offence under section 76 of the Criminal Justice and Public Order Act 1994 (failure to comply with interim possession order);
- unlawfully at large and whom he is pursuing; and for the purpose of saving life or limb or preventing serious damage to property (section 17(1)). (In the case of *D'Souza v DPP* (1992) it was held that there is no power to enter premises to arrest a person unlawfully at large unless an immediate, active pursuit is ongoing eg the escapee is actually being chased.)

In respect of the exercising of a power of arrest for the offences under the Criminal Law Act 1977 and the Criminal Justice and Public Order Act 1994 referred to a constable must be in uniform; although in respect of the other offences it will often be good practice to have a uniformed presence so as to allay unnecessary suspicion and anxieties.

Q: To whom does the expression 'unlawfully at large' extend?
A: While the expression is not defined in the Act it includes persons who have escaped from prison, the custody of a court, the custody of the police and those who have absconded from detention in mental hospitals and other establishments of compulsory detention.

It is worth bearing in mind that the offence of escape at common law, though not extending to all persons unlawfully at large, is an arrestable offence and thus in respect of such a person the power may be exercised on two fronts.

Q: The power seems wide. Are there any restrictions to prevent unnecessary interference with the liberty of the individual?
A: Yes. Except insofar as section 17(1) of the Act refers to saving life or limb or preventing serious damage to property, the power of entry is exercisable if the constable has reasonable grounds for believing that the person sought is on the premises. The power is also limited in relation to premises consisting of two or more separate dwellings, for example bed-sit flats and maisonettes. In such cases the power to enter and search is limited to:

(a) any parts of the premises which the occupiers of any dwelling comprised in the premises use in common with the occupier of any other such dwelling; and
(b) such dwellings in which the constable has reasonable grounds for believing that the person sought may be (section 17(2)).

It follows that while a police officer may enter and search communal areas of blocks of flats he cannot enter every flat or maisonette and search them on a process of elimination. He may only search a dwelling if he has reasonable grounds for believing that the person is in that specific dwelling.

On a more general footing, the Code of Practice for the Searching of Premises by the Police, which applies to searches effected under a variety of circumstances, including those conducted under section 17 of the Act, is designed to provide a balance between the needs of the police to investigate crime and arrest offenders and the rights of members of the public not to be subjected to interference without just cause.

Q: Having gained access to premises to arrest someone, what is there to prevent the police rummaging about?
A: The power of search is only a power to search to the extent that is reasonably required for the purpose for which the power of entry is exercised (section 17(4)). A constable is thus restricted to that which is necessary to search for and arrest a person. The power does not sanction a general 'fishing expedition'.

Q: What effect, if any, does the Act have on a constable's power at common law to enter premises without a warrant?
A: All such powers of entry are repealed by the Act with the exception of a constable's power of entry to deal with or prevent a breach of the peace (section 17(5) and (6)). Police practice is further controlled by the code of practice in this respect.

Entry and search after arrest

Q: For what purpose and in what circumstances may a constable enter and search a person's premises after his arrest?
A: He may enter and search any premises occupied or controlled by a person who is under arrest for an arrestable offence, as defined in section 24 of the Act, if he has reasonable grounds for suspecting that there is on the premises evidence, other than items subject to legal privilege, which relates to that offence or to some other arrestable offence which is connected with or similar to that offence. The powers may not be exercised unless an officer of the rank of inspector or above has authorised them in writing. That authority should (unless wholly impracticable) be given on the Notice of Powers and Rights.

A constable may exercise the power of entry and search without the authorisation of an officer of the rank of inspector, before taking the arrested person to a police station if the presence of that person at a place other than a police station is necessary for the effective investigation of that offence (section 18(1)(4) and (5)). It follows that while as a general rule an inspector's authority is pre-requisite to the exercise of the power, such authority is not necessary where, for example; upon being arrested elsewhere than at a police station, the person makes admissions say, in respect of the stolen property being at his home, a weapon being hidden in his loft, having just stabbed his wife at his home etc. Similarly it may be necessary for the officer to enter and search premises occupied by the arrested person to discover evidence which may help to establish his innocence.

Q: What does the expression 'evidence' mean for the purposes of this power?

A: It is not restricted to the fruits of the crime. The term will incorporate not only such property, but also the instrument by which the crime was committed or other evidence, documentary or otherwise, which helps to prove the commission of the crime for which the person has been arrested, or some other arrestable offence connected with it or similar to it.

Q: What does the inclusion of the expression 'to some other arrestable offence which is connected with or similar to that offence' contemplate?

A: The provision clearly envisages a person being arrested for an arrestable offence which is identifiable with another offence or a series of other offences. The effect of the provision is, for example, that in the event of a bogus official, a fraudster or burglar being arrested for a particular offence, search can be effected not only to secure evidence in respect of the offence giving rise to his arrest, but also with a view to securing evidence of other similar offences which may be attributable to him.

Q: Does the power merely provide the police with an opportunity to go on a 'fishing expedition' in premises occupied by every person arrested for an offence?

A: No. First of all the power is restricted to persons arrested for an 'arrestable offence'. Furthermore the power cannot be utilised by whim or by fancy or as a matter of routine. Reasonable grounds must always exist to found suspicion that admissible evidence is on the premises. A further safeguard to prevent abuse of the power is found in section 18(3) of the Act which declares that the power of search is restricted to the extent that is reasonably required for the purpose of discovering such evidence. Clearly, what is reasonable in the circumstances will depend on the evidence which is sought and the section in no way provides police officers with a licence to ransack property. Neither can one look into a jewellery box in a search for a stolen washing machine.

Q: What obligations are placed on the constable who lawfully exercises the power of entry and search without the authority of an inspector or above?

A: He shall inform an officer of the rank of inspector or above that he has made the search as soon as practicable after he has made it (section 18(6)).

Q: Do any provisions exist to measure the use made of the power and to satisfy the need for accountability?

A: Yes. An officer who:

(a) authorises a search; or
(b) is informed of a search effected without the authorisation of an inspector or above, shall make a record in writing:
  (i) of the grounds for the search; and
  (ii) of the nature of the evidence that was sought.

If the person who was in occupation or control of the premises at the time of the search is in police detention at the time the record is to be made, the officer shall make the record as part of his custody record (section 18(7) and (8)).

Q: What about seizure of items found?

A: The Act caters for the obvious. A constable may seize and retain anything for which he may search by virtue of the power conferred on him (section 18(2)).

Q: Does the power contained in section 18 of the Act constitute an extension to police powers?

A: As well as enjoying specific powers of seizure under various enactments the police have always held powers of seizure at common law. Prior to the Act coming into force it was settled law (*Ghani v Jones* (1969); *Elias v Passmore* (1934)) that where the police are searching premises under a warrant or have arrested a person lawfully or entered premises lawfully, they may seize articles found on his person or on his premises which they reasonably believe to be evidence of the offence for which he was arrested or other offences.

In respect of seizure, section 18 of the Act does nothing more than re-state common law principles in a clearer form. Reference in the section to searching premises 'controlled by a person who is under arrest' seemingly constitutes an extension to the former law which was readily identifiable with searching only the home of an arrested person. Clearly, section 18 extends beyond that and will authorise for example, a police officer to search the school of a headmaster arrested for indecency offences, or for misappropriation of school funds; or both the home and the shop premises of a person arrested for receiving stolen cigarettes. At common law there was no coercive power of entry. By virtue of section 18, entry can now be effected to the premises specified without the consent of the occupier/person in control of them and, indeed, against his will. Reasonable force may be used in the exercise of the power.

Seizure

Section 19 of the Act confers on the police a general power to seize articles suspected of being unlawfully obtained and evidence of offences in circumstances when they are lawfully on premises. The power is supplemented by section 20 of the Act which is concerned with information contained in a computer. Access to and the copying of articles seized is facilitated by section 21 of the Act whilst section 22 is confined to the retention of items seized. In addition the code of practice details various procedural steps which must be adhered to in exercising the powers and gives directions in relation to access considerations and the retention of property.

Q: What powers of general seizure are entrusted to police officers by the Act?

A: Where a constable is lawfully on any premises, he may seize anything which is on the premises if he has reasonable grounds for believing:

- (a) that it has been obtained in consequence of the commission of an offence; and
- (b) that it is necessary to seize it in order to prevent it being concealed, lost, damaged, altered or destroyed.

Additionally a constable may seize anything which is on the premises if he has reasonable grounds for believing:

- (a) that it is evidence in relation to an offence which he is investigating or any other offence; and
- (b) that it is necessary to seize it in order to prevent the evidence being concealed, lost, altered or destroyed (section 19(1) to (3)).

One can only speculate as to why the risk of damage being caused is a criterion in respect of property obtained in consequence of the commission of the offence but is not regarded as a relevant consideration in respect of a matter which is 'evidence'. It seems a mistake has been made by the legislators especially since the relevant code of practice does not draw such a distinction.

The provisions of sections 8 (warrant for evidence), 18 (search of premises after arrest) and 32 (search upon arrest), and a warrant issued under Schedule 1 to the Act all contain their own powers of seizure. The powers detailed in section 19 of the Act above, are additional to these specific powers of seizure.

While section 19 clarifies the common law powers and presents them in a more clear and precise form, reference in section 19 to it being necessary to seize the article 'to prevent the evidence being lost etc' is a qualification which did not exist hitherto. Section 19 thus introduces a 'necessity principle' and eradicates temptation for officers to seize evidence as a matter of course.

Whilst section 19 of the Act incorporates the wide aspect of a police officer being lawfully on premises, the Code of Practice for the Searching of Premises by Police Officers provides a limited power of seizure and retention in respect of officers searching premises under a statutory power or with the consent of the occupier.

Q: In what circumstances may a police officer be regarded as being lawfully on premises?

A: A police officer may be lawfully on premises by virtue of his being there under the authority of a warrant issued under any enactment; a search order; while exercising a statutory right of entry, such as the power of entry conferred on constables under section 17 of the Police and Criminal Evidence Act 1984; or by virtue of his being on the premises with the express or implied permission of the occupier of them. It follows that if a constable, whilst executing a search warrant for controlled drugs were to discover stolen property he would be entitled to seize the stolen property.

Q: Does the legality of lawfully searching for one commodity but seizing another allow the police to embark on a 'fishing expedition'?

A: No. In the course of a lawful search of premises, under the authority of a warrant or otherwise, the search may only be 'to the extent that is reasonably required for that purpose'. The general power of seizure under section 19 authorises officers to seize evidence of other offences they might stumble upon during their lawful presence on the premises. Obviously the police cannot be expected to wilfully ignore property obtained in consequence of crime or evidence of offences which is not the principal object of the search. The section does little more than give statutory effect to the previous common law authorities of *Elias v Passmore* (1934) and *Ghani v Jones* (1969).

Q: How much elasticity is there in the expression 'obtained in consequence of the commission of an offence'?

A: The term obviously includes the fruits of the crime irrespective of what that crime may be. In respect of the Theft Act 1968, whether goods have been obtained in circumstances amounting to theft, criminal deception or blackmail, they will be seizable. Goods directly or indirectly representing in whole or in part, the fruits of the crime can also be regarded as being 'obtained in consequence of the commission of an offence'. It follows that a motor cycle bought with stolen money is liable to seizure. Money realised from the unlawful supply of drugs is obtained 'in consequence of the commission of an offence' and it follows that the expression will include property bought with that money since such property directly represents the money.

As indicated, the provision is not confined either to the Theft Act 1968 or the Misuse of Drugs Act 1971. The power of seizure extends to anything obtained in consequence of the commission of an offence and thus the term allows the seizure of money or tangible commodities offered as a bribe, money or other reward paid to a person for 'minding' stolen goods or 'laundering' stolen money; intoxicating liquor obtained in breach of the Licensing Act 1964; an offensive weapon bought in consequence of a sale in breach of the Restriction of Offensive Weapons Act 1959; or cigarettes or fireworks bought from a retailer by a person under the relevant permitted ages.

Q: What will constitute evidence?
A: This expression goes far beyond the term 'obtained in consequence of the commission of an offence'. It will include such material as the con-man's disguise, the long-firm fraudster's false references, the assailant's weapon, the burglar's tools, the drug dealer's scales and wraps. It could also be something far less sinister such as a receipt or a ticket or even control samples. The term evidence thus means all descriptions of admissible relevant material.

Q: How may a police officer seize evidence if it is stored in a computer?
A: The Police and Criminal Evidence Act 1984 and the codes of practice have taken legislation into the technological era and specifically provides that a constable may require any information which is contained in a computer and is accessible from the premises to be produced in a form in which it can be taken away and in which it is visible and legible if he has reasonable grounds for believing:

(a) that:
  (i) it is evidence in relation to an offence which he is investigating or any other offence; or

  (ii) it has been obtained in consequence of the commission of
       an offence; and
  (b) that it is necessary to do so in order to prevent it being con-
      cealed, lost, tampered with or destroyed (section 19(4)).

While section 19 is concerned with the general power of seizure,
section 20 of the Act extends powers of seizure conferred on constables by other statutes to allow the seizure of computerised information.

By virtue of the provision, powers of seizure under:

- any other enactment, passed before or after the Police and
  Criminal Evidence Act 1984;
- section 8 of the Act (justice's search warrant for evidence);
- section 18 of the Act (search of premises after arrest);
- schedule 1, para 12 (Circuit Judge's warrant);

shall be construed as including a power to require any information
contained in a computer and accessible from the premises to be produced in a form in which it can be taken away and in which it is visible and legible (section 20). Being given a floppy disc thus falls short
of an officer's entitlement.

Q: Section 8 of the Act prevents a police officer seizing items which are subject to legal privilege. Does section 19 provide the means of circumventing that prohibition?

A: No. On the contrary it prevents the seizure under any power of
seizure conferred on a constable under any enactment of an item
which the constable has reasonable grounds for believing to be subject to legal privilege (section 19(6)). This provision provides additional protection to minimise the chances of the police gaining access
to material which might disclose details of the defence which an
accused person was seeking to depend upon at his trial. The rules of
evidence have always afforded special protection to legally privi-
leged items and the Police and Criminal Evidence Act 1984 brings
forward that protection to the investigative stages of an enquiry.

Q: What rights are afforded to the person from whom property is seized?

A: The Police and Criminal Evidence Act 1984 recognises that hitherto the rights of owners of property were inadequate. The 'necessity
principle' of seizure enunciated in section 19 of the Act should help
to reduce the risk of a person being deprived of his property without
just cause. Other provisions of the Act specifically designed in the
interests of the owners of property include the fact that a constable

who seizes anything in the exercise of a power conferred by any enactment, including an enactment contained in an Act passed after this Act shall, if so requested by a person showing himself:

(a) to be the occupier of premises on which it was seized; or
(b) to have had custody or control of it immediately before the seizure;

provide that person with a record of what he seized. The record must be provided within a reasonable time from the making of the request for it (section 21(2) and (3) and Code B).

Q: The seizure and retention of property can disrupt business life and personal habits. How does the Act seek to reduce the likelihood of this?
A: By facilitating access to and the copying of the material seized. If something has been seized and retained by a constable, the person who had custody or control of it before it was seized, or a person acting on such person's behalf, may make a request for access to the seized material. The request should be made to the officer in charge of the investigation who must allow access to the material under the supervision of a constable. The general right of access is subject to an exception concerning such access adversely affecting investigations or the course of justice.

The Act also facilitates a person who may lawfully seek access, requesting the officer in charge of the investigation to be allowed to photograph or copy the material seized. Again, subject to the exception in respect of it prejudicing investigations, the officer in charge of the investigation must allow the person making the request access to the material under the supervision of a constable for the purpose of photographing or copying it. Alternatively, the police may photograph or copy it on behalf of the person making the request and supply it to him, within a reasonable time (section 21 and Code B).

Effectively, the provisions of this section are designed to ensure that legitimate activities, whether personal or business, are not harmed or interfered with unnecessarily.

Q: Will allowing access and copying by persons who had custody or control of a seized item immediately before it was seized allow defences and alibis to be sometimes manufactured?
A: The Act endeavours to prevent the right of access and copying prejudicing investigations and any subsequent proceedings. It specifically declares that there is no duty to grant access to, or to supply a photograph or copy of, anything if the officer in charge of the inves-

tigation for the purposes of which it was seized has reasonable grounds for believing that to do so would prejudice:

(a) that investigation;
(b) the investigation of an offence other than the offence for the purposes of investigating which the thing was seized; or
(c) any criminal proceedings which may be brought as a result of:
  (i) the investigation of which he is in charge; or
  (ii) the investigation as is mentioned in paragraph (b) above (section 21(8)).

Q: Are the police empowered to photograph or copy material?

A: Yes, provided the material is liable to seizure (section 21(5)). Effectively, this provision, when read in conjunction with section 22(4) of the Act – which dictates that seized items may not be retained if a copy or photograph would be sufficient – dilutes the common law 'best evidence' rule that secondary evidence will only be admissible if there is good reason for the primary evidence not being available.

Q: Having seized material in exercise of the powers conferred upon him by section 19 of the Act, or having required computerised information to be produced in visible and legible form under either section 19 or 20 of the Act, for how long may a constable retain the material?

A: So long as is necessary. Without prejudice to the generality of the statement, anything seized for the purposes of a criminal investigation may be retained;

(i) for use as evidence at a trial for an offence; or
(ii) for forensic examination or for investigation in connection with an offence;

unless a photograph or copy would be sufficient for either of these purposes (section 22(1) (2) and (4)). Again, without prejudice to the generality of section 22(1) of the Act, anything may be retained in order to establish its lawful owner, where there are reasonable grounds for believing that it has been obtained in consequence of the commission of an offence (section 22(2) and Code B).

While no arbitrary rules as to time limits can be laid down to cater for general circumstances, the Act is specific in respect of items seized from persons in custody on the grounds that the article may be used to cause physical injury to any person; to damage property; to interfere with evidence; or to assist in escape from police detention or lawful custody.

In such circumstances the article cannot be retained once the person is no longer in police detention; or in the custody of the court or whilst in the custody of the court has been released on bail (section 22(3)). The provisions of section 22 do not prejudice any power of a court to make an order under the Police (Property) Act 1897 in respect of property coming into the possession of the police as a result of their investigation into a suspected offence. Such proceedings could be instituted by the police or any other interested party.

With the exception of diluting the 'best evidence' rule by specifying that an article may not be retained for evidential, forensic, or investigative purposes if a photograph or copy would be sufficient, section 22 does little more than give statutory affect to common law principles and long-established police procedures.

Q: Can the powers of seizure and retention be exercised in respect of things in the possession of persons who are not in any way implicated in the offence under investigation?
A: Yes, but that is not to say the powers will be utilised in every case. For instance, the powers could be utilised in respect of a stolen cycle found in possession of a second-hand dealer who bought the cycle in good faith. In the event of the dealer giving a satisfactory explanation and it being apparent that it is unnecessary to seize the cycle on the grounds specified in section 19(2) of the Act, the cycle may not be seized.

In this connection the code of practice dictates that where an officer decides that it is not appropriate to seize property because of an explanation given by the person holding it, but who has reasonable grounds for believing that it has been obtained in consequence of the commission of an offence by some person, he shall inform the holder of his suspicions and shall explain that, if he disposes of the property, he may be liable to civil or criminal proceedings. This provision is designed not only to safeguard the property for any future proceedings but to prevent such possessors of property from possibly committing criminal offences by disposing of the property.

Q: Are the provisions of section 21 and 22 only applicable to the investigation of offences?
A: No. By virtue of the Drug Trafficking Act 1994, for the purpose of the provision of section 21 (access and copying) and section 22 (retention) of PACE, an investigation into drug trafficking shall be treated as if it were an investigation of or in connection with an offence, and material produced under the Drug Trafficking Act 1994 shall be treated as if it were material seized by a constable.

Q: What remedy may be available to a person whose property has been wrongfully seized?

A: Apart from the question of police disciplinary proceedings, a person claiming property seized by the police may apply to a magistrates' court under the Police (Property) Act 1897 for its possession and should, where appropriate, be advised of this procedure (Code B). He may also have redress before the civil court.

Q: How are the police made accountable in respect of searches?

A: Records must be made. The code of practice stipulates that specific action must be taken after the following searches have been effected:

(a) searches of premises undertaken for the purposes of an investigation into an alleged offence with the occupier's consent other than routine scenes of crime searches and searches following the activation of burglar or fire alarms or bomb threat calls, and certain consensual searches outlined in Code B.

(b) searches of premises under the powers conferred by sections 17,18 and 32 of the Police and Criminal Evidence Act 1984;

(c) searches of premises undertaken in pursuance of a search warrant issued in accordance with section 15 of or Schedule 1 to that Act, or Schedule 7 to the Prevention of Terrorism (Temporary Provisions) Act 1989.

The code of practice dictates that where premises have been searched in the above circumstances other than in 'consensual searches' effected without written consent because of disproportionate inconvenience being caused, the officer in charge of the search shall, on arrival at a police station, make or have made a record of the search. The record shall include:

(i) the address of the premises searched;

(ii) the date, time and duration of the search;

(iii) the authority under which the search was made – where the search was made in the exercise of a statutory power to search premises without warrant, the record shall include the power under which the search was made; and where the search was made under warrant, or with written consent, a copy of the warrant or consent shall be appended to the record or kept in a place identified in the record;

(iv) the names of all the officers who conducted the search (except in the case of inquiries linked to the investigation of terrorism, in which case the record shall state the warrant or other identification number and duty station of each officer concerned);

(v) the names of any persons on the premises if they are known;
(vi) either a list of any articles seized or a note of where such a list is kept and, if not covered by a warrant, the reason for their seizure;
(vii) whether force was used and, if so, the reason why it was used;
(viii) details of any damage caused during the search and the circumstances in which it was caused.

These details must be recorded in the search register maintained at each sub-divisional police station. Additionally the code reiterates the provisions of the Act which demand the endorsement of search warrants and the return of both executed and unexecuted warrants to the clerk of the justices or appropriate officer of court as the case may be.

Code of practice for the searching of premises and seizure of property

Q: What provisions exist to regulate the conduct of police officers exercising powers of search under section 8 (search warrant for evidence); section 17 (entry and search of premises without warrant to arrest persons etc); section 18 (entry and search of premises without warrant after arrest) and section 32 (search of persons and premises without warrant on arrest) or any other statute?
A: The Act is regulatory in itself. Additionally, the Code of Practice for the Searching of Premises by Police Officers and the Seizure of Property found by Police Officers on Persons or Premises makes adequate provision to ensure that the powers of search are used prudently and judiciously and, above all else, with courteous regard to the occupiers of premises. The avoidance of unnecessary interference with the liberty of the individual and an acute awareness of the sensitivity of searches are issues more than adequately catered for by the code of practice.

The code of practice applies to the following searches of premises:

(a) searches of premises undertaken for the purposes of an investigation into an alleged offence, with the occupier's consent, other than routine scenes of crime searches and searches following the activation of burglar or fire alarms or bomb threat calls;
(b) searches of premises under the powers conferred by sections 17, 18 and 32 of the Police and Criminal Evidence Act 1984;

(c) searches of premises undertaken in pursuance of a search warrant issued in accordance with section 15 of, or Schedule 1 to, that Act or Schedule 7 to the Prevention of Terrorism (Temporary Provisions) Act 1989. The Code does not apply to the exercise of a statutory power to enter premises or to inspect goods, equipment or procedures if the exercise of that power is not dependent on the existence of grounds for suspecting that an offence may have been committed and the person exercising the power has no reasonable grounds for such suspicion.

As section 15 of the Act relates to all search warrants, it necessarily follows that the code of practice applies not only to search warrants issued under the authority of the Act but also those to enter and search premises issued under any other enactment such as the Theft Act 1968 (to search for stolen goods); Criminal Damage Act 1971 (to search for articles used/intended to be used for causing damage); Scrap Metal Dealers Act 1964 (to ascertain whether the Act is being complied with); Firearms Act 1968 (to search for firearms/ammunition); Misuse of Drugs Act 1971 (to search for controlled drugs); etc.

Q: How does the code of practice seek to control and direct police behaviour?

A: Some reference has been made already to selected aspects of the code of practice. So far as entry without warrant is concerned, the code specifies that in respect of entry for the purpose of arrest the conditions under which an officer may enter and search premises without warrant are set out in section 17 of the Act.

The code then lays down that the powers of an officer to search premises in which he has arrested a person are set out in section 32 of the Act and finally that the powers of an officer to search premises occupied or controlled by a person who has been arrested for an arrestable offence are set out in section 18 of the Police and Criminal Evidence Act 1984.

The code reiterates the provision of the Act. It makes it clear that the powers provided by section 18 of the Act may not (unless section 18(5) applies – search of premises prior to taking person to police station) be exercised unless an inspector or above has given written authority. That authority should (unless wholly impracticable) be given on the Notice of Powers and Rights.

The record of the search required by section 18(7) of the Act shall be made in the custody record where there is one. In the case of inquiries linked to the investigation of terrorism the authorising officer shall use his warrant or other identification number.

Section 67(10) of the Act declares that failure on the part:

(a) of a police officer to comply with any provision of a code of practice, or
(b) of any person other than a police officer who is charged with the duty of investigating offences or charging offenders to have regard to any relevant provision of such a code in the discharge of that duty,

shall not of itself render him liable to any criminal or civil proceedings. However, a police officer may be liable under the discipline code for failing to comply with a provision of a code of practice. It follows, therefore, that a police officer whose conduct does not meet the standards prescribed in the relevant sections or who breaches any conditions or restrictions specified in the relevant sections shall be liable to disciplinary proceedings and consequential risk of dismissal, requirement to resign, demotion, fine, reprimand or caution.

Q: In what other ways is the behaviour of the police and others charged with the responsibility of investigating offences governed?
A: In all criminal and civil proceedings any code of practice shall be admissible in evidence; and if any provision of such a code appears to the court or tribunal conducting the proceedings to be relevant to any question arising in the proceedings it shall be taken into account in determining that question (section 67(11)).

It follows that non-compliance with a code of practice could result in evidence obtained being rendered inadmissible.

Q: What provisions exist in the code of practice concerning the search of premises with consent?
A: In this respect the aim of the code is to ensure that consenting parties are apprised of their rights and such searches are only undertaken with the true consent of the occupier of the premises. Where premises are to be searched with consent, consent must be given, where practicable, in writing on the Notice of Powers and Rights. The officer conducting the search must establish that the person providing the consent is in a position to do so.

Prior to requesting consent the person approached must be told the nature of the search to be carried out, that he is under no obligation to give his consent and that if anything is seized during the course of the search it may be used as evidence. If the person from whom consent is sought is not suspected of committing any offence, he must be informed accordingly.

In necessarily stating the obvious, the code directs that if consent is provided under duress or the person who has provided consent changes his mind part way through, then the search cannot be carried out or continued as the case may be.

It is unnecessary to seek the consent of the person entitled to grant entry, where in the circumstances the seeking of consent would cause disproportionate inconvenience. While extending common courtesy is to be applauded, seeking consent in every case could do more harm than good.

The exception as to consent not being necessary would be applicable where in the early hours of the morning a burglar is disturbed and following a chase he is lost and a search is undertaken of open gardens, yards or basement areas to find him, or, following the arrest of such person, searching the premises mentioned – for premises includes 'any place' – for the fruits of his crime; his housebreaking implements or other incriminating evidence. In such circumstances it is reasonable to assume that innocent occupiers would agree to, and expect that, police should take the proposed action.

Examples are where the suspect has fled from the scene of a crime to evade arrest and it is necessary quickly to check surrounding gardens and readily accessible places to see whether he is hiding; or where police have arrested someone in the night after a pursuit and it is necessary to make a brief check of gardens along the route of the pursuit to see whether stolen or incriminating articles have been discarded.

It is worthy of reiteration that the immediately foregoing provisions of the code of practice do not apply to routine searches of scenes of crime and searches effected consequential upon intruder alarm calls or bomb threat calls.

Q: The Act dictates that a search warrant must be executed within one month from the date of issue of the warrant and will authorise entry on one occasion only. What risk does a police officer run if he breaches these issues?
A: The matters are reiterated and somewhat clarified in the code of practice which provides that searches made under warrant must be made within one calendar month from the date of issue of the warrant. In addition, searches must be made at a reasonable hour unless this might frustrate the purpose of the search.An officer breaching the provisions will expose himself to the risk of disciplinary proceedings.

Q: Must a police officer announce his identity and intention before endeavouring to gain entry other than with consent, ie under the authority of any of the coercive powers to which the code applies?

A: The code seeks to minimise any interference or annoyance caused in consequence of a police officer exercising any of the powers of entry falling within its purview. Accordingly code B provides a balanced approach to the conduct of non-consensual searches. Unless the target premises are known to be occupied, or the occupier or person who is able to consent to access if known to be away from the premises or that the object of the search might be thwarted or danger might be caused if there is an attempt to communicate with such a person, the first step should be an approach explaining the authority granted to search the premises and to request entry.

In circumstances where the object of the search may be thwarted or danger caused by attempting to communicate and obtain consent first, and where the premises are known to be occupied, officers carrying out the search must identify themselves and, if not wearing uniform, must produce their warrant cards. The purpose of the search and the reason why it is being conducted must be explained before the search commences.

Q: Does the code of practice make any reference to the use of reasonable force or consideration for the occupier?

A: While it does not describe what might constitute 'reasonable force' the code of practice is clear when it may be used. The code stipulates that reasonable force may be used if necessary to enter premises if the officer in charge is satisfied that the premises are those specified in any warrant or in the exercise of the powers provided by sections 17, 18 and 32 of the Act and where:

(i) the occupier or any other person entitled to grant access has refused a request to allow entry to his premises;

(ii) it is impossible to communicate with the occupier or any other person entitled to grant access; or

(iii) the premises are known to be unoccupied; or the occupier and any other person entitled to grant access are known to be absent; or there are reasonable grounds for believing that to alert the occupier or any other person entitled to grant access by attempting to communicate with him would frustrate the object of the search or endanger the officers concerned or other persons. The code thus preserves the notion that alacrity and secrecy are vitally important to some police operations.

So far as the second issue is concerned, that of consideration being shown to the occupier of the premises, the code stipulates that searches must be conducted with due consideration for the property and privacy of the occupier of the premises searched, and with no more disturbance than necessary. Reasonable force may be used only where this is necessary because the co-operation of the occupier cannot be obtained or is insufficient for the purpose.

Q. Are the police required to provide the occupier of the premises with any kind of documentation?

A: Yes. If an officer conducts a search to which the code applies, he shall, unless it is impracticable to do so, provide the occupier with a copy of a 'Notice of Powers and Rights'. This notice which is in a standard format should:

(i) specify whether the search is made under warrant, or with consent, or in the exercise of the powers described in sections 17, 18 or 32 of the Act (the format of the notice provides for the authority or consent to be indicated where appropriate);

(ii) summarise the extent of the powers of search and seizure conferred in the Act;

(iii) explain the rights of the occupier, and of the owner of property seized in accordance with paragraphs 6.1 to 6.5 and 6.8 of the code;

(iv) explain that compensation may be payable in appropriate cases for damage caused in entering and searching premises, and giving the address to which an application for compensation should be directed; and

(v) state that a copy of the code of practice is available to be consulted at any police station.

Unless the officer who is in charge of the search is of the view that it would thwart the search or cause danger to police officers or others, a copy of the Notice of Powers and Rights and of the warrant should, if practicable, be handed to the occupier of the target premises before the search commences. Where the occupier is absent, copies must be left in a prominent place in the premises or appropriate part. The copies must be endorsed with the name of the officer who was in charge of the case. This does not apply to those searches carried out in connection with a terrorism investigation where an officer's identity need not be disclosed. Instead, his warrant number must be included. In addition, the name of the officer's police station and the date and time of the search must be endorsed on the Notice and on the warrant.

Q: Must a search in pursuance of a warrant cease once all the articles specified in it have been found?
A: Yes. It must also cease once the officer in charge of the search is satisfied that the articles sought are not on the premises.

Q: May the occupier or person entitled to grant entry have a 'friend' present during a search of his premises?
A: Yes, the code accommodates such action. However, if the officer in charge of the search has cause to suspect that the presence of a neighbour or friend would seriously hinder the investigation or cause danger to either the police officers involved or others, he may refuse the request. A search cannot be unreasonably delayed in order that a request of this nature can be complied with.

Q: If forcible entry has been gained what onus is placed on the police to remedy any breach of security caused by such entry?
A: Neither the Act nor the code makes provision for financial recompense in such circumstances but the code of practice imposes on the officer in charge of the search a duty before leaving the premises to satisfy himself that they are secure either by arranging for the occupier or his agent to be present or by any other appropriate means.

Q: What provision does the code of practice make concerning searches effected under a warrant issued by a circuit judge under Schedule 1 to the Act for excluded or special procedure material?
A: Due to the sensitivity of such searches an officer of the rank of inspector or above shall take charge of the search and be present at any search under a warrant issued under Schedule 1 or under Schedule 7 to the Prevention of Terrorism (Temporary Provisions) Act 1989. The code of practice dictates that the officer is responsible for ensuring that the search is conducted with discretion and in such a manner as to cause the least possible disruption to any business or other activities carried on in the premises. That is not the end of the officer's responsibilities.

No doubt because of the sensitive nature of searches of this type, the code provides almost a step-by-step series of instructions to the officer carrying out the search. After ensuring that no material can be removed from the premises he shall ask for the production of the documents or records. He is also empowered, if he thinks fit, to inspect the index of files kept there. By the same token, any files which according to the index, appear to hold any of the material for which the search is being conducted, may be examined.

A more thorough search of the premises can then take place but

2: Entry, search and seizure

only if certain conditions prevail. These are, that there is a refusal by the person concerned to produce the material or to grant sight of the index, or the index is flawed or if, for any reason the officer in charge reasonably believes that a more extensive search is necessary to find what he is looking for.

A rather more obvious note of guidance advises that officers who are requesting the production of documents should ensure that they ask for a person in authority who has responsibility for the documents sought.

Q: Is any restriction placed upon the times of day at which a warrant may be executed?

A: No, but the 'Notes of Guidance' contained within the code of practice suggest that in deciding when a search should be conducted, the officer in charge should address his mind to such considerations as the time when the occupier is likely to be on the premises and a search should not be made when such a person or others on the premises, are likely to be asleep, unless of course the object of searching the premises is likely to be frustrated.

Q: What if the police enter the wrong premises when executing a warrant?

A: The only reference in Code B is contained in a note of guidance which provides that where a mistake has been made, every effort should be made as soon as possible to make amends and, where appropriate, guidance should be provided to enable compensation to be made.

CHAPTER 3

ARREST

Part III of the Police and Criminal Evidence Act 1984 makes sweeping changes in the law relating to arrest. It re-defines the meaning of 'arrestable offence', creates the new classification of a 'serious arrestable offence', abolishes most powers of arrest exercisable by a constable; provides a new general conditional power of arrest; outlines procedures which must be adhered to when a person is arrested and makes statutory provision for persons attending police stations voluntarily.

Q: In many of the powers contained in the Police and Criminal Evidence Act 1984 the commission or suspicion of an arrestable offence is a prerequisite. What is an 'arrestable offence'?
A: Section 24 of the Act provides the definition of an arrestable offence as any offence:

(a) for which the sentence is fixed by law;
(b) for which a person of or over the age of 21 years (not previously convicted) may be sentenced to imprisonment for a term of five years (or might be so sentenced but for restrictions imposed by section 33 of the Magistrates' Courts Act 1980, ie criminal damage offences where the value involved is small);
(c) for which a person may be arrested under the Customs and Excise Acts (defined in section 1(1) of the Customs and Excise Management Act 1979);
(d) under the Official Secrets Act 1920 which is not an arrestable offence by virtue of the term of imprisonment for which a person may be sentenced in respect of it;
(e) under any provision of the Official Secrets Act 1989 except section 8(1) (4) or (5);
(f) under section 22 (causing prostitution of women) or 23 (procuration of girl under 21) of the Sexual Offences Act 1956;
(g) under section 12(1) (taking a motor vehicle or other conveyance without authority etc) or 25(1) (going equipped for stealing etc) of the Theft Act 1968;
(h) any offence under the Football (Offences) Act 1991.
(i) an offence under section 2 of the Obscene Publications Act 1959 (publication of obscene matter);
(j) an offence under section 1 of the Protection of Children Act 1978

(indecent photographs and pseudo photographs of children);

(k) an offence under section 19 of the Public Order Act 1986 (publishing etc. material intended or likely to stir up racial hatred);

(l) an offence under section 166 of the Criminal Justice and Public Order Act 1994 (sale of tickets by unauthorised persons);

(m) an offence under section 167 of the Criminal Justice and Public Order Act 1994 (touting for hire car services);

(n) conspiring, attempting, inciting, aiding, abetting, counselling or procuring offences under (c) to (g) above, other than attempting to commit an offence under section 12(1) of the Theft Act 1968.

By virtue of the Offensive Weapons Act 1996, the following are arrestable offences:

– an offence under section 1 of the Prevention of Crime Act 1953 (possessing offensive weapon without lawful authority or reasonable excuse);

– an offence under section 139 of the Criminal Justice Act 1988 (having article with blade or point in public place);

– an offence under section 139A(1) or (2) of the Criminal Justice Act 1988 (having article with blade or point or offensive weapon on school premises);

and, by virtue of the Protection from Harassment Act 1997, an offence under section 2 of that Act (harassment) (when brought into force).

Q: What powers of arrest exist to arrest a person for an arrestable offence?

A: Powers of arrest in this respect are divided into two categories; those which any person may exercise and those which can only be effected by a constable.

The Act provides that any person may arrest without a warrant:

(a) anyone who is in the act of committing an arrestable offence;

(b) anyone whom he has reasonable grounds for suspecting to be committing such an offence.

Where an arrestable offence has been committed, any person may arrest without a warrant:

(a) anyone who is guilty of the offence;

(b) anyone whom he has reasonable grounds for suspecting to be guilty of it.

Where a constable has reasonable grounds for suspecting that an arrestable offence has been committed, he may arrest without a warrant anyone whom he has reasonable grounds for suspecting to be guilty of the offence.

A constable may arrest without warrant:

(a) anyone who is about to commit an arrestable offence;

(b) anyone whom he has reasonable grounds for suspecting to be about to commit an arrestable offence.

The powers of arrest entrusted to 'any person' obviously extend to a constable.

Q: What provisions are contained in the Act to enable arrests to be made for offences which are not 'arrestable offences' within the meaning of the Act?

A: The Police and Criminal Evidence Act 1984 recognises that many powers of arrest developed at random. In order to tidy up the law the Act repeals the great majority of a police officer's powers of arrest which existed prior to the Act becoming operative and replaces them with a general conditional power of arrest which applies to all offences. Under the general power of arrest where a constable has reasonable grounds for suspecting that any offence which is not an arrestable offence has been committed or attempted, or is being committed or attempted, he may arrest the relevant person if it appears to him that service of a summons is impracticable or inappropriate because any of the general arrest conditions is satisfied (section 25(1)).

The 'relevant person' is described as any person whom the constable has reasonable grounds to suspect of having committed or having attempted to commit the offence or of being in the course of committing or attempting to commit it.

Prior to exercising the power of arrest the existence of any one of the following general arrest conditions must be established:

(a) that the name of the relevant person is unknown to, and cannot be readily ascertained by, the constable;
(b) that the constable has reasonable grounds for doubting whether a name furnished by the relevant person as his name is his real name;
(c) that:
  (i) the relevant person has failed to furnish a satisfactory address for service; or
  (ii) the constable has reasonable grounds for doubting whether an address furnished by the relevant person is a satisfactory address for service;
(d) that the constable has reasonable grounds for believing that arrest is necessary to prevent the relevant person:
  (i) causing physical injury to himself or any other person;
  (ii) suffering physical injury;
  (iii) causing loss of or damage to property;
  (iv) committing an offence against public decency (an arrest is not authorised under this particular paragraph except where members of the public going about their normal

> business cannot reasonably be expected to avoid the per-
> son to be arrested); or
>   (v) causing an unlawful obstruction of the highway;
> (e) that the constable has reasonable grounds for believing that
>   arrest is necessary to protect a child or other vulnerable person
>   from the relevant person (section 25(3)).

Effectively the 'general arrest conditions' give statutory effect to the long established principle that a power of arrest should only be utilised where a summons will not suffice. This statutory presumption that the summons procedure must be used wherever possible does not apply to the powers of arrest for 'arrestable offences' in section 24 of the Act.

Q: What will constitute a satisfactory address for the service of a summons?
A: If it appears to the constable:

(a) that the relevant person will be at it for a sufficiently long peri-
    od for it to be possible to serve him with a summons; or
(b) that some other person specified by the relevant person will
    accept service of a summons for the relevant person at it.

Q: Are not the homeless disadvantaged by the general power of arrest for 'non-arrestable offences'?
A: No. It will be noted that section 25(3) makes no reference to a 'home address'. The nub of the issue is the provision of a satisfactory address for service of a summons. Theoretically, a person could tender that of his probation officer; the Social Services Department etc.

Q: If an offender who initially refused to give his name or address were to cooperate with the police officer on his way to the police station and give the necessary details, would such action secure his release?
A: Yes. A person arrested by a constable at a place other than a police station shall be released if a constable is satisfied, before the person arrested reaches a police station, that there are no grounds for keeping him under arrest (section 30(7)).

Q: Mention has been made of the Act repealing many powers of arrest but yet preserving a handful. Which powers of arrest are preserved?
A: Among the most common of those powers which have been pre-served are:

- section 7(3) Public Order Act 1936 – offences relating to public order.
- section 49 Prison Act 1949 – persons unlawfully at large.
- section 1(3) Street Offences Act 1959 – common prostitute soliciting for the purposes of prostitution.
- section 7 Bail Act 1976 – failing to answer bail etc.

A full list of the offences appears in Schedule 2 to the Act.

Q: What effect, if any, has section 25 of the Act – general arrest conditions – on those powers of arrest outside the section's purview?
A: It does not prejudice them (section 25(6)).

Q: When a person has been arrested, what information must the police supply to him?
A: The answer is contained in section 28 of the Act which gives statutory effect to the decision in *Christie v Leachinsky* (1947) and other decided cases on what constitutes a lawful arrest. The section provides that where a person is arrested, otherwise than by being informed that he is under arrest, the arrest is not lawful unless the person arrested is informed that he is under arrest as soon as is practicable after his arrest (section 28(1)). Where a person is arrested by a constable this principle is still of application regardless of whether the fact of the arrest is obvious (section 28(2)).

The requirement to notify an arrested person does not require a person to be informed: (a) that he is under arrest; or (b) of the ground for the arrest if it was not reasonably practicable for him to be so informed by reason of his having escaped from arrest before the information could be given (section 28(5)).

Not only must a person be informed of the fact that he is under arrest, he must also be told of the grounds. Subject to it not being reasonably practicable for him to be so informed by reason of his having escaped from arrest before the information could be given, no arrest is lawful unless the person arrested is informed of the ground for the arrest at the time of, or as soon as practicable after, the arrest (section 28(3)).

Q: One often learns from the media that 'a person is helping the police with their enquiries'. Does the Police and Criminal Evidence Act 1984 affect this practice?
A: The Act preserves the decisions in the cases of *R v Wattam* (1952) and *R v Inwood* (1973) that there is nothing wrong with the practice

of inviting a person to attend at a police station of his own free will to assist with police inquiries. The Act recognises the propriety of such practices and improves the necessary safeguards for the individual by providing that where for the purpose of assisting with an investigation a person attends voluntarily at a police station or at any other place where a constable is present or accompanies a constable to a police station or any such other place without having been arrested:

(a) he shall be entitled to leave at will unless he is placed under arrest;

(b) he shall be informed at once that he is under arrest if a decision is taken by a constable to prevent him from leaving at will (section 29).

Q: What provisions exist to make sure that the police do not hoodwink a person who is at a police station of his own accord?

A: The code of practice relating to the detention, treatment and questioning of persons reiterates the provisions of section 29 of the Act and goes on to dictate that if it is decided that he would not be allowed to leave then he must be informed at once that he is under arrest and brought before the custody officer. If he is not placed under arrest but is cautioned in accordance with paragraph 10 of the code of practice the officer who gives the caution must at the same time inform him that he is not under arrest, that he is not obliged to remain at the police station but that if he remains at the police station he may obtain legal advice if he wishes.

Q: The term 'serious arrestable offence' is applicable to many aspects of the Act's provisions; such as road checks; the extended detention of persons not charged; the taking of intimate samples and the delaying of a detained person's legal rights. How is such an offence defined?

A: The Police and Criminal Evidence Act 1984 introduces 'serious arrestable offence' as a new classification of offence. It cannot be over-emphasised that this is not a term of academic interest or relevant only to procedural or sentencing matters. It is of the utmost importance to common operational matters and cannot be divorced from the investigation of crime. In simplistic terms, whether an offence is a serious arrestable offence will determine the powers available and may affect the direction an enquiry may take.

The definition of the term is contained in section 116 of the Act and in the 5th Schedule to the Act, by virtue of which the following arrestable offences are always serious:

(a) (whether at common law or under any enactment) the offences of:
- treason
- murder
- manslaughter
- rape
- kidnapping
- incest with a girl under the age of 13
- buggery with a person under the age of 16;
- indecent assault which constitutes an act of gross indecency:

(b) any of the offences mentioned in paragraphs (a) to (d) of the definition of 'drug trafficking offence' in section 1 of the Drug Trafficking Act 1994 viz:

(1) an offence under section 4 (2) or (3) or 5(3) of the Misuse of Drugs Act 1971 (production, supply and possession for supply of controlled drugs),

(2) an offence under section 20 of that Act (assisting in or inducing commission outside United Kingdom of offence punishable under a corresponding law);

(3) an offence under:

(i) section 50(2) or (3) Customs and Excise Management Act 1979 (improper importation);

(ii) section 68(2) of that Act (exportation); or

(iii) section 170 of that Act (fraudulent evasion); in connection with a prohibition or restriction on importation or exportation having effect by virtue of section 3 of the Misuse of Drugs Act 1971;

(4) an offence under section 24 of the Act (assisting another to retain the benefit of drug trafficking):

(c) an offence under the following enactments: *Explosive Substances Act 1883*, section 2 (causing explosion likely to endanger life or property): *Sexual Offences Act 1956*, section 5 (intercourse with a girl under the age of 13): *Firearms Act 1968*, section 16 (possession of firearms with intent to injure), section 17(1) (use of firearms and imitation firearms to resist arrest), section 18 (carrying firearms with criminal intent): *Taking of Hostages Act 1982*, section 1 (hostage-taking): *Aviation Security Act 1982*, section 1 (hi-jacking): *Road Traffic Act 1988*, section 1 (causing death by dangerous driving), section 3 (causing death by careless driving while under the influence of drink and drugs): *Criminal Justice Act 1988*, section 134 (torture): *Aviation and Maritime Security Act 1990*, section 1 (endangering safety at aerodromes), section 9 (hijacking of ships), section 10 (seizing or exercising control of fixed platforms): *Protection of Children Act 1978,* section 1 (indecent photographs and pseudo-photographs of children *Obscene Publications Act 1959,* section 2 (publication of obscene matter).

The foregoing are pure serious arrestable offences at all times.

Section 116 of the Act creates circumstances when an 'arrestable offence' may become a 'serious arrestable offence' because of aggravating circumstances. The section continues that any other arrestable offence may be classified as a serious arrestable offence only if the commission of it has led to or is intended to lead to or is likely to lead to any of the following consequences:

(a) serious harm to the security of the State or to public order;
(b) serious interference with the administration of justice or with the investigation of offences or of a particular offence;
(c) the death of any person;
(d) serious injury to any person;
(e) substantial financial gain to any person; and
(f) serious financial loss to any person (section 116(3) and (6)).

It follows that whilst assault occasioning actual bodily harm is not in itself a serious arrestable offence, it could become one if coupled with a threat that the victim should not give evidence in forthcoming judicial proceedings.

Similarly while, for example, theft, robbery, burglary are not serious arrestable offences in themselves, they could be so regarded if any one of the aggravating circumstances exist. In this respect it should be borne in mind that 'substantial financial gain' is not synonymous with 'serious financial loss'.

'Loss' is serious for the purposes of the section if, having regard to all the circumstances, it is serious for the person who suffers it (section 116(7)). A novel legalistic contrivance is thus created to differentiate between loss suffered by one as against loss suffered by another.

'Injury' is defined as including any disease and any impairment of a person's physical or mental condition (section 116(8)).

The classification of 'serious arrestable offences' extends even further. An arrestable offence which consists of making a threat is serious if carrying out the threat would be likely to lead to any of the consequences described in (a) to (f) above. It follows that offences of threats to kill (section 16 Offences Against the Person Act 1861) and, in some circumstances the offence of threats to commit damage (section 3 Criminal Damage Act 1971) may be classified as serious arrestable offences.

For the sole purpose of section 56 (right to have someone informed of person's arrest) and section 58 (right of access to legal advice) of the Police and Criminal Evidence Act 1984, sections 2, 8, 9, 10 or 11 of the Prevention of Terrorism (Temporary Provisions) Act 1989 (and attempts and conspiracies to commit them) will always be 'serious arrestable offences'.

Q: Once a person has been arrested what procedures must be followed?

A: Where a person:

(a) is arrested by a constable for an offence; or
(b) is taken into custody by a constable after being arrested for an offence by a person other than a constable; at any place other than a police station he shall be taken to a police station by a constable as soon as practicable after the arrest (section 30(1)). This general statement is subject to two provisos. Firstly, a person arrested by a constable at a place other than a police station shall be released if a constable is satisfied, before the person arrested reaches a police station, that there are no grounds for keeping him under arrest (section 30(7)).

This provision will be of application where the innocence of the person may be established en route to the police station or where, after initially not co-operating with the police he provides his name or a satisfactory address for service of summons. A constable releasing a person in these circumstances must record that fact as soon as is practicable after the release.

Secondly, nothing in subsection (1) above shall prevent a constable delaying taking a person who has been arrested to a police station if the presence of that person elsewhere is necessary in order to carry out such investigations as it is reasonable to carry out immediately (section 30(10)). This provision gives statutory effect to the decision in *Dallison v Caffery (1964)* and recognises that in some instances, with a view to establishing guilt or innocence, immediate enquiries are essential, for example to check out an immediately verifiable alibi tendered on arrest. Any delay in taking an arrested person to a police station shall be recorded (section 30(11)).

Q: Can an arrested person be taken to any police station?

A: He should be taken to a designated police station, ie a police station for the time being designated under section 35 of the Act as being a police station to be used for detaining arrested persons (section 30(2)).

However, if he is working in a locality covered by a police station which is not a designated police station, a constable may take an arrested person to any police station unless it appears to the constable that it may be necessary to keep the arrested person in police detention for more than six hours. This exception also applies to constables belonging to police forces not maintained by a police authority, for example the British Transport Police and Ministry of Defence Police (section 30(3) and (4)). A further exception to the rule that a person must be taken to a designated police station is provided by section 30(5) of the Act which declares that any constable may take an arrested person to any police station if:

(a) either of the following conditions is satisfied: (i) the constable has arrested him without the assistance of any other constable and no other constable is available to assist him; (ii) the constable has taken him into custody from a person other than a constable without the assistance of any other constable and no other constable is available to assist him; and

(b) it appears to the constable that he will be unable to take the arrested person to a designated police station without the arrested person injuring himself, the constable or some other person (section 30(5)).

Q: Can a person be detained at a non-designated police station indefinitely?

A: No. He must be taken to a designated police station not more than six hours after his arrival at the first police station unless he is released previously (section 30(6)).

Q: Once a person is under arrest, his detention is under continuous scrutiny in order that he may be released as expeditiously as possible. What is there to prevent an officer from arresting a person for a further offence once the person is released in order to gain more time to interview him?

A: The Act prohibits officers keeping offences up their sleeves and ensures that a detained person knows exactly what he is in custody for. It provides that where:

(a) a person:
    (i) has been arrested for an offence; and
    (ii) is at a police station in consequence of that arrest; and

(b) it appears to a constable that if he were released from that arrest he would be liable to arrest for some other offence, he shall be arrested for that offence (section 31).

Arrest for fingerprinting

Section 27 of the Act empowers a constable to require certain offenders to attend police stations in order that fingerprints may be taken.

Q: What is the extent of the power?
A: If a person:

(a) has been convicted of a recordable offence;
(b) has not at any time been in police detention for the offence; and
(c) has not had his fingerprints taken:
   (i) in the course of the investigation of the offence by the police; or
   (ii) since the conviction,

any constable may at any time not later than one month after the date of the conviction require him to attend a police station in order that his fingerprints may be taken (section 27(1)).

It will be noted that the power is conditional upon a number of factors, not least of which is the fact that the power cannot be invoked in respect of a person who has been in police detention for the recordable offence for which he was convicted. The term 'recordable offence' means an offence which is listed in regulations as being 'recordable' for the purposes of the National Identification Bureau.

Q: Can a person be required to attend there and then?
A: No. A requirement to attend a police station for fingerprints to be taken shall give the person a period of at least seven days within which he must attend and may direct him to attend at a specified time of day or between specified times (section 27(2)). It follows that provided the requirement is made within the one month period the fingerprints could be taken outside that period.

Q: What can be done in respect of a person who fails to comply with such a requirement?
A: He may be arrested without warrant (section 27(3)) and taken to a police station where his fingerprints may be taken.

Search upon arrest

Section 32 of the Police and Criminal Evidence Act 1984 empowers a constable to search arrested persons in certain circumstances for dangerous articles, those which may assist an escape and for evidence. The section also caters for the search, by police officers, of premises where a person was at the time of his arrest or immediately prior to it.

Q: What is the extent of the power?

A: A constable may search an arrested person, in any case where the person to be searched has been arrested at a place other than a police station, if the constable has reasonable grounds for believing that the arrested person may present a danger to himself or others. A constable shall also have the power:

(a) to search the arrested person for anything:
    (i) which he might use to assist him to escape from lawful custody; or
    (ii) which might be evidence relating to an offence; and
(b) to enter and search any premises in which he was when arrested or immediately before he was arrested for evidence relating to the offence for which he has been arrested.

One of the constant themes of the Police and Criminal Evidence Act 1984 is that of reasonableness and thus to avoid public embarrassment or humiliation, the power to search for escape articles or evidence is restricted to that which is reasonably required for the purpose of discovering any such thing or any such evidence (section 32(1)-(3)).

The section provides additional safeguards for preserving the liberty and dignity of the individual by providing that before commencing a search the constable must have reasonable grounds for believing that the person to be searched may have concealed on him an article he might use to facilitate escape or is evidence; as the case may be. The power of search cannot thus be used as a matter of routine practice (section 32(5) and (6)).

By virtue of section 166(5) of the Criminal Justice and Public Order Act 1994, the provisions of section 32 are specifically declared to apply to offences under section 166 which relate to ticket touts. Section 166(5) provides that section 32 of the Police and Criminal

Evidence Act 1984 (search of persons and premises (including vehicles) upon arrest) shall have effect, in its application in relation to an offence under the section, as if the power conferred on a constable to enter and search any vehicle extended to any vehicle which the constable has reasonable grounds for believing was being used for any purpose connected with the offence.

Q: In consequence of the powers of search in section 32 could a police officer almost strip search an arrested person?

A: The section stipulates that the powers are not to be construed as authorising a constable to require a person to remove any of his clothing in public other than an outer coat, jacket or gloves but they do authorise a search of a person's mouth (section 32(4)).

It will be noted that this restriction applies only to the compulsory removal of the specified items in public. Elsewhere than in public and provided reasonable grounds exist to justify the action, an arrested person could be required to remove additional items of clothing.

While the Code of Practice for the Exercise by Police Officers of Statutory Powers of Stop and Search does not apply to a search conducted under the authority of section 32 of the Act it is suggested that it would be sensible to adhere to the principles enunciated in that code of practice, so far as they relate to the power being used responsibly, and with due consideration being given to the person being searched.

It is worthy of note that the restriction contained in section 32(4), does not preclude an arrested person from voluntarily forfeiting his statutory protection and removing additional items of clothing of his own accord.

Q: What will be deemed to be a search in public?

A: The Act gives no hint nor is any detailed meaning attributed to it in any of the codes of practice. Nonetheless whilst the Code of Practice for Stop and Search is of no application to the power under review, a note of guidance in that code offers the view, which is perhaps an obvious one, that 'a search in a street should be regarded as being in public even though it may be empty at the time the search begins'.

It is suggested that for the purposes of the restriction and the similar one applicable to the stop and search powers conferred by section 1 of the Act, it would be useful to apply the definitions of 'public places' found in the Public Order Act 1986 and the Prevention of Crime Act 1953.

Q: For the purpose of entry to and search of premises, how far will the phrase 'immediately before he was arrested' extend?

A: Immediacy is a relative issue. The spirit of the provision is to authorise a constable to search premises in which the prisoner may have been hidden or visited immediately prior to arrest in order that he, the constable, may search for evidence which the person may have secreted or disposed of. It will thus include the searching of a person's home, if he is arrested at home or the search of licensed premises where the arrest was effected but it is stressed that in all such circumstances the power is qualified by the necessity for a reasonable belief that the items mentioned in the section are to be found on the premises.

Q: What will amount to 'premises' for the purposes of this power?

A: 'Premises' includes any place, and in particular includes

(a) any vehicle, vessel, aircraft or hovercraft;
(b) any offshore installation and
(c) any tent or movable structure.

Q: To what extent does the section ensure that the sanctity of the home is not unjustifiably intruded upon?

A: It imposes stringent control by providing that insofar as the power of search of the place where a person was when arrested or immediately before he was arrested related to premises consisting of two or more separate dwellings, it is limited to a power to search:

(a) any dwelling in which the arrest took place or in which the person arrested was immediately before his arrest; and
(b) any parts of the premises which the occupier of any such dwelling uses in common with the occupiers of any other dwellings comprised in the premises (section 32(7)).

It follows that if the arrested person lives in a block of flats, a maisonette or a bed-sit the search provisions are restricted to the flat, a bed-sit occupied by him, or such place where he was immediately before arrest, and any communal parts such as landings, stairways, yards, utility rooms etc.

Q: What provisions are there in respect of the seizure of items discovered in the course of a search carried out under the section?

A: A constable searching a person because he reasonably believes the person may present a danger to himself or others may seize and retain anything he finds, if he has reasonable grounds for believing that the person searched might use it to cause physical injury to himself or to any other person.

A constable searching a person because he reasonably believes the person may have concealed on him articles which he might utilise in an escape or articles which might be evidence of an offence, may seize and retain anything he finds, other than an item subject to legal privilege, if he has reasonable grounds for believing:

(a) that he might use it to assist him to escape from lawful custody; or
(b) that it is evidence of an offence or has been obtained in consequence of the commission of an offence (section 38(2) and (9)).

Analysis of section 32 reveals no power of seizure and retention of articles found in consequence of a search of premises where the accused was or had been immediately prior to his arrest. The authority for seizing and retaining items so discovered is found in section 19 of the Act which in its entirety is concerned with the general principles of seizure by police officers lawfully on premises.

However, an officer searching premises under the power conferred by section 32 may, by virtue of the Code of Practice for the Searching of Premises by Police Officers, seize anything (other than items of legal privilege) which he has reasonable grounds for believing is evidence of an offence or has been obtained in consequence of the commission of an offence. Such items may only be seized where it is necessary to prevent their concealment, alteration, loss, damage or destruction.

Provisions also exist in the Code of Practice to facilitate the retention of seized property.

Q: What will constitute 'reasonable grounds' to justify utilisation of the power of search?

A: Things said or done by the arrested person immediately or at the time of arrest will often be a sound foundation for such suspicion. But there is no reason why suspicion should not be founded on information from an independent witness or other source or, indeed, from police intelligence sources. While 'reasonableness' is a common thread throughout the web of the Police and Criminal Evidence Act 1984, each case must be judged on its merits and the lawfulness of police conduct must be determined by the facts prevailing at the time and not with the benefit of hindsight.

Although the guidance provided in the code of practice relating to stop and search about 'reasonable grounds for suspicion' does not apply to the exercise by police officers of the powers to search persons and premises, it would no doubt be regarded as prudent practice to observe that particular guidance.

Q: In exercise of the power may a constable use force?

A: The officer may use reasonable force, if necessary. Such force may be used against the person, or to gain entry to the premises in which the arrested person was when arrested or immediately before he was arrested (section 117 and Code B).

Q: To what extent does the power to search persons upon arrest give statutory effect to the common law?

A: Tradition and common law authorities seemingly established that it was right and proper for a police officer in certain circumstances to search a person upon arrest. It was always thought that searching every prisoner was lawful in order that the prisoner may be prevented from harming himself and to provide for the safe custody of his property.

The lawfulness of such action was challenged in the cases of *R v Naylor (1979)* and *Lindley v Rutter (1981)*. Both cases give a positive indication that prisoners cannot be searched as a matter of course and that to effect a lawful search of a prisoner, a police officer must have formed the opinion in good faith that there was real necessity for the search to be carried out. In many ways section 32 of the Act re-affirms the decision in the cases of *Naylor*, and *Lindley v Rutter* and in particular in respect of preventing the routine searching of persons upon arrest. The power detailed in section 32 is, however, innovative in respect of the entry and search of premises where the arrested person was at the time of or immediately before his arrest.

CHAPTER 4

DETENTION

Part IV of the Police and Criminal Evidence Act 1984 introduces radical reforms to the law. It imposes limitations on police detention; creates the concept of 'designated police stations'; makes provision for the appointment of 'custody officers' and details their duties; prescribes general responsibilities in relation to detained persons; creates a system of reviewing the detention of persons held in police custody; imposes limitations in respect of persons held without charge; details the circumstances when a person may be detained after charge and provides a miscellany of other associated issues relating to persons in police custody.

Q: What are the principal aims of the provisions of the Act so far as relates to detention?
A: To introduce a 'necessity principle' in respect of a person's detention whether charged or not; to ensure that persons in police detention are dealt with diligently and expeditiously; and that persons held in police detention are treated fairly and without oppression. In addition the detention provisions make police officers accountable for their actions and decisions in respect of detained persons.

Q: When will a person be deemed to be in police detention for the purposes of the Act?
A: If:

(a) he has been taken to a police station after being arrested for an offence; or after being arrested under section 14 of the Prevention of Terrorism (Temporary Provisions) Act 1989 or under paragraph 6 of Schedule 5 to that act by an examining officer who is a constable, or

(b) he is arrested at a police station after attending voluntarily at the station or accompanying a constable to it, and is detained there or is detained elsewhere in the charge of a constable, except that a person who is at a court after being charged is not in police detention for those purposes (section 118(2)).

For the purposes of Part IV of the Act, which contains the detention provisions, a person who returns to a police station to answer to his bail or is arrested under section 46A of the Act (failure to answer police bail) shall be treated as arrested for an offence and the offence in connection with which he was granted bail shall be deemed to be that offence.

This qualifying provision introduced by the Criminal Justice and Public Order Act 1994 removes any doubt about the status of a person who returns to a police station to surrender to his bail or is arrested for failing to surrender to a police station when bailed. In both sets of circumstances the person is in police detention for the original offence.

Q: Is the period of a person's detention in police custody controlled?
A: The Act distinguishes between the grounds for which a person may be held without charge and those which will allow detention to continue after charge. If at any time a custody officer becomes aware that the grounds for the detention of a person have ceased to apply; and is not aware of any other grounds on which the continued detention of that person could be justified, it shall be the duty of the custody officer to order his immediate release from custody, unless the person is unlawfully at large (section 34(2) and (4)).

Q: If a person is arrested without warrant for a non-arrestable offence solely on the grounds that he refused to disclose his name and address and, on being accepted into custody decides that he will, after all, supply these details, is the custody officer bound to release him?
A: Yes. The grounds for his detention have ceased to apply and unless the custody officer is aware of any other grounds to justify his further detention he must release him.

Q: If a person is taken to a police station under arrest without warrant solely because he has failed to supply his personal details and there is sufficient evidence to charge him, can a charge be preferred without his identity etc being known?
A: Yes. Section 38(1) clearly contemplates a charge being preferred

in such circumstances. If after he has been charged, his personal details become known, the custody officer must release him under the provisions of section 34 because the grounds of his detention have ceased to apply, unless, of course, other grounds exist to justify his further detention.

Q: What procedure must be utilised when the grounds of detention have ceased to apply?

A: In such circumstances the person shall be released without bail unless it appears to the custody officer:

(a) that there is need for further investigation of any matter in connection with which he was detained at any time during the period of his detention; or

(b) that proceedings may be taken against him in respect of any such matter, and if it so appears, he shall be released on bail (section 34(5)).

This provision may be equated with the need to await the outcome of further inquiries being made, witnesses being interviewed etc or until the result of forensic or similar examination of articles is known or to evaluate any alibi supplied by the detainee. In addition, the provision enables a person to be bailed to appear at a police station at a later date in order that a decision may be made whether or not he should be prosecuted.

Q: What do the expressions 'designated police station' and 'custody officer' entail?

A: Chief officers of police for each police area are bound to designate police stations in their respective areas which are to be used for the purpose of detaining arrested persons. A 'designated police station' is such a police station and, subject to a number of exceptions, an arrested person must always be taken and detained in such a station (section 35).

'Custody officers' of at least the rank of sergeant must be appointed for each designated police station (section 36). Officers holding such posts have, in effect, a statutory job description involving a number of mandatory and discretionary statutory responsibilities. However, the Act does recognise that a custody officer will not always be readily available at every second of the day and accordingly provides that an officer of any rank may perform the functions of a custody officer at a designated police station if a custody officer is not readily available to perform them (section 36(4)).

Q: In respect of the custody officer's functions which may be performed by an officer 'of any rank' could the person investigating the offence for which the person has been arrested fall into that category?

A: To ensure that a conflict of interests does not arise and to make certain that impartiality is preserved, none of the functions of the custody officer in relation to a person shall be performed by an officer who, at the time when the function falls to be performed is involved in the investigation of an offence for which that person is in police detention at that time (section 36(5)).

This broad principle is subject to the further provisions of section 36 applying to non-designated police stations and to those occasions when a detained person is, for one reason or another, removed from the custody officer's immediate care (section 39(2)).

Although avoiding conflict of interests and impartiality are paramount, the custody officer is afforded some leeway in the performance of some duties under the Act or code of practice which may be regarded as investigative by their very nature; carrying out identification procedures or carrying out the procedures contained in section 7 of the Road Traffic Act 1988 (section 36(6)).

Q: Upon arrest a person may, in some circumstances, be taken to a 'non-designated police station'. What procedures must be implemented at the police station in such an eventuality?

A: The functions in relation to him which at a designated police station would be the functions of a custody officer shall be performed:

(a) by an officer who is not involved in the investigation of an offence for which he is in police detention, if such an officer is readily available; and

(b) if no such officer is readily available, by the officer who took him to the station or any other officer (section 36(7)).

Additionally, in such circumstances, the officer who took him to the station and who is to perform the functions of a custody officer shall, as soon as is practicable, inform an officer of at least the rank of inspector at a designated police station that he is to so act (section 36(9) and (10)).

Reference in the provisions of the Act following section 36(8) to 'custody officer' includes those officers who are performing the functions of a custody officer by virtue of the fact that a custody officer is not readily available (section 36(4)) or by the officer who takes a person to a non-designated police station (section 36(7)).

Q: What responsibilities in respect of a person's continued detention are placed on a custody officer when an arrested person arrives at a police station?

A: He must decide whether there is sufficient evidence to charge the person. The Act stipulates that where a person is arrested for an offence:

(i) without a warrant; or

(ii) under a warrant not endorsed for bail,

the custody officer at each police station where he is detained after his arrest shall determine whether he has before him sufficient evidence to charge that person with the offence for which he was arrested and may detain him at the police station for such period as is necessary to enable him to do so (section 37(1)).

The duty imposed on a custody officer by this provision must be carried out as soon as is practicable after a person arrives at a police station, or in the case of a person arrested at a police station, as soon as is practicable after the arrest.

In the event of the custody officer deciding that there is sufficient evidence to charge, the person must be charged or released without charge, on bail or otherwise. If released on bail and a decision as to proceedings has not been taken, the person must be informed of this.

If the person is not in a fit state to be dealt with, for example due to him being under the influence of drink, violent, or in threatening rage or temper, or perhaps hallucinating on drugs, he may be kept in police detention until he is fit to be dealt with; his detention being reviewed by the 'review officer' in the interim period to determine whether he is yet in a fit state to be released (section 37(7)-(9)).

If the person is charged, the procedures detailed in section 38 of the Act must be implemented and, in particular, the custody officer must decide whether the person's continued detention is necessary.

Q: May the police detain a person in respect of whom there is insufficient evidence to charge?

A: A conditional yes.

If the custody officer determines that he does not have such evidence before him, the person arrested shall be released either on bail or without bail, unless the custody officer has reasonable grounds for believing that his detention without being charged is necessary to secure or preserve evidence relating to an offence for which he is under arrest or to obtain such evidence by questioning him, in which case he may authorise the person to be kept in police detention. Upon making such an authorisation the custody officer must make a written record of the grounds for the person's detention in the presence of the detainee who must also be informed of the grounds. The obligations in respect of the detainee being present and apprised do not apply where the person is at that time:

(a) incapable of understanding what is said to him;
(b) violent or likely to become violent; or
(c) in urgent need of medical attention (section 37(2)-(6)).

While the Act recognises that detention without charge is permissible in order to conduct further enquiries or obtain evidence by questioning the suspect, the Act and the relevant code of practice prescribe conditions designed to ensure the fair treatment of the suspect and that any interview is not conducted in oppressive circumstances.

Q: For how long may a person be detained without charge?

A: As a general rule 24 hours but in cases of 'serious arrestable offences' this may be extended up to 36 hours on the authority of an officer of the rank of superintendent or above; or beyond such period by a warrant of further detention issued by a magistrates' court, or an extension to it; again granted after magisterial examination.

Q: Is there a maximum limit for which a person may be detained without charge?

A: Yes. While research shows that 98 per cent of all arrested persons are released within 24 hours, prior to the Act coming into force there was no precise limitation on how long a person could be held without charge. The only controlling influence was the possibility of a writ of *habeas corpus* being applied for to a High Court Judge. The Act ensures that a person cannot be detained without charge for more than 96 hours.

Such lengthy detention may only be achieved following recurring reviews not least of which are those touched upon in the preceding question. On each and every occasion a person's detention without charge is reviewed; the reviewing authority be he 'review officer', superintendent or magistrate must be satisfied, amongst other things, that the investigation is being conducted diligently and expeditiously and that further detention is warranted.

Q: Once a person in police detention has been charged, what provisions exist in respect of the person's continued detention?

A: His continued detention is governed by the 'necessity principle' which the Act embodies. More specifically the Act dictates that where a person arrested for an offence otherwise than under a warrant endorsed for bail is charged with an offence, the custody officer shall subject to section 25 of the Criminal Justice and Public Order Act 1994 order his release from police detention, either on bail or without bail, unless:

(a) if the person arrested is not an arrested juvenile:
   (i) his name or address cannot be ascertained or the custody officer has reasonable grounds for doubting whether a name or address furnished by him as his name or address is his real name or address;
   (ii) the custody officer has reasonable grounds for believing that the person arrested will fail to appear in Court to answer bail;
   (iii) in the case of a person arrested for an imprisonable offence, the custody officer has grounds for believing that the detention of the person arrested is necessary to prevent him committing an offence;
   (iv) in the case of a person arrested for an offence which is not an imprisonable offence the custody officer has reasonable grounds for believing that the detention of the person arrested is necessary to prevent him from causing physical injury to any other person or from causing loss of or damage to property;
   (v) the custody officer has reasonable grounds for believing that the detention of the person arrested is necessary to prevent him from interfering with the administration of justice or with the investigation of offences or of a particular offence; or
   (vi) the custody officer has reasonable grounds for believing that the detention of the person arrested is necessary for his own protection.
(b) if he is an arrested juvenile:
   (i) any of the requirements of paragraph (a) above is satisfied; or
   (ii) the custody officer has reasonable grounds for believing that he ought to be detained in his own interests (section 38(1)).

The criteria mentioned in this provision are readily identifiable with those operated by the courts in considering applications for bail and thus the provision ensures that police and magisterial procedures are similar. This is made clear by section 38(2A) which provides that the custody officer in taking the decisions required by section

38(1)(a) and (b) above (except (a)(i) and (vi) and (b)(ii) shall have regard to the same considerations as those which a court is required to have regard to in taking the corresponding decisions under paragraph 2 of Part 1 of the Bail Act 1976.

However, it will be noted that the foregoing apply to all charges irrespective of how grave they may be. The Act does not distinguish between say theft and murder for the purposes of the provision but obviously detention being necessary for the detainee's own protection is more relevant to the latter than it is to the former.

Reference in the section to a juvenile being detained in his own interests contemplates matters beyond detention being necessary for his own protection. Falling within the scope of the provision would be the case of an arrested juvenile who is reported as being missing from home being detained until his parents arrive to collect him or that of a juvenile who is exposed to moral danger.

If not released in accordance with the provisions of section 38(1), the custody officer may authorise him to be kept in police detention and must, as soon as practicable, make a written record of the grounds for the detention (section 38(2) and (3)). The written record shall be made in the presence of the person charged who at that time shall be informed of the grounds of his detention unless the person is:

(a) incapable of understanding what is said to him;
(b) violent or likely to become violent; or
(c) in urgent need of medical attention (section 38(4) and (5))

Q: What are the provisions referred to which are contained in section 25 of the Criminal Justice and Public Order Act 1994?

A: The section removes the right to bail of persons with previous convictions for particular offences who are charged with repeats of those offences.

Section 25(1) and (2) provide that a person who in any proceedings has been charged with or convicted of an offence of murder, attempted murder, manslaughter, rape or attempted rape, shall not be granted bail in those proceedings if that person has been previously convicted by or before a court in any part of the United Kingdom of any such offence or of culpable homicide and, in the case of a previous conviction of manslaughter or of culpable homicide, if he was then sentenced to imprisonment or, if he was then a child or young person, to long-term detention under any of the relevant enactments.

The section applies whether or not an appeal is pending against conviction or sentence.

In section 25(5), the terms conviction and relevant enactments are further defined. Conviction includes:

(a) a finding that a person is not guilty by reason of insanity;
(b) a finding under section 4A(3) of the Criminal Procedure (Insanity) Act 1964 (cases of unfitness to plead) that a person did the act or made the omission charged against him; and
(c) a conviction of an offence for which an order is made placing the offender on probation or discharging him absolutely or conditionally.

The 'relevant enactment' means:

(a) as respects England and Wales, section 53(2) of the Children and Young Persons' Act 1933;
(b) as respects Scotland, sections 205 and 206 of the Criminal Procedure (Scotland) Act 1975;
(c) as respects Northern Ireland, section 73(2) of the Children and Young Persons (Northern Ireland) Act 1968.

It is also interesting to note that a defendant need not be granted bail if he is charged with an indictable offence or an offence triable either way and it appears to the court that he was on bail in criminal proceedings on the date of the offence.

Q: Do any special provisions exist in respect of juveniles detained after charge?

A: Yes. There has been considerable discussion regarding the interpretation of the word 'impracticable' which was contained in the original provision of the Act.

The custody officer was apparently very restricted in the way he dealt with a juvenile who persistently offended and escaped from local authority accommodation. In the case of *R v Chief Constable of Cambridgeshire ex parte M* (1990) it was decided that if the custody officer was not satisfied with the proposed arrangements of the local authority for the secure detention of the juvenile he was entitled to refuse to transfer him into the care of the local authority.

This was particularly so if the only accommodation available for the detention of a juvenile is insufficient to avoid the very consequences which led to the original decision to refuse him bail.

The decision of the court has been reinforced somewhat by the substitution of a new section 38(6) by the provisions of section 59 of the Criminal Justice Act 1991.

The section as further amended by the Criminal Justice and Public

Order Act 1994 now provides that where a custody officer authorises an arrested juvenile to be kept in police detention under section 38(1), the custody officer shall, unless he certifies:

(a) that by reason of such circumstances as are specified in the certificate, it is impracticable to do so; or

(b) in the case of an arrested juvenile who has attained the age of 12 years, that no secure accommodation is available and that keeping him in other local authority accommodation would not be adequate to protect the public from serious harm from him,

secure that the arrested juvenile is moved to local authority accommodation.

The certificate must be produced to the court at which he next appears (section 38(7)).

Q: Who is responsible for persons held in police detention?

A: It is the duty of the custody officer to ensure:

(a) that all persons in police detention at that station are treated in accordance with the Act and any code of practice issued under it and relating to the treatment of persons in police detention; and

(b) that all matters relating to such persons which are required by the Act or by such codes of practice to be recorded are recorded in the custody records relating to such persons (section 39(1)).

Q: Can the custody officer be held responsible for a prisoner while he is in the custody of the investigator or some other person?

A: The custody officer does not have vicarious liability. If the custody officer transfers or permits the transfer of a person in police detention:

(a) to the custody of a police officer investigating an offence for which that person is in police detention; or

(b) to the custody of an officer who has charge of that person outside the police station, the custody officer shall cease in relation to that person to be responsible for the duties specified in section 39(1). In such eventuality it becomes the duty of the officer to whom the transfer is made to ensure that the prisoner is dealt with in accordance with the Act and the relevant codes of practice (section 39(2)).

The transfer of responsibility can thus be associated with a prisoner being put in the charge of another police officer to be interviewed about the offence for which he is under arrest, or in respect of any other matter; to be interviewed as a witness in respect of an earlier incident; or those instances where a prisoner is taken out of the police station in the custody of another officer to be taken to court, hospital or to identify houses which he has burgled, or to indicate where stolen property is located etc.

As the provision is concerned with accountability some formality of the transfer of responsibility is necessary; a matter emphasised by section 39(3) of the Act which provides that if the person detained is subsequently returned to the custody of the custody officer it shall be the duty of the officer investigating the offence to report to the custody officer as to the manner in which this section and the codes of practice have been complied with while that person was in his custody.

Q: The custody officer is responsible for making many decisions concerning persons in police detention, not least of which are those concerning whether a person should be charged or released, on bail or otherwise. What is there to prevent a higher ranking officer overruling him?
A: The Act contemplates such an eventuality by providing that where:

- (a) an officer of higher rank than the custody officer gives directions relating to a person in police detention; and
- (b) the directions are at variance: (i) with any decision made or action taken by the custody officer in the performance of a duty imposed on him under this Act; or (ii) with any decision or action which would, but for the directions, have been made or taken by him in the performance of such a duty, the custody officer shall refer the matter at once to an officer of the rank of superintendent or above who is responsible for the police station for which the custody officer is acting as custody officer (section 39(6)).

Q: Once it has been decided to keep a person in custody, by whom must his detention be reviewed?
A: In the case of a person who has been arrested and charged, by the custody officer; and in the case of a person who has been arrested but not charged, by an officer of at least the rank of inspector who has not been directly involved in the investigation. Such officer is referred to in the Act as the 'review officer' (section 41(1) and (2)).

Q: What are the review officer's specific responsibilities?

A: He is responsible under section 40 of the Act (or, in terrorist cases, under Schedule 3 to the Prevention of Terrorism (Temporary Provisions) Act 1989) for determining whether or not a person's detention continues to be necessary. Before conducting a review, the review officer must ensure that the detained person is reminded of his entitlement to free legal advice as is mentioned in section 6 of Code C. It is the responsibility of the review officer to ensure that all such reminders are noted in the custody record. In addition, a record shall be made as soon as is practicable of the outcome of each review and application for a warrant of further detention or its extension.

Q: Has a detained person any right to make representations when the statutory reviews are undertaken?

A: Yes. Before determining whether to authorise a person's continued detention the review officer shall give:

(a) that person (unless he is asleep); or

(b) any solicitor or an appropriate adult representing him who is available at the time of the review, an opportunity to make representations to him about the detention. The representations may be made orally or in writing but the review officer may refuse to receive oral representations from the prisoner if he considers that the person is unfit to do so by reason of his condition or behaviour (section 40(12)-(14) and code of practice).

The possibility of a review officer having to reason with drunken and truculent prisoners is thus obviated. The relevant code of practice affords the review officer a discretion to allow other people having an interest in the detainee's welfare to make representations about the detention. The same people may make representations to the officer determining whether further detention should be authorised under section 42 of the Act or under Schedule 3 to the Prevention of Terrorism (Temporary Provisions) act 1989.

After hearing any representations, the review officer or officer determining whether further detention should be authorised shall note any comment the person may make if the decision is to keep him in detention. The officer shall not put specific questions to the suspect regarding his involvement in any offence, nor in respect of any comments he may make in response to the decision to keep him in detention. Such an exchange is likely to constitute an interview as defined in the Code of Practice and would require the associated safeguards included in section 11 of Code C. Any written representations shall be retained.

Q: What should the review officer do if the review time falls half way through the rest period?

A: A note of guidance to the code of practice advises that if the detained person is likely to be asleep at the latest time when a review of detention or an authorisation of continued detention may take place, the appropriate officer should bring it forward so that the detained person may make representations without being woken up.

Q: How often must reviews be undertaken by the review officer?

A: The first review shall not be later than six hours after the detention was first authorised; the second review shall not be later than nine hours after the first; subsequent reviews shall be at intervals of not more than nine hours (section 40(3)).

Before conducting a review the review officer must ensure that the detained person is reminded of his entitlement to free legal advice. It is the responsibility of the review officer to ensure that all such reminders are noted in the custody record. The Act recognises that in some circumstances it will be neither practicable nor appropriate for a review to be carried out. A review may be postponed if, having regard to all the circumstances prevailing at the latest time specified for it, it is not practicable to carry out the review at that time.

More specifically, a review may be postponed if:

(i) at that time the person in detention is being questioned by a police officer and the review officer is satisfied that an interruption of the questioning for the purpose of carrying out the review would prejudice the investigation in connection with which he is being questioned; or

(ii) at that time no review officer is readily available. Where a review is postponed it must be carried out as soon as practicable. A postponement does not delay the time of any subsequent reviews and the review officer must record any reasons for postponement on the detainee's custody record with the extent of the delay (section 40(4)-(7) and Code C).

Q: If a review of a person's detention is postponed say, until eight hours after he has first been accepted into custody, when must the next review take place?

A: The postponement has no effect. Accordingly it must take place no later than 15 hours from the relevant time.

Q: If a review takes place after a person has been in detention for only three hours, the next review must take place before the twelfth hour. Is that correct? A: Yes.

Q: In conducting the review of a person who is detained without charge, what criteria must the reviewing inspector apply?

A: He must apply the principles detailed in section 37(1)-(6) of the Act (duties of a custody officer before charge), ie review whether there is sufficient evidence to charge, whether detention is necessary to secure or preserve evidence, or obtain such evidence by questioning him. The review officer must similarly record the grounds for authorising continued detention and notify the detainee of them unless he is incapable of understanding what is said to him, is violent or likely to become violent or is in urgent need of medical attention.

Q: When reviewing the detention of a person who has been charged, to what issues must the custody officer address his mind?

A: The same issues which he considered immediately after the person was charged, ie those matters defined in section 38(1)-(6) of the Act. The 'necessity principle' is applicable to all reviews and thus upon conducting a review a custody officer must release the person unless the prisoner's name or address are unknown or he, the custody officer, has reasonable grounds to believe that detention is necessary because there are reasonable grounds for believing the person will fail to appear at court, in the case of a person arrested for an imprisonable offence, detention is necessary to prevent him committing further offences, in respect of a person arrested for a non-imprisonable offence the custody officer believes with reasonable grounds that detention is necessary to prevent him from causing physical injury to any other person or from causing loss of or damage to property, there are reasonable grounds for believing that detention is necessary to prevent him from interfering with the administration of justice or with the investigation of offences or of a particular offence or detention is necessary for his own protection.

If the person is a juvenile, any of the foregoing considerations apply or the custody officer has reasonable grounds for believing that he ought to be detained in his own interests (section 38(1) to (6).

It is reiterated that in taking the decisions required by section 38(1)(a) and (b) (except (a)(i) and (vi) and (b)(ii) the custody officer shall have regard to the same considerations as those which a court is required to have regard to in taking the corresponding decisions under paragraph 2 of Part 1 of the Bail Act 1976 (section 38(2A))

Q: Are the police entitled to grant bail to a person subject to conditions?

A: Yes. Section 47(1) of the Police and Criminal Evidence Act 1984 (as amended) provides that a release on bail of a person under Part

IV of the Act shall be a release on bail granted in accordance with sections 3, 3A, 5 and 5A of the Bail Act 1976 as they apply to bail granted by a constable.

Section 47(1A) stipulates that the normal powers to impose conditions of bail shall be available to him where a custody officer releases a person on bail under section 38(1) (including that subsection as applied by section 40(10)) but not in any other cases.

The expression "the normal powers to impose conditions of bail" has the same meaning as that given in section 3(6) of the Bail Act 1976. Amendments have accordingly been made to the Bail Act 1976 and to the Magistrates' Courts act 1980 to reflect the extension of the custody officer's powers to impose conditions of bail and for those conditions to be varied by a custody officer or by a magistrates' court.

Prior to these amendments, the police were restricted in imposing conditions of bail to instances where a surety or the provision of a security could be required.

The new provisions permit conditions to be imposed if they appear necessary to secure his surrender to custody, does not commit an offence whilst on bail and does not interfere with witnesses or otherwise obstruct the course of justice whether in relation to himself or any other person. There is no power to require a person to live at a bail hostel.

By virtue of section 3(8) of the Bail Act 1976, where a custody officer has granted bail in criminal proceedings he or another custody officer serving at the same police station may, at the request of the person to whom it was granted, vary the conditions of bail; and in doing so he may impose conditions or more onerous conditions.

Section 5 of the Bail Act has necessarily been amended to reflect the new situation by requiring the reasons for imposing or varying conditions of bail to be recorded by the custody officer on the person's custody record. A note of the decision must also be supplied to the person bailed.

Section 5(3) as amended provides that where a custody officer, in relation to any person:

(a) imposes conditions in granting bail in criminal proceedings, or
(b) varies any conditions of bail or imposes conditions in respect of bail in criminal proceedings, the custody officer shall, with a view to enabling that person to consider requesting him or another custody officer, or making an application to a magistrates' court, to vary the conditions, give reasons for imposing or varying the conditions.

Section 5(4) directs that a custody officer who is, by virtue of section 5(3) required to give reasons for his decision, shall include a note of those reasons in the custody record and shall give a copy of that note to the person in relation to whom the decision was taken.

The powers of the court in relation to the imposition of bail conditions by the police has not been overlooked and a supervisory function has been grafted into the Magistrates' Courts Act 1980. Section 43B(1) of that Act provides that where a custody officer :

(a) grants bail to any person under Part VI of the Police and Criminal Evidence Act 1984 in criminal proceedings and imposes conditions, or

(b) varies, in relation to any person, conditions of bail in criminal proceedings under section 3(8) of the Bail Act 1976, a magistrates' court may, on application by or on behalf of that person, grant bail or vary the conditions.

Where such an application is made and the court grants bail and imposes conditions or if it varies the conditions, it may impose more onerous conditions (section 43B (2)). By virtue of section 43B(3) on determining an application under section 43B(1) the court shall remand the applicant, in custody or on bail in accordance with the determination and, where the court withholds bail or grants bail the grant of bail made by the custody officer shall lapse.

As the person bailed has further access to the magistrates' court, a similar provision exists in relation to the prosecutor who, by virtue of section 5B of the Bail Act 1976, may apply to the court for bail to be varied, withheld or for conditions to be imposed.

Q: What is there to prevent a review officer's decision being overruled by an officer of higher rank?
A: An identical provision to that which prevents a custody officer's decision or intention being overruled. The variance must be referred to an officer of the rank of superintendent or above who is responsible for the police station.

Q: What are the precise provisions regarding the length of time a person may be detained without charge?
A: As a general principle for not more than 24 hours but this period may be extended by a superintendent's authorisation of continued detention for a period of up to 36 hours (section 42) or by a warrant of further detention for a further period of 36 hours (section 43). The persons referred to in the previous answer may also make representations to the officer determining whether further detention should be

authorised under section 42 of the Act or under Schedule 3 to the Prevention of Terrorism (Temporary Provisions) Act 1989.

An extension to the warrant of further detention may be obtained to continue detention for up to a further 36 hours (section 44), provided that the total period does not extend beyond 96 hours. Subject to his detention being lawfully extended a person who has not been charged at the expiry of twenty-four hours shall be released at that time either on bail or without bail (section 41(7)).

Q: From which time is a period of detention calculated?
A: This will be dependent on where the person was arrested, whether he was arrested in one police area and transferred to another and if he was questioned about the offence in the first area after being arrested and other similar issues (section 41).

Q: From when will the period of detention be calculated in respect of a person who is arrested on the streets and taken to the local police station?
A: Even though that police station may not be a designated police station, the time at which he arrives at the first police station to which he is taken after his arrest (section 41(2)(d)).

Q: From when will the period of detention be calculated in respect of a person who is arrested at a police station after having attended there voluntarily or having accompanied a constable there without being arrested?
A: From the time of his arrest (section 41(2)(c)).

Q: In the case of a person arrested outside England and Wales from when will his detention period be calculated?
A: The time at which that person arrives at the first police station to which he is taken in the police area in England or Wales in which the offence for which he was arrested is being investigated; or the time 24 hours after the time of that person's entry into England and Wales, whichever is the earlier (section 41(2)(b)).

Q: A prisoner is arrested, say in Cambridgeshire, by officers of that force, having been circulated by another police force, say, Greater Manchester. He is taken to the Greater Manchester area. From when will the period of detention of this prisoner be calculated?
A: Provided he is not questioned in the area in which he is arrested in order to obtain evidence in relation to an offence for which he is arrested, the time at which the person arrives at the first police sta-

tion to which he is taken in the area in which his arrest was sought or 24 hours after his arrest, whichever is the earlier.

In the event of the person being questioned in the area where he was arrested in respect of the offence for which he was arrested, the time shall be calculated from when he arrived at the first police station to which he was taken after his arrest (section 41(2)(a),(d) and (3)).

The restriction on questioning should not be construed as applying to any questioning which took place prior to arrest, the operative words in section 41(3) being 'he is not questioned in the area...in relation to an offence for which he is arrested'. This clearly restricts the provision to questioning which takes place following arrest and not questioning prior to arrest to establish identity, ownership of a vehicle etc.

Q: A person is arrested, say, in Hampshire for a petty theft. While he is in custody for that offence it is discovered he is wanted by another police force, say, South Yorkshire, for aggravated burglary. He is subsequently taken to South Yorkshire. From when will this prisoner's detention period in respect of the aggravated burglary be calculated?
A: Twenty-four hours after the time he leaves the place where he was first detained in the first police area; or the time at which he arrives at the first police station to which he is taken in the second police area, whichever is the earlier (section 41(5)).

Q: A person has been arrested and is in police detention. While at the police station he is placed under arrest for another offence, in accordance with the requirements of section 31 of the Act. In what way, if any, does the subsequent arrest affect the time from which the person's detention is calculated?
A: It does not affect it. The time from which the period of detention is calculated is on the basis of the offence for which he was originally arrested (section 41(4)).

Q: Are any periods excluded from the period of police detention?
A: Yes. When a person who is in police detention is removed to hospital because he is in need of medical treatment, any time during which he is being questioned in hospital or on the way there or back by a police officer for the purpose of obtaining evidence relating to an offence shall be included in any period which falls to be calculated for the purposes of this Part of this Act, but any other time while he is in hospital or on his way there or back shall not be so included (section 41(6)).

Q: What rights has a detained prisoner in connection with the superintendent's decision-making process?

A: Before determining whether to authorise the keeping of a person in detention the superintendent shall give:

(a) that person; or

(b) any solicitor or appropriate adult representing him who is available at the time when it falls to the officer to determine whether to give the authorisation, an opportunity to make representations to him about the detention. Other people having an interest in the person's welfare may make representations at the superintendent's discretion.

The representations may be made either orally or in writing. The superintendent may refuse to hear oral representations from the prisoner if he considers that the detainee is unfit to make such representations by reason of his condition or behaviour.

Where continued detention is authorised, the superintendent must inform the detained person of the grounds for the continued detention and record those grounds in the person's custody record (section 42(5)-(8) and Code C). It will be noted that the superintendent's obligation is to provide an opportunity for representations to be made.

The Act and Code of Practice C demand a listening or reading role and, whilst he must notify the detainee of the grounds of detention and record his decision the section does not demand that the superintendent enters into discussions or legal argument with the prisoner or his legal representative.

Code C directs that after the review officer/officer determining further detention has listened to any representations made to him, he must make a note of anything said by the detainee where the decision made is that he should remain in custody. He must not solicit a reply and must be careful not to ask him any questions which might place the conversation within the restrictions relating to interviews.

Where an authorisation of continued detention is made and at that time the detainee has not exercised his right to have someone informed when arrested (under section 56); or his right of access to legal advice (under section 58) the superintendent:

(i) shall inform him of that right;

(ii) shall decide whether he should be permitted to exercise it;

(iii) shall record the decision in his custody record; and

(iv) if the decision is to refuse to permit the exercise of the right, shall also record the grounds for the decision in that record (section 42(9)).

Q: Can reviews be conducted over the telephone?
A: That depends on the type of review. A note of guidance advises that if in the circumstances the only practicable way of conducting a review is over the telephone then this is permissible, provided that the requirements of section 40 of the Act or of Schedule 3 to the Prevention of Terrorism (Temporary Provisions) Act 1989 are observed.

However, a review to decide whether to authorise a person's detention under section 42 of the Act must be done in person rather than on the telephone.

Q: What must happen if a person held without charge remains not charged when the superintendent's authorisation expires?
A: Unless continued detention has been authorised by a warrant of further detention, he shall be released with or without bail. Upon being released the person cannot be re-arrested for the same offence unless new evidence has come to light since his release (section 42(10)-(11)). This does not prevent an arrest for failing to surrender at a police station to police bail.

Q: In the event of a person who has not been charged being released from custody at the expiry of 24 hours, what is there to prevent him being re-arrested for the same offence?
A: This is prohibited by section 41(9), unless new evidence justifying a further arrest has come to light since his release.This does not prevent an arrest for failing to surrender at a police station to police bail.

Q: On what grounds and for how long may a superintendent authorise the keeping of a person who has not been charged beyond 24 hours?
A: If he has reasonable grounds for believing that:
- (a) the detention of that person without charge is necessary to secure or preserve evidence relating to an offence for which he is under arrest or to obtain such evidence by questioning him;
- (b) an offence for which he is under arrest is a serious arrestable offence; and
- (c) the investigation is being conducted diligently and expeditiously, he may authorise the keeping of the person in detention for a period expiring at or before 36 hours from the relevant time from which the person's detention is being calculated (section 42(1)). Even if further detention is authorised, the person's detention is still subject to the review officer's scrutiny.

All three conditions are pre-requisite to the exercise of the power. In the event of the superintendent authorising the continued detention of the person for a period less than the maximum he is permitted to authorise, he may make a subsequent authorisation (provided the necessary conditions still exist) extending the period to the maximum to which he is entitled to authorise, ie 36 hours from the time from which the prisoner's detention is being calculated (section 41(1) and (2)).

To prevent premature authorisation being given, no authorisation may be given before the second review of the person's detention has been conducted (section 42(4)). An authorisation cannot be made more than 24 hours after the relevant time of the person's detention.

In respect of a prisoner whom it is proposed to move to another police area, in determining whether or not to make an authorisation, the superintendent shall have regard to the distance and the time the journey would take (section 42(3)). This provision serves no more than a reminder to superintendents to take account of all relevant issues.

Q: When may a magistrates' court issue a warrant of further detention?
A: Where, on an application on oath made by a constable and supported by an information, the court is satisfied that there are reasonable grounds for believing that the further detention of the person to whom the application relates is justified, it may issue a warrant of further detention authorising the keeping of that person in police detention. A court may not hear an application for a warrant of further detention unless the person to whom the application relates: (a) has been furnished with a copy of the information; and (b) has been brought before the court for the hearing (section 43(1) and (3)).

For the purpose of this section a magistrates' court must comprise of two or more justices, sitting otherwise than in open court (section 45(1)).

Q: On what grounds may the justices consider the application to be justified?
A: On exactly the same grounds that a superintendent may authorise continued detention ie if satisfied that:

- (a) his detention without charge is necessary to secure or preserve evidence relating to an offence for which he is under arrest or to obtain such evidence by questioning him;
- (b) an offence for which he is under arrest is a serious arrestable offence; and
- (c) the investigation is being conducted diligently and expeditiously (section 43(4)).

Q: What legal rights has a person held in police detention in respect of an application to a magistrates' court for a warrant of further detention?
A: He must be furnished with a copy of the information and brought before the court for the hearing. Additionally the person has a right to be legally represented and, in the event of him wishing to be represented, the court must adjourn the hearing to enable him to obtain such representation (section 43(2) and (3)).

Q: Before applying for a warrant of further detention must the police have utilised a superintendent's authorisation of continued detention?
A: Not necessarily. An application may be made at any time before the expiry of 36 hours from the time his detention period is being calculated. In a case where:

(i) it is not practicable for the magistrates' court, to which the application will be made to sit at the expiry of 36 hours after the relevant time; but

(ii) the court will sit during the six hours following the end of that period, the application may be made at any time before the expiry of the said six hours.

Where the 36-hour period is breached without an application being made, but one is made under the foregoing provision within the specified six-hour period, the person may be kept in police custody. The fact that the person was so detained and the reasons for it must be recorded by the custody officer on the prisoner's custody record (section 43(5) and (6)). In the event of an application being made after the expiry of the 36 hour period and it appears to the court that it would have been reasonable for the police to have made the application before the end of that period, that court shall dismiss the application (section 43(7)). This measure effectively reinforces the responsibility of the police to deal with detention matters expeditiously at all times and discourages the police from seeking to abuse the 'six hour' rule by delaying potentially weak applications. The strength of the judicial reviews cannot be underestimated.

Q: What must a magistrates' court do if not satisfied that an application for a warrant of further detention is justified?
A: The court must refuse the application or adjourn the hearing of it until a time not later than 36 hours after the relevant time. If the court adjourns, the person may be kept in police detention during the adjournment (section 43(8) and (9)).

Q: Will a warrant of further detention automatically authorise detention for a period of 36 hours?
A: No. The period stated in a warrant of further detention shall be such period as the magistrates' court thinks fit, having regard to the evidence before it, but it shall not be longer than 36 hours.

The warrant will state the time of issue and refer to the period authorised (section 43(10)-(12)). Unless charged, a person must be released, on bail or otherwise, at the expiry of the warrant and once released a person cannot be re-arrested unless new evidence has come to light since his release (section 43(18) and (19)). This does not prevent an arrest for failing to surrender at a police station to police bail.

Q: What matters must be incorporated in an information laid for a warrant of further detention?
A: The following;

- (a) the nature of the offence for which the person to whom the application relates has been arrested;
- (b) the general nature of the evidence on which that person was arrested;
- (c) what enquiries relating to the offence have been made by the police and what further inquiries are proposed by them;
- (d) the reasons for believing the continued detention of that person to be necessary for the purposes of such further enquiries (section 43(14)).

Q: What must occur if the magistrates refuse an application for a warrant of further detention?
A: The detained person must be charged forthwith or released but he need not be released before the expiry of 24 hours from the time from which his detention is being calculated or before the expiry of any period of continued detention authorised by a superintendent (section 43(15) and (16)).

Q: Once a warrant of further detention has been refused can the police make a further application?
A: Yes, but only if it is supported by evidence which has come to light since the refusal (section 43(17)).

Q: How is an extension to a warrant of further detention obtained?
A: In an identical manner to that utilised to obtain the warrant, ie application on oath, supported by an information (section 44(1)).

Q: By what period may the magistrates extend the warrant?
A: For such period as they think fit but the period shall not be longer than 36 hours or end later than 96 hours from the relevant time of the person's detention. Once the magistrates have extended the warrant they may further extend it up to a time no later than the maximum permitted period of 96 hours upon application being made, in which case the warrant must be endorsed with details of the further extension (section 44(2) - (5)).

Q: On what grounds and in what form may an application for an extension to a warrant of further detention be made and what legal rights does the detainee have in respect of the hearing of the application?
A: Exactly the same as those applicable to the application for the warrant itself.

Q: What must happen if the magistrates' court refuses an application for an extension to a warrant of further detention?
A: The detained person must be charged or released from custody, with or without bail but he need not be released before the expiry of any period remaining for which a warrant of further detention in respect of him has been extended or further extended on a previous application under the section (section 44(7) and (8)).

It would seem, therefore, that if the magistrates refuse an initial application for an extension to a warrant of further detention the person must be charged or released and thus the magistrates, by refusing the application, cancel any time remaining in the warrant itself. It is doubtful whether Parliament intended this consequence.

Q: What records are required to be kept about reviews and extensions?
A: The code of practice directs that a record shall be made as soon as practicable of the outcome of each review and application for a warrant of further detention or its extension.

Q: Will the courts be sitting 24 hours a day in order to issue warrants of further detention?
A: No. A 'Note of Guidance' in the code of practice states that an application for a warrant of further detention or its extension should be made between 10 am and 9pm and if possible during normal court hours. It will not be practicable to arrange for a court to sit specially outside the hours of 10am to 9pm. If it appears possible that a special sitting may be needed (either at a weekend, Bank/Public Holiday or

on a weekday outside normal court hours but between 10am and 9pm) then the clerk to the justices should be given notice and informed of this possibility, while the court is sitting if possible.

Q: Times seem vitally important to a person's detention. Is the Act to a minute or two?

A: Any reference in Part IV of the Act (which relates to detention) to a period of time or a time of day is to be treated as approximate only.

Q: What procedure must be followed in bringing before a magistrates' court a person who has been charged with an offence and kept in police custody?

A: If he is to be brought before a magistrates' court for the petty sessions area in which the police station at which he was charged is situated, he shall be brought before such a court as soon as is practicable and in any event not later than the first sitting after he is charged with the offence.

If no magistrates' court for that area is due to sit either on the day on which he is charged or on the next day, the custody officer for the police station at which he was charged shall inform the clerk to the justices for the area that there is a person in police detention awaiting to be brought before the court (section 46(2) and (3)).

If the person charged is to be brought before a magistrates' court for a petty sessions area other than that in which the police station at which he was charged is situated, he shall be removed to that area as soon as is practicable and brought before such a court as soon as is practicable after his arrival in the area and in any event not later than the first sitting of a magistrates' court for that area after his arrival in the area (section 46(4)).

If no magistrates' court for that area is due to sit either on the day on which he arrived in the area or on the next day:

(a) he shall be taken to a police station in the area; and
(b) the custody officer at that station shall inform the clerk to the justices for the area that there is a person in the area to whom subsection (4) applies (section 46(4)).

In cases where no court is sitting either on the day the person is charged or the next day or the day the person arrives in the police area or the next day, as the case may be; upon being informed of the person's detention the clerk to the justices must arrange for a court to sit not later than the day following the day he was charged or the day he arrived in the area. If such day is Christmas Day, Good Friday or Sunday, the clerk to the justices must arrange a court to sit on the next day which is not one of those days (section 46(7) and (8)). If for example a person is charged on a Saturday and cannot be brought before a court on that day, then although a court may sit each Monday, it is nonetheless the duty of the custody officer to inform the clerk to the justices of the circumstances.

Q: Can a person who has been released on bail in order that further investigations may be made be re-arrested without warrant before he is due to answer to his bail at the police station?
A: Yes, provided new evidence justifying a further arrest has come to light since his release. The provisions of the Act apply to him as though he were arrested for the first time (section 47(2) and (7)).

Q: What procedures exist in respect of a person granted bail subject to a condition to attend at a police station?
A: The person must attend the police station unless he receives notice in writing from the custody officer that his attendance at the police station is not required. It is reiterated that for the purposes of Part IV of the Act, which contains the detention provisions, a person who returns to a police station to answer to his bail or is arrested under section 46A of the Act (failure to answer police bail) shall be treated as arrested for an offence and the offence in connection with which he was granted bail shall be deemed to be that offence.

This qualifying provision introduced by the Criminal Justice and Public Order Act 1994 removes any doubt about the status of a person who returns to a police station to surrender to his bail or is arrested for failing to surrender to a police station when bailed. In both sets of circumstances the person is in police detention for the original offence.

Q: What provisions apply in respect of the person who fails to attend at a police station in answer to police bail?
A: Section 46A of the Act was inserted by the Criminal Justice and Public Order Act 1994 to lay to rest the debate as to whether a person could be arrested for the 'original offence' if he failed to surrender after being bailed to return to a police station.

The section provides that a constable may arrest without a warrant any person who, having been released on bail under this Part of this Act subject to a duty to attend at that police station, fails to attend at that police station at the time appointed for him to do so (section 46A(1)).

A person so arrested shall be taken to the police station appointed as the place 'at which he is to surrender to custody as soon as practicable after the arrest' (section 46A(2)).

For the purposes of section 30 (subject to the obligation in section 46A(2)) and section 31, an arrest under this section shall be treated as an arrest for an offence.

Where a person who has been granted bail and either has attended at the police station in accordance with the grant of bail or has been arrested under section 46A is detained at a police station, any time during which he was in police detention prior to being granted bail shall be included in calculating the period for which he may be detained (section 47(6)).

Q: Does the Act in any way affect three day remands in custody to police cells made in respect of a person charged with an offence?

A: Yes. The Act amends section 128 of the Magistrates' Courts Act 1980 and adds the following subsection (8): 'Where a person is committed to detention at a police station under section 128(7):

(a) he shall not be kept in such detention unless there is a need for him to be so detained for the purposes of enquiries into other offences;

(b) if kept in detention, he shall be brought back before the magistrates' court which committed him as soon as that need ceases;

(c) he shall be treated as a person in police detention to whom the duties under section 39 of the Police and Criminal Evidence Act 1984 (responsibilities in relation to persons detained) relate;

(d) his detention shall be subject to a periodic review at the times set out in section 40 of that Act (review of police detention)'.

The effect of the provision is two-fold. Firstly a person remanded under the provision will be treated as though he was a person detained after arrest and secondly the three day period will be a maximum rather than a defined period. The length of detention will be subject to constant review and continuing examination on the criterion of the need for him to be so detained for the purposes of enquiries into other offences. Once this need no longer exists he must be brought back before the court. A juvenile may be remanded to police custody for a period of 24 hours.

Q: How can police conduct in respect of the Act's provisions concerning detention be scrutinised?

A: Every Annual Report of a Chief Constable under the Police Act 1964 or Annual Report made by the Commissioner of Police of the Metropolis must contain information about the following matters:

(a) the number of persons kept in police detention for more than 24 hours and subsequently released without charge;
(b) the number of applications for warrants of further detention and the results of the applications; and
(c) in relation to each warrant of further detention: (i) the period of further detention authorised by it; (ii) the period which the person named in it spent in police detention on its authority; and (iii) whether he was charged or released without charge.

CHAPTER 5

QUESTIONING AND TREATMENT OF PERSONS BY POLICE

A substantial proportion of the provisions of the Police and Criminal Evidence Act 1984 and the Codes of Practice are directed specifically towards the manner in which persons are dealt with while in police custody and the various processes utilised to gather evidence. A balance is sought to preserve the dignity and the rights of the individual whilst affording adequate provision to regularise and authorise the obtaining of admissible evidence.

Code of Practice

Q: The Act makes detailed provisions in respect of the detention and treatment of persons by police officers. How may the police be disciplined in respect of those measures?
A: The Code of Practice for the Detention, Treatment and Questioning of Persons by Police Officers makes adequate provision in respect of the rights and liberty of the individual. Failure to comply with any part of the code of practice may breach the police discipline code.

In many respects the code of practice reiterates the provisions of the Act itself, thus rendering a police officer liable to the risk of discipline proceedings for not complying with the Act's procedural requirements.

Q: What general matters are covered in the code of practice for the protection of persons?
A: The code stipulates that all persons in custody must be dealt with

expeditiously and released as soon as the need for detention has ceased to apply.

All the functions detailed in the Code must be carried out as soon as practicable by the custody officer. If a delay arises the codes are not breached if it is justifiable and every effort was made to avoid it. Any delay must be recorded in the custody record with reasons.

A note of guidance explains that on occasions there are bound to be delays especially when processing a number of persons who may have been arrested at a football match or following a drugs raid. Delays may also be occasioned if interview rooms are occupied or efforts to get hold of solicitors or appropriate adults are being met with some difficulty.

Q: How should people with apparent mental disabilities be treated?
A: Where an officer believes or if he is told by someone else in good faith that a person he is dealing with may be mentally disordered or mentally handicapped or mentally incapable of understanding what the officer is saying to him or his replies, he must be treated as a mentally disordered or mentally handicapped person for the purposes of Code C.

A note of guidance provides that the generic term ''mental disorder'' is used throughout the code. ''Mental disorder'' is defined by the Mental Health Act 1983 as ''mental illness, arrested or incomplete development of mind, psychopathic disorder and any other disorder or disability of mind.'' It should be noted that ''mental disorder'' is different to ''mental handicap'' although the two forms of disorder are dealt with similarly throughout the code.

Q: What arrangements must be made for juveniles?
A: A person shall be treated as a juvenile if he appears to be under 17 and there is nothing to indicate that he is older.

Q: Does the Code of Practice cater for those who have sight, speech or hearing difficulties?
A: Persons appearing to be blind or seriously visually handicapped, deaf, unable to read or speak or unable to speak properly because of a speech impediment must be acknowledged as having such difficulties and dealt with accordingly.

Q: How does the Code of Practice deal with those who might not be in a position to understand what is going on around them?
A: Where a person is, at the time, incapable of understanding what is

being said to him or he is either violent or likely to become so, or is in urgent need of medical attention, the information he must be given need not be given whilst he is in that condition but as soon as practicable thereafter

Q: Does the Code of Practice apply to everyone detained in police custody?

A: With the exception of persons who fall into the following categories of prisoner:

(a) those arrested in Scotland under the cross-border powers under section 137(2) of the Criminal Justice and Public Order Act 1994;

(b) those arrested under section 3(5) of the Asylum and Immigrations Appeals Act 1993 for fingerprinting;

(c) those served with a notice telling them that they have been detained under the Immigration Act 1971;

(d) prisoners either convicted or on remand in police cells held there on behalf of the prison service under the provisions of the Imprisonment (Temporary Provisions) Act 1980;

Code C is of application to all persons in custody at police stations whether or not they have been arrested for an offence. It applies also to those who have been taken to a police station as a place of safety under sections 135 and 136 of the Mental Health act 1983. It is important to realise, however, that persons falling within categories (a) to (d) above are covered by sections 8 and 9 of Code C which incorporate the conditions for detention and treatment of detained persons. They must,in fact, be considered as the minimum standards which must be applied.

Section 15 of Code C which relates to reviews and extensions of detention only applies to persons who are classed as being in police detention within the true definition of the expression i.e. those arrested for an offence whether brought to the police station afterwards or arrested there after having attended voluntarily.

Persons in custody include those prisoners detained under section 14 of the Prevention of Terrorism (Temporary Provisions) Act 1989 or under paragraph 6 of Schedule 5 to the Act.

Q: The Act requires that a number of matters be recorded on a person's 'custody record'. What provision does the code of practice make in respect of such a document?

A: Where a person is arrested and taken to a police station or is arrested there after attending voluntarily, a separate custody record must be commenced and all the information which the Act and the Codes of Practice require to be recorded must be recorded in it as soon as is practicable. Where there are audio or visual recording facilities in custody suites they are not regarded as part of the custody record. Where some specific authority is required from an officer holding a specified rank e.g. the search of a person's home or the delaying of legal advice, the name and rank of the officer concerned must be noted in the custody record.

There is an exception in respect of officers who are conducting inquiries regarding people who they have arrested under the provisions of the Prevention of Terrorism (Temporary Provisions) Act 1989. Their warrant or other identifying numbers and their stations must be recorded instead.

Q: Is a solicitor allowed access to the custody record?

A: When a solicitor or appropriate adult arrives at a police station he must be allowed to inspect his client's custody record as soon as practicable. Copies of the custody record of persons released or taken to court must be supplied on request as soon as practicable. This right lasts for 12 months.

When a person leaves police detention, he, the appropriate adult or legal representative must be allowed to inspect the original custody record provided that reasonable notice is given. Any such inspection must be recorded in the custody record.

Q: Must entries in the custody record be signed to identify the person making them?

A: Yes, they must be signed and timed and, in the case of computerised custody suites entries must be timed and the operator's identification number endorsed. There is again, an exception for those dealing with terrorist offenders where warrant or other identification numbers must be used in relation to prisoners in custody under the Prevention of Terrorism (Temporary Provisions) Act 1989.

Q: What about awkward prisoners who refuse to sign the custody record?

A: Any refusal by a person to sign a custody record must be recorded, along with the time.

Q: How does the code of practice cater for an arrested person's statutory rights to have someone informed of his arrest or right to legal advice or right to consult codes of practice?

A: First of all it must be pointed out that the right to consult the codes of practice does not entitle a person to delay unreasonably any necessary investigative or administrative action while he does so. In particular the procedures under the Road Traffic Act 1988 requiring samples of blood, urine or breath need not be delayed.

The custody officer must give the person a written notice setting out the above three rights, the right to a copy of the custody record and the caution in the terms prescribed by the code. The notice must also explain the arrangements for obtaining legal advice. The custody officer must also give the person an additional written notice briefly setting out his entitlements whilst in custody. The custody officer shall ask the person to sign the custody record to acknowledge receipt of this notice and any refusal to sign must be recorded on the custody record.

A note of guidance advises that the notices should also be available in Welsh, the main ethnic minority languages and the principal European languages whenever they are likely to be helpful.

Q: What does the additional notice of entitlements contain?

A: A note of guidance prescribes its form and contents. Whilst the notice of rights sets out a person's rights under the Act and the Codes of Practice, the Notice of Entitlements lists the rights which are set out in Code C which are in addition to those detailed in the notice of rights. The form should incorporate details of permitted visits and contacts with outside parties, including specific arrangements for foreigners, the standard of comfort, food and drink, washing and toilet arrangements, clothing and medical attention and exercise where there are facilities.

The Notice of Entitlements should also detail arrangements as to interviews, appropriate adults and their involvement and the prisoner's right to make representations at those stages where his detention is subject to review.

Q: What provision exists to ensure that a person is aware of the grounds of his detention?

A: The Code reiterates the provisions of the Act. It requires the custody officer to note in the custody record anything said by the prisoner after the arresting officer's version of events has been given. He should not invite any comment from the prisoner.

Once the custody officer has decided to authorise detention, the grounds for doing so must be explained as soon as practicable and, in any event, before questioning commences. Any comment made about the decision to detain him shall be noted but a response should not be invited.

In this situation, the custody officer is in a somewhat precarious situation and needs to be quite circumspect in carrying out his duties without getting involved in the investigation. He must not ask the prisoner any direct questions about being involved in the commission of any offence. In addition, he should not involve himself in developing any comments which the prisoner has already made either after hearing the arresting officer's account or following his decision conveyed to the prisoner about keeping him in custody.

If the custody officer were to open up lines of inquiry at either of these stages with the prisoner, there would no doubt be an argument in any subsequent proceedings that the conversation amounts to an interview and that the safeguards outlined in section 11 of Code C had not been complied with. In essence, any evidence obtained in such circumstances would probably be regarded as inadmissible.

The grounds for a person's detention shall be recorded, in his presence if practicable.

Where video cameras have been fitted in custody suites, a prominent notice must be displayed indicating that cameras are in use. The cameras must not be switched off notwithstanding requests from prisoners or anyone else.

The person shall be asked to sign on the custody record to signify whether or not he wants legal advice at this point. The custody officer is responsible for ensuring that the person signs the custody record in the correct place to give effect to his decision.

Q: Does the code of practice make any special provision for special groups such as the deaf, juveniles, the mentally handicapped and the blind?

A: There are occasions when custody officers are faced with some difficulty when they are unable to establish a meaningful rapport with a prisoner. This might occur where the prisoner seems to be deaf or his hearing ability seems questionable or he does not appear to be able to understand English. In such cases the custody officer is required to summon the assistance of an interpreter as soon as practicable and ask him to provide the information which is required to be given to a prisoner on his behalf.

When dealing with juveniles, the custody officer must, where it is practicable, find out who is responsible for his welfare. It may be a parent or guardian or the care authority or voluntary organisation where he is in care.

It may be someone else who, for the time being has assumed responsibility for his welfare. Once the person has been identified, he must be told as soon as practicable. that the juvenile has been arrested, the reason why and where he is. It is worth mentioning at this stage that a juvenile cannot be kept incommunicado and the foregoing is in addition to that proviso.

There are frequent occasions when a juvenile who is in the care of the local authority actually lives with his parents etc. Unless suspected of being involved in an offence with a juvenile, arrangements should be made for them to be informed as well as the care authority. Similarly, even though he is in care, consideration should be given to informing his parents what is happening to him.

Where the person arrested is a juvenile or is either mentally disordered or mentally handicapped, the custody officer must, as soon as practicable have an appropriate adult informed of the grounds for detention and ask him to come to the police station.

According to Code C, it is imperative that a mentally disordered or mentally handicapped person detained under section 136 of the Mental Health Act 1983 shall be assessed as soon as possible. Where an assessment is to take place at a police station an interview with an approved social worker and a registered medical practitioner must be arranged. Once that interview has been concluded and suitable arrangements made for his care, the person cannot be further detained under the section. However, he must not be released until he has been seen by both the social worker and the doctor.

If the appropriate adult is already at the police station when information is given to the person as to his legal rights and the grounds for his detention then the information must be given to the detained person in his presence. If the appropriate adult is not at the police station when the information is given then the information must be given to the detained person again in the presence of the appropriate adult once that person arrives.

The prisoner must be told by the custody officer that, where applicable, the appropriate adult is there at the police station to assist and advise him and that if he wishes he can consult privately with him at any time. If, having been informed of the right to legal advice, the appropriate adult or the person detained wishes that legal advice should be taken, then the prescribed action provided by section 6 of the code should be put in train.

A note of guidance puts the foregoing paragraph into perspective by advising that the provision is for the protection of the rights of vulnerable people such as juveniles, the mentally disordered or mentally handicapped, who may not be able to comprehend what is going on around them. If a person in one of these categories requests legal advice, the appropriate action should be taken straight away and not delayed pending the arrival of the appropriate adult.

Q: Who is the appropriate adult?

A: In the code 'the appropriate adult' means:

(a) In the case of a juvenile:
   (i) his parent or guardian (or, if he is in care, the care authority or voluntary organisation); The term 'in care' is used in Code C to cover all cases in which a juvenile is 'looked after' by a local authority under the terms of the Children Act 1989,
   (ii) a social worker; or
   (iii) failing either of the above, another responsible adult aged 18 or over who is not a police officer or employed by the police.

(b) In the case of a person who is mentally disordered or mentally handicapped:
   (i) a relative, guardian or other person responsible for his care or custody;
   (ii) someone who has experience of dealing with mentally disordered or mentally handicapped people but who is not a police officer or employed by the police (such as an approved social worker as defined by the Mental Health Act 1983 or a specialist social worker); or
   (iii) failing either of the above, some other responsible adult aged 18 or over who is not a police officer or employed by the police.

There are obvious exceptions to when a person may or may not be an appropriate adult. A father who goes out burgling with his son is not a suitable person to act as an appropriate adult when the procedures relating to his son are taking place. Similarly, if a person has assaulted his mother, she should not be the appropriate adult because she is the victim. Following this line of reasoning, a social worker who has received a confession from a person in his care to the effect that he is responsible for burning down the community home where he was living, should not participate in the investigation into the allegation of arson, as the appropriate adult.

In short, a person, no matter what his relationship with the juvenile may be, should not act as the appropriate adult if he is suspected of being criminally involved in the crime, is the victim or a witness, is involved in the investigation or has received admissions.

Where a juvenile's family has split up, an estranged parent should not be the appropriate adult if the juvenile objects.

To place matters beyond doubt about the position of social workers, a note of guidance adds that should a juvenile make an admission either to him or in his presence at a time other than when he is acting as appropriate adult for him, another social worker should replace him.

A solicitor or a lay visitor who happens to be at a police station in their official capacities cannot be utilised as appropriate adults.

So far as mentally disordered or mentally handicapped persons are concerned, a note of guidance suggests that it may be more appropriate for a person with knowledge or experience of such persons, rather than a relative who has no knowledge in this area, should act as the appropriate adult. However, the wishes of the prisoner are paramount and if he prefers the relative to act, his wishes should be observed where it is practicable to do so.

Where the appropriate adult and the solicitor are present at the police station, the prisoner must be given the facilities to consult privately with the solicitor without the appropriate adult being present.

A note of guidance points out the importance of a custody officer reminding the appropriate adult and the prisoner of the right to legal advice under section 6 of Code C. Where it is refused, the reasons must be recorded.

The Code of Practice develops the issue of vulnerable prisoners and the safeguarding of rights by a provision relating to persons who are blind, seriously visually handicapped or unable to read. So far as such persons are concerned, the custody officer must ensure that either his solicitor, a relative, the appropriate adult or some other person likely to take an interest in him and who is not involved in the inquiry is available to assist in checking out the documentation.

In situations where either written consent or a signature is required, the person assisting may sign on his behalf where appropriate. A blind or seriously visually handicapped person might, for obvious reasons, be rather reluctant to sign police documents. If the representative signs instead, the integrity of both the police system and the interests of the prisoner are thereby preserved.

Reasonable steps should be taken to inform the supervising officer of a juvenile who is the subject of a supervision order what is happening in his case.

Action which is taken in respect of persons who fall into the specified special groups must be recorded.

Q: Does the code of practice make any provision in respect of persons attending a police station voluntarily?

A: Yes. It reiterates the principles enunciated in section 29 of the Act. Additionally it stipulates that persons attending police stations voluntarily to assist with an investigation should be treated with no less consideration (eg offered refreshments at appropriate times) and enjoy an absolute right to obtain legal advice or communicate with anyone outside the police station.

Whilst the foregoing generalisation is contained in a note of guidance which features in the preamble to Code C, the Code contains a more definitive provision regarding volunteers.

Initially that provision explains that a person who voluntarily attends a police station to assist with an investigation may leave whenever he wishes unless he is told that he is under arrest. Once a police officer determines that a voluntary attender will not be allowed to leave, he must tell him that he is under arrest and must take him before the custody officer. The custody officer is then responsible for advising him of his rights.

If the volunteer is not arrested but the caution is administered to him, he must also be told that he is not under arrest, is not bound to stay at the police station but that if he does stay, he may obtain free and independent legal advice if he so desires. It should also be made clear that the entitlement to legal advice includes the right to speak with a solicitor on the telephone and he should be asked if he wishes to do so.

If the volunteer asks about legal advice, he must be given a notice explaining the arrangements.

Q: What responsibilities are imposed on custody officers by the code of practice in respect of the property of a detained person?

A: It is the responsibility of the custody officer to discover what a detained person has in his possession when he arrives at a police station whether he arrives under arrest, on being detained after answering bail, on commitment to prison after being ordered there or sentenced by a court, or on being lodged at a police station prior to being produced in court after transfer from another police station or from hospital or on detention under sections 135 or 136 of the Mental Health Act 1983.

The responsibility also extends to determining what he might have obtained which might be used for an unlawful or harmful purpose whilst in custody. The safekeeping of a prisoner's property which has been taken from him and which remains at a police station also comes within the custody officer's responsibility.

In accordance with his responsibilities in this respect, the custody officer may either search the prisoner himself or give authority for him to be searched as far as he considers it necessary. It should be borne in mind, however, that the search of the intimate parts of the prisoner's body or a search which involves him taking off more than outer clothing must be carried out in accordance with the relevant provisions contained in Annex A of Code C. Any search may be carried out only by an officer of the same sex as the prisoner.

Section 54(1) of the Police and Criminal Evidence Act 1984 and section 4.1 of Code C combine to provide the custody officer with a requirement to search a person when it is apparent that he will have a continuing duty in respect of him or where his behaviour or the offence for which his detention was authorised make an inventory of his property appropriate.

The provisions do not provide a hard and fast rule directing that all persons in custody must be searched, far from it. A person who is expected to be in custody for only a short period of time and is not to be placed in a cell, for example a breathalyser prisoner, does not have to be searched. But the decision is the custody officer's. Quite simply, in such cases, the custody record is marked 'not searched' and the prisoner is asked to sign the entry. If he refuses, the custody officer will conduct a search to find out what he has in his possession.

(Annex A repeats the provisions of section 55 of the Act (re intimate searches) and makes further provision in respect of juveniles, the mentally disordered or mentally handicapped. These considerations are dealt with separately).

Q: What may a prisoner be allowed to retain in his possession by virtue of the code of practice?

A: Clothing and personal effects can be retained by the prisoner at his own risk but this may be denied if the custody officer believes that he might use them to harm himself or someone else, interfere with evidence, cause damage, escape or if they are required as evidence. It would be foolhardy indeed to allow a person arrested for recently smashing a shop window with his fist to retain the clothing he was wearing at the time which might provide valuable forensic evidence. Similarly, a person who is known to have previously attempted suicide should be treated with great care where property and personal possessions are concerned.

Q: What are regarded as personal effects?

A: The expression personal effects is developed in Code C which determines that they are items which might be lawfully needed, used or referred to by a prisoner whilst he is in detention. It does not include cash or other items of value.

The code repeats the Act's requirements detailed in section 54 to record items in a detained person's possession and stipulates that the detained person shall be allowed to check and sign the record as correct. Any refusal to sign should be recorded. Notes of Guidance add that the custody officer is not required to record property in the arrested person's possession if, by its nature, quantity or size, it is not practicable to remove it to a police station.

In addition, items of clothing worn by the detainee need not be recorded unless the custody officer withholds them. If a detained person is not allowed to keep any article of clothing or personal effects the reason must be recorded.

Code of Practice C –
detention of persons in police custody

Q: What protection does the code of practice offer in respect of the detention of citizens of independent Commonwealth countries or foreign nationals in police detention?
A: Such person may communicate at any time with his High Commission, Embassy or Consulate. He must be informed of this right as soon as practicable. He must also be informed as soon as practicable of his right upon request to have his High Commission, Embassy or Consulate told of his whereabouts and the grounds for his detention. Such a request should be acted upon as soon as practicable.

If a citizen of an independent Commonwealth country or a national of a foreign country with which a bilateral consular convention agreement is in force requiring notification of arrest is detained, the appropriate High Commission, Embassy or Consulate shall be informed as soon as practicable. However, when the person is a political refugee (whether for reasons of race, nationality, political opinion or religion) or is seeking political asylum, a consular officer shall not be informed of the arrest of one of his nationals or given access to or information about him except at the person's express request.

Consular officers may visit one of their nationals who is in police detention to talk to him and, if required, to arrange for legal advice. Such visits shall take place out of the hearing of a police officer. A record shall be made when a person is informed of his rights under this section and of any communications with a High Commission, Embassy or Consulate.

A note of guidance advises that the exercise of the rights outlined above may not be interfered with even though Annex B applies (Delay in notifying arrest or allowing access to legal advice.)

Q: Does the code of practice make any stipulations as to conditions of a person's detention?

A: Yes, section 8 of Code C details what may be regarded as the basic creature comforts which must be extended to a person in police custody. Unless it is impracticable a prisoner should have a cell to himself. Cells must be adequately heated, ventilated, cleaned and lit with a dimming facility which will serve to both allow the prisoner to sleep and to enable safety and security.

There must be no additional restraints used unless this is absolutely necessary and then they should only be suitable handcuffs.

Great care must be exercised in the case of mentally disordered or mentally handicapped people as to whether handcuffs should be used at all.

Where blankets, mattresses, pillows and other bedding is supplied to a prisoner in a cell, they must be of a reasonable standard and in a clean and sanitary condition. There must be provision for toilet and washing facilities.

In circumstances where a person's clothes are taken from him either for forensic examination or other reason associated with an investigation, or if they are removed for hygiene or health reasons or if they are to be cleaned, they must be replaced by clothing of a reasonable standard of comfort and cleanliness. A person cannot be interviewed unless such clothing has been offered to him. The watchword here, of course, is offered rather than supplied.

The provision of overalls which is becoming more common, seems to fit well within this provision of the Code.

So far as food is concerned, at least two light meals and one main meal should be offered to a prisoner in any period of 24 hours and at the recognised meal times. Drinks should accompany meals and may be supplied between meals if requested.

If the custody officer is in any doubt about medical or dietary matters, he should seek help from the police surgeon. The meals that are provided shall offer a varied diet and should meet any special dietary requirement to conform to any religious beliefs the prisoner may have.

Q: Is it permissible for food to be brought in for prisoners?

A: The Code provides that meals can be provided by his family or friends at their own expense.

Q: Are longer-term prisoners afforded any special treatment?

A: A qualified yes, as a useful note of guidance points out that bedding and a varied diet are of particular importance in the case of prisoners in custody for offences under the Prevention of Terrorism (Temporary Provisions) Act 1989 and those who are detained under immigration rules or persons who are likely to be detained for lengthy periods. For example, a person who has been remanded to police cells for 3 days should be seen to have a reasonable standard of comfort in his cell and more particular attention paid to his diet.

Q: What provisions are there about daily exercise?
A: If it is practicable, prisoners should be offered daily exercise.

Q: What special measures are there to cater for juveniles?
A: They are afforded slightly different rules in that they must not be put in a cell unless there is no other accommodation available which is secure and the custody officer determines that it is impracticable to supervise him if he is not put in a cell. He may also be of the view that a cell is more comfortable than the alternative. There is also a strict ban on juveniles being placed in cells with detained adults.

Q: When may reasonable force be used?
A: It may be used in order to make sure that reasonable instructions are complied with, which includes those which are given in accordance with Code C, or to prevent escape, injury, damage to property or the destruction of evidence.

Q: What are the rules about prisoners being visited to make sure they are alright?
A: Code C directs that all prisoners must be visited every hour and those who are drunk every half hour. A person who is drunk and asleep must be woken up and spoken to on each visit. If the custody officer becomes worried about a prisoner's condition, for example, when roused his responses are unusual, he must arrange for medical treatment.

   Juveniles and other people at risk should be visited more frequently than other prisoners.

Q: What records are required to be kept?
A: Details of replacement clothing and meals offered must be recorded. The fact that a juvenile is placed in a cell must be recorded along with the reasons.

Q: How should complaints or perceived mistreatment of prisoners be dealt with?
A: Where a detained person makes a complaint about his treatment

since being arrested or if an officer finds out that a prisoner has been mistreated, he must report the matter as soon as practicable to an officer of inspector rank or above who is not involved with the case. If there is some suggestion of assault or unlawful or unnecessary force, the police surgeon should be summoned.

Q: There are numerous instances reported in the newspapers about people who die in police custody. What arrangements exist to cater for the provision of early medical attention to prisoners?

A: If a person detained at a police station or brought to a police station appears to be suffering from physical injury or mental disorder; is injured; seems unable to respond normally to questions posed or to a normal conversation, unless this is caused through sheer drunkenness alone; or in any other way seems to require medical attention, the custody officer must call the police surgeon immediately. If the requirement for medical attention seems more immediate, for example, there is some problem with the prisoner's signs of sensibility or awareness, the custody officer must despatch him to hospital or call the nearest doctor.

The foregoing provision must be applied whether or not there is a request for medical attention by the prisoner and whether he has already had treatment elsewhere or not, unless, of course, he is taken to a police station directly from hospital.

According to the Code of Practice, the foregoing provisions are not intended to delay the transfer of a person to a place of safety in accordance with the Mental Health Act 1983. In the case of a person who is to be assessed under the Act at the police station, the custody officer has a discretion not to call out the police surgeon if he is of the opinion that the assessment by a doctor can take place without delay.

The obvious problems which can be met in carrying out the somewhat inflexible provisions of the Codes of Practice is recognised and a note of guidance advises that where the prisoner has a minor ailment or an injury which does not need attention, he is not required to call the police surgeon. There is a rider that all such ailments or injuries must be recorded in the custody record. As a back-up, the note suggests that any doubt should be settled by calling out the police surgeon.

Q: Are there any provisions regarding a prisoner who has an infectious disease?

A: Yes, the Code of Practice contains a specific provision in this respect. When the infectious disease is of any significance, the custody officer must attempt to isolate the prisoner and his property whilst a medical diagnosis can take place and directions received as to how the prisoner should be dealt with. There should also be directions sought and complied with regarding fumigation and the treatment of those who have had or will have contact with the prisoner.

Q: What is the position where a person asks for a medical examination?

A: The police surgeon must be summoned as soon as practicable. A prisoner may have his own doctor called out provided that he pays for the visit and examination.

Q: Does the Code make any provision regarding prisoners and medications?

A: Yes. Where a person who has been prescribed medication etc. prior to being detained, the custody officer should seek the police surgeon's advice about its use in police detention.

The custody officer is, of course, responsible for safeguarding the medicine and for supervising its taking or applying by the prisoner with the obvious duty of making it available to him at the material times.

A police officer is not authorised to administer any medicine which is a controlled drug and which falls within the scope of the Misuse of Drugs Act 1971. This may, however, be administered by the prisoner under the watchful eye of the police surgeon. If the custody officer consults the police surgeon, by telephone or otherwise, and they both agree that the prisoner may administer the drug to himself and that this will not expose the prisoner, any police officer, or anyone else to the risk of harm or injury, he may be allowed to do so on the authority of the police surgeon. If the custody officer has any doubt, he should request the police surgeon to attend the police station. A consultation of this nature must be recorded on the custody record.

A further provision of the Code of Practice extends this question to the prisoner who may be in possession of or may say that he needs medication for a heart condition, diabetes, epilepsy or similar ailment. In such circumstances, the police surgeon must be consulted and his advice obtained in all cases, no matter what.

Q: A prisoner may act strangely even though he does not appear to be ill. Does the Code have anything to say about this?

A: Yes, a note of guidance points out that it should not be overlooked that a person who may appear to be drunk or is behaving in an abnormal way might be ill or suffering from the effects of drugs. Indeed, he may have suffered an injury to his head which is not outwardly obvious. In addition, a person who needs or is addicted to certain drugs may display disturbing withdrawal symptoms and experience harmful effects even though he has been deprived of his supply for only a short period of time. When in doubt about such people, the police surgeon must be contacted and the police officer concerned should act with some degree of urgency.

Q: Does the police surgeon's findings need to be recorded?
A: Yes, either on the custody record or there must be some form of note on the custody record as to where they are recorded.

Searches and intimate searches

Q: What rights and responsibilities have the police in respect of searching prisoners at police stations and safeguarding their property?
A: The Police and Criminal Evidence Act 1984 clarifies the uncertainties as to the extent of police powers which were highlighted in the cases of *R v Naylor* (1979) and *Lindley v Rutter* (1981). The conducting of 'intimate' body searches is also restricted.

The Act specifies that the custody officer at a police station shall ascertain and record or cause to be recorded everything which a person has with him when he is:

(a) brought to the station after being arrested elsewhere or after being committed to custody by an order or sentence of a court; or
(b) arrested at the station or detained there as a person falling within section 34(7), under section 37 (above) (i.e. returning to police station in answer to bail) or arrested under section 46A for failing to answer bail to a police station.

The officer may seize and retain items in the prisoner's possession but clothes and personal effects may only be seized if the custody officer:

(a) believes that the person from whom they are seized may use them:
 (i) to cause physical injury to himself or any other person;
 (ii) to damage property;
 (iii) to interfere with evidence; or
 (iv) to assist him to escape; or
(b) has reasonable grounds for believing that they may be evidence relating to an offence.

The Act therefore gives statutory effect to well-established police procedures designed to minimise disputes and allegations in respect of the fabrication of evidence. The person from whom property is seized must be told the reason unless he is violent or likely to become violent; or incapable of understanding what is said to him (section 54(1)-(5)).

The foregoing provisions of the Act contemplate a detained person cooperating with the custody officer or his delegatee but the Act also recognises that search may be necessary to ensure that the person does not retain articles which he could use to harm himself or others, help in escape or articles which comprise evidence of the offence for which he is detained or other offences. Accordingly the Act provides that a person may be searched if the custody officer considers it necessary to enable him to carry out his duty to ascertain and record a prisoner's property.

The search may be conducted to the extent that the custody officer considers it necessary for that purpose but this does not extend to conducting an intimate search of the person. The search must be carried out by a constable of the same sex as the detainee (section 54(6)-(8)).

It will be noted that the Act does not licence the routine searching of all persons taken into police custody, a matter mentioned in a note of guidance in the code of practice. Searching is conditional upon it being considered necessary for the specific duties imposed but may be carried out at any time e.g. where a person in detention is moved from one place to another either within a police station or, perhaps, to a hospital.

Q: What records must be kept of searches of persons detained in police custody?

A: In addition to the Act's provisions in respect of written authorisations being required in certain cases and records being kept the code of practice stipulates that in the case of an intimate search the custody officer shall as soon as practicable record which parts of the person's body were searched, who carried out the search, who was present, the reasons for the search and its result. It continues that in the case of a strip search he shall record the reasons for the search, those present and its result. If an intimate search is carried out by a police officer, the reason why it is impracticable for a suitably qualified person to conduct it must be recorded.

Q: Are the police entitled to strip search persons detained in police custody?

A: Yes, but such a search defined in the code of practice as a search involving the removal of more than outer clothing may take place only if the custody officer considers it to be necessary to remove an article which the detained person would not be allowed to keep and the officer reasonably considers that the person might have concealed such an article. Strip searches shall not be routinely carried out where there is no reason to consider that articles have been concealed.

Q: Do any measures exist to protect the modesty of persons detained in police custody when they are searched?

A: Yes. Where an intimate search or a strip search is carried out by a police officer, the officer must be of the same sex as the person searched. No person of the opposite sex who is not a medical practitioner or nurse shall be present, nor shall anyone whose presence is unnecessary but a minimum of two people, other than the person searched, must be present during the search. The search shall be conducted with proper regard to the sensitivity and vulnerability of the person in these circumstances.

Q: How are strip searches regulated by Code C?

A: Annex A of Code C contains detailed provisions relating to the carrying out of strip searches. Paragraph 11 lays down the following procedures:

(a) the police officer must be of the same sex as the prisoner;
(b) the prisoner should be out of sight of officers, including those who do not need to be present, and any person of the opposite sex. This does not include an appropriate adult of the opposite sex who has been specifically requested to be present by the prisoner;
(c) unless it is an urgent matter where there is a risk of serious harm to the prisoner or others, in cases where a strip search involves revealing the intimate parts of the body, two people at least must be present in addition to the prisoner. If the subject is a juvenile or a mentally disordered or mentally handicapped person, one of those people must be the appropriate adult. Except in urgent cases, as outlined already, a search of a juvenile may take place without the appropriate adult being present if he prefers it and the appropriate adult consents. A record of this decision and the appropriate adult's consent must be signed by both of them. The presence of more than two people other than the appropriate adult will only be permitted in the most exceptional circumstances.

(d) a search must be carried out with due consideration to the sensitivity and vulnerability of the prisoner in such circumstances and there should be efforts made to obtain the prisoner's co-operation and to reduce embarrassment to the minimum. A person should not be requested to remove all his clothes at once, for example, a man should be allowed to put his shirt on before he takes off his trousers. Similarly, a woman should be allowed to replace her upper garments before she takes off anything else.

(e) if it is considered necessary the prisoner can be required to hold his arms up or to stand with legs apart and to bend forward so that his genital and anal areas may be viewed. There must be no physical contact made with any body orifice.

(f) if anything is found the prisoner shall be asked to hand it over. If found within a body orifice other than the mouth and the prisoner refuses, removal of the article would constitute an intimate search which needs to be conducted under Part A of Annex A to Code C.

(g) the conduct of a strip search must be completed as soon as possible and the prisoner allowed to get dressed as soon as the procedures are complete.

Q: What records are needed in respect of strip searches?

A: A record of a strip search must be made in the custody record and must contain the reasons why it was considered necessary to carry it out, the persons present and the result.

Q: Are the police empowered to search juveniles and the mentally handicapped detained in police custody?

A: Yes, but they are afforded special protection. The Code of Practice dictates that an intimate search of a juvenile or a mentally disordered or mentally handicapped person can only be conducted whilst an appropriate adult of the same sex is present. It should be borne in mind however, that a juvenile may specifically request the presence of an appropriate adult who is of the opposite sex who can be called upon there and then, for example, a 14 year old boy may ask for his mother to be present.

Where the prisoner is a juvenile a search may take place without the attendance of the appropriate adult if the juvenile elects in the appropriate adult's presence that this is what he would prefer and the adult consents.

A record needs to be made of the decision which must be signed by the appropriate adult.

Q: What is an 'intimate search'? By whom and on what grounds may such a search be conducted?

A: The Act recognises that persons detained in police custody have been known to conceal articles, usually weapons, in their body orifices and authorises intimate searches to be effected. But in doing so the Act imposes strict limitations as to the extent of the power. An 'intimate body search' means a search which consists of the physical examination of a person's body orifices other than the mouth (section 65 Police and Criminal Evidence Act 1984). The expression, therefore, includes searches of the anus, vagina, nostrils and ears. An intimate search may only be carried out under the authority of an officer of at least the rank of superintendent who may only authorise it if he has reasonable grounds for believing:

(a) that a person who has been arrested and is in police detention may have concealed on him anything which: (i) he could use to cause physical injury to himself or others; and (ii) he might so use while he is in police detention or in the custody of a court; or

(b) that such a person: (i) may have a Class A drug concealed on him, and (ii) was in possession of it intending to unlawfully supply it or with the intention of exporting it with intent to evade a prohibition or restriction.

It will be noted that the grounds upon which an intimate body search may be authorised are very restrictive and there is no power to authorise such a search for evidence unless it is in respect of the trafficker's 'Class A' drugs.

The superintendent must have reasonable grounds for believing that the item cannot be found without such a search. His authorisation may be given orally or in writing, but if given orally, he must confirm it in writing as soon as is practicable (section 55(1) - (3)).

An intimate search which is only a drugs offence search must be by way of examination by a suitably qualified person, ie a registered medical practitioner or a registered nurse. It may not be carried out at a police station (section 55(4), (9) and (17)).

The Act recognises that while it is desirable for intimate searches to be conducted by a medically qualified person this will not always be practicable. The Act therefore provides that, except in the case of a drugs search, which must always be conducted by a suitably qualified person, an intimate search shall be by way of examination by a suitably qualified person unless an officer of at least the rank of superintendent considers that this is not practicable, in which case the search will be carried out by a constable of the same sex as the person searched (section 55(5)(7)).

The exception allowing for a search to be effected by a constable thus caters for those instances where no suitably qualified person is available or likely to be available in the immediate future; or such qualified persons refuse to assist the police on the grounds of professional ethics.

A general restriction, applying to intimate searches, is that they must be conducted at a police station; at a hospital; at a registered medical practitioner's surgery; or at some other place used for medical purposes, subject to the exception that a drugs only search cannot be carried out at a police station (section 55(8) and (9)).

If an intimate search of a person is carried out, the custody record relating to him shall state which parts of his body were searched and why they were searched. The record must be made as soon as practicable after the search.

Q: Does Code C make reference to intimate searches?
A: Yes. The Act's provisions are mirrored in Annex A to Code C.

Q: May force be used when conducting an intimate body search?
A: Section 117 of the Act provides that where any provision of the Act confers a power on a constable and does not provide that the power may only be exercised with the consent of some person, other than a police officer, the officer may use reasonable force if necessary.

It follows that on the face of it no statutory authority exists for a registered medical practitioner or registered nurse to use force. Two options emerge, it could be argued that an accompanying constable could exercise any necessary force on behalf of the registered medical practitioner or nurse in accordance with the power conferred by section 117. Alternatively, the necessity to use force could be sufficient reason for it not being practical for the search to be conducted by a suitably qualified person and carried out by a constable in accordance with section 55(6). The latter argument has greater strength but it is stressed that it could not be invoked in respect of a drugs search which must be conducted by a suitably qualified person on every occasion.

Q: What articles may an officer seize in consequence of an intimate body search?
A: He may seize and retain anything he believes that the person from whom it is seized may use:

   (a) to cause physical injury to himself or any other person;
   (b) to damage property;

(c) to interfere with evidence; or
(d) to assist him to escape;

or if he has reasonable grounds for believing that it may be evidence relating to an offence (section 55(12)).

It will be noted that the powers of seizure extend to items beyond that for which the search was authorised. The person from whom property is seized shall be told the reason for the seizure unless he is violent or likely to become violent; or incapable of understanding what is said to him.

Q: What provisions exist to ensure that the police do not abuse the power to conduct an intimate body search?

A: The provisions of section 55 of the Act are repeated in the code of practice and thus any misuse of the coercive power will constitute a discipline offence.

Q: What measures exist to monitor police use of the coercive power to carry out intimate body searches?

A: Annual Reports of Chief Officers of Police must include:

(a) the total number of searches;
(b) the number of searches conducted by way of examination by a suitably qualified person;
(c) the number of searches not so conducted but conducted in the presence of such a person; and
(d) the result of the searches carried out.

Drugs searches and their results must be itemised separately (section 55(14) - (16)).

Right to have someone informed when arrested

Section 56 of the Act details the right of a person to have someone informed of his arrest and of his whereabouts.

Q: What is the extent of a person's right to have someone informed of his arrest?

A: Where a person has been arrested and is being held in custody in a police station or other premises, he shall be entitled, if he so requests, to have one friend or relative or other person who is known to him or who is likely to take an interest in his welfare told, as soon as is practicable except to the extent that delay is permitted by the section, that he has been arrested and is being detained there (section 56(1)).

Delay may be permitted in the case of a person who is in detention for a serious arrestable offence but only if authorised by an officer of at least the rank of superintendent who must have reasonable grounds for believing that telling the named person of the arrest:

(a) will lead to interference with or harm to evidence connected with a serious arrestable offence or interference with or physical injury to other persons; or

(b) will lead to the alerting of other persons suspected of having committed such an offence but not yet arrested for it; or

(c) will hinder the recovery of any property obtained as a result of such an offence (section 56(2) and (5)).

An officer may also authorise delay where the serious arrestable offence is a drug trafficking offence or an offence to which Part VI of the Criminal Justice Act 1988 applies (offences in respect of which confiscation orders may be made) and the officer has reasonable grounds for believing

(a) where the offence is a drug trafficking offence, that the detained person has benefited from drug trafficking and that the recovery of the value of that person's proceeds of drug trafficking will be hindered by telling the named person of the arrest; and

(b) where the offence is one to which Part VI of the Criminal Justice Act 1988 applies, that the detained person has benefited from the offence and that the recovery of the value of the property obtained by that person from or in connection with the offence or of the pecuniary advantage derived by him from or in connection with it will be hindered by telling the named person of the arrest (section 56(5A)).

No further delay is permitted once the reason for authorising the delay ceases to subsist (section 56(9)).

Where delay is authorised, the person in custody must be allowed to exercise the right within 36 hours from the time from which his detention is being calculated and must be told as soon as practicable, of the reason for the delay being authorised (section 56(3) and (6)).

The superintendent may authorise the right being delayed orally or in writing but if the former he must confirm it in writing as soon as practicable. The reason for authorising delaying the right must be entered on the prisoner's custody record as soon as practicable (section 56(4), (6) and (7)).

The rights conferred on a detained person are exercisable whenever he is transferred from one place to another in police custody (section 56(8)).

The provisions of delaying a person's right to have someone informed of his arrest apply with modifications to persons arrested under the Prevention of Terrorism (Temporary Provisions) Act 1989 (section 56(10) and (11) and Annex B of code C).

The Code of Practice for the Detention, Treatment and Questioning of Persons specifies that any person arrested and held in custody at a police station or other premises may on request have one person known to him or who is likely to take an interest in his welfare informed at public expense of his whereabouts as soon as practicable. If the person cannot be contacted the person who has made the request may choose up to two alternatives. If they too cannot be contacted the person in charge of detention or of the investigation has discretion to allow further attempts until the information has been conveyed.

The code reiterates the provisions of section 56 of the Act in respect of the circumstances when the exercise of the right to have someone informed may be delayed under the authority of a superintendent. The code also provides that the right may be exercised every time the prisoner is removed from one police station to another.

In addition, the Code of Practice directs that a person is in the hands of the custody officer when the question of visits arises. While he should allow visits when possible, he must have regard to the availability of sufficient manpower to supervise them and any possible hindrance a visit might have on the inquiry. The matter is at his discretion.

If a friend, relative or person having an interest in the prisoner's welfare makes an inquiry as to the whereabouts of a prisoner, the information should be provided if he agrees, unless a superintendent has sanctioned a delay under the terms of section 56 of the Act. It is recognised in the Code of Practice that it may not always be appropriate to discuss information regarding prisoners over the telephone.

Further provisions exist to allow further privileges to the prisoner provided that delay of the right not to be held incommunicado has not been authorised. He must be provided with writing materials and be allowed to talk with one person for a reasonable time on the telephone. This is above and beyond the telephone call advising a person of his detention or to summon legal advice.

There is a proviso which enables an officer of the rank of inspector or above to deny or delay these privileges in certain circumstances where the writing of a letter or the making of a telephone call is considered to be likely to interfere with evidence etc. The right to deny or delay applies where the prisoner is in custody for an arrestable or serious arrestable offence.

A further proviso enables an officer of that rank to delay or deny the privileges if he believes it will interfere with the gathering of information about terrorism and the prisoner is detained in accordance with the provisions of the Prevention of Terrorism (Temporary Provisions) Act 1989.

Following the general principles of the Act and the Codes of Practice, documentation is required. Records must be kept of requests made and the resulting action; letters, messages, telephone calls which are made or received or any visits; and any refusal of a prisoner to allow disclosure about himself or his whereabouts to a person making an inquiry about him. Prisoners should be asked to countersign the record and any refusal to do so should itself be recorded.

Q: Is an interpreter allowed to make a telephone call or write a letter on a person's behalf?
A: Yes. This is provided for in a note of guidance.

Q: Does the code of practice cater for persons who may not have anyone available to help them?
A: Solitude and loneliness experienced by persons in police custody is recognised in the Code of Practice. A note of guidance advises that if a prisoner does not know anyone who can provide him with advice or support or he is unable to get in touch with a friend or relative, the custody officer should be conscious of the fact that there are various local voluntary organisations who may be able to help in such circumstances. If it is legal advice that is required, the provisions relating to legal advice should, of course, be acted upon.

Q: Can the police intercept communications emanating from a person held in police detention?
A: Yes, there is implicit approval for messages etc to be listened to or read. It should be borne in mind that prisoners should be told that whatever he says in a letter, telephone call or other message is likely to be listened to or read. A telephone call which has been authorised may be cut off if it is being abused.

Q: Who pays for these calls or messages?
A: They can be at public expense but this is a matter for the custody officer to decide.

Q: Are any special responsibilities imposed on the police in respect of arrested juveniles?

A: Yes. Where a child or young person is in police detention, such steps as are practicable shall be taken to ascertain the identity of a person responsible for his welfare, ie his parent, guardian or any other person who has for the time being assumed responsibility for his welfare. If it is practicable to ascertain the identity of that person he shall be informed, unless it is not practicable to do so:

(a) that the child or young person has been arrested;

(b) why he has been arrested; and

(c) where he is being detained (section 57(2) - (5)).

If it is practicable to give the information this must be given as soon as it is practicable (section 57(6)). The Act defines the expression 'parent or guardian' and also stipulates that in the case of a person under supervision his supervisor be informed (section 57(7) - (8)).

A note of guidance to Annex B of Code C advises that even if the provisions of Annex B are satisfied, in respect of delaying notification or legal advice, in the case of a juvenile (or a person who is mentally disordered or mentally handicapped) action to inform the appropriate adult (and the person responsible for a juvenile's welfare, if that is a different person) must nevertheless be taken in accordance with paragraphs 3.7 and 3.9 of the code of practice.

Access to legal advice

Section 58 of the Act makes provision for access to legal advice.

Q: Does the Act confer on persons in police detention a statutory right of access to such advice?

A: Yes, the Act and the code of practice provide detailed provisions regarding a person's right to legal advice.

Whilst it is made demonstrably clear that persons should be told of and regularly reminded of the right, the Act and code of practice recognise that occasions will arise from time to time where the interests of justice override the interest of individuals. Accordingly, a person's right to legal advice may be delayed by a superintendent or above in certain stringent circumstances.

The Act dictates that a person arrested and held in custody in a police station or other premises shall be entitled, if he so requests, to consult a solicitor privately at any time.

Any request made shall be recorded on the person's custody

record unless it is made at a time while he is at court after being charged with an offence (section 58(1) - (3)).

A person making the request must be permitted to consult a solicitor as soon as practicable but this right may be delayed for up to 36 hours from the time his detention is being calculated:

(a) in the case of a person who is in police detention for a serious arrestable offence; and

(b) if an officer of at least the rank of superintendent authorises it.

The delay may be authorised orally or in writing, but if the former must be confirmed in writing as soon as is practicable (section 57(6) - (7)).

An officer may only authorise delay where he has reasonable grounds for believing that the exercise of the right conferred:

(a) will lead to interference with or harm to evidence connected with a serious arrestable offence or interference with or physical injury to other persons; or

(b) will lead to the alerting of other persons suspected of having committed such an offence but not yet arrested for it; or

(c) will hinder the recovery of any property obtained as a result of such an offence (section 58(8)).

In section 58(8) the word 'will' is deliberately restrictive and the denial of access to legal advice is confined to those narrow limits. Having reasonable grounds for merely believing that the consequences would or may assist will not suffice (*R v Samuel (1988)* and *R v Alladice* (1988))

A note of guidance contained in the code of practice provides that the effect of the foregoing is that the officer may authorise delaying access to a specific solicitor only if he has reasonable grounds to believe that specific solicitor will, inadvertently or otherwise, pass on a message from the detained person or act in some other way which will lead to any of the three results outlined at (a), (b) or (c) coming about. In these circumstances the officer should offer the detained person access to a solicitor (who is not the specific solicitor referred to above) on the duty solicitor scheme.

The case of *R v Dunford* concerned a person who was denied access to a solicitor but showed by his conduct that he was aware of his rights and it was considered that a solicitor's advice would not have added anything to his knowledge of his rights. Accordingly his admissions were held to have been properly admitted even though there had been a breach of section 58.

An officer may also authorise delay when the serious arrestable offence is a drug trafficking offence or an offence to which Part VI of the Criminal Justice Act 1988 applies (offences in respect of which confiscation orders may be made) and the officer has reasonable grounds for believing:-

(a) where the offence is a drug trafficking offence, that the detained person has benefited from drug trafficking and that the recovery of the value of that person's proceeds of drug trafficking will be hindered by the exercise of the right conferred by section 58(1); and

(b) where the offence is one to which Part VI of the Criminal Justice Act 1988 applies, that the detained person has benefited from the offence and that the recovery of the value of the property obtained by that person from or in connection with the offence or of the pecuniary advantage derived by him from or in connection with it will be hindered by the exercise of the right conferred by section 58(1) (section 58(8A)).

If delay is authorised the detained person must be told the reason for it and this must be recorded on the custody record.

These responsibilities must be met as soon as is practicable (section 58(9) - (10)).

The provisions with some special adaptations which allow consultation with a solicitor in the sight and hearing of a police officer, apply to persons arrested under the provisions of the Prevention of Terrorism (Temporary Provisions) Act 1989.

A person detained in police detention has thus an effective right to legal advice. Both the Act and the relevant code of practice demand that a suspect be made fully aware of the right. It will be noted that whilst the exercise of the right may be delayed it cannot be denied totally, and in no case beyond 36 hours after the relevant time. If the grounds for delay cease to apply within this time, the person must as soon as practicable be asked if he wishes to exercise his rights under section 56 or 58, the custody record must be noted accordingly, and action must be taken in accordance with the relevant section of the code of practice.

The Act is reinforced by the code of practice which reiterates the section's contents and further provides comprehensive detail regarding a person's right to legal advice. Section 6 of the code sets the scene with a reminder that subject to the provisos contained in Annex B of Code C, all people in police detention must be informed that they may at any time consult and communicate privately, whether in person, in writing or on the telephone, with a solicitor and that independent legal advice is available free of charge from the duty solicitor.

Q: What is the initial procedure for finding out who the prisoner wants to represent him?

A: First of all, it is reiterated that when a person arrives at a police station and is seen by the custody officer, one of the officer's immediate responsibilities is to tell him about his right to free legal advice.

Where a person indicates that he wishes to avail himself of the right, a note of guidance advises that he must be allowed to consult a solicitor he requests, a solicitor from the same practice, or the duty solicitor. If advice in accordance with this process is unavailable and the prisoner does not wish to see the duty solicitor, he should be allowed to select a solicitor from a list. If the solicitor he then chooses is not available he can select up to two others. If all this fails, the custody officer has the discretion to work through the solicitors' list until he finds one who is available.

Q: Can't the custody officer simply recommend one to the prisoner?

A: No, there is a rider to the note of guidance stressing that police officers should not recommend specific solicitors to prisoners.

Q: If the suspect asks to speak to his solicitor on the telephone, can he do so in private?

A: Yes, unless it is impracticable to do so because of the layout of the custody suite or in view of the fact that the telephones are not suitably sited.

Q: What steps must the custody officer take to secure legal advice?

A: The right to legal advice can only be delayed by a superintendent if the conditions laid down in Annex B of Code C are met. If Annex B does not apply a person who asks for legal advice the custody officer must take immediate steps to carry out his wish. Where a person is told or is reminded that he has a right to legal advice and he says that he does not wish to talk to a solicitor face-to-face, the custody officer must tell him that he can speak instead on the telephone if he wishes to do so. If the prisoner persists with his decision not to obtain legal advice, the custody officer must ask him for his reasons and record them on the custody record or the record of interview.

Q: The Code of Practice seems to bend over backwards in relation to legal advice for suspects and there seems to be a number of occasions when reminders have to be given even though legal advice has been declined in the first place. Why is this?

A: The right to legal advice is acknowledged as a fundamental right to a person who finds himself in the alienating world of a police station. During the procedures which take place in the police station, for example from initial detention to cell, from cell to interview, from interview to identification procedure, he must be reminded of his right to legal advice. They are mentioned in paragraphs 3.5, 11.2 and 15.3 of Code C and paragraphs 2.15(ii) and 5.2 of Code D.

When it becomes obvious that the prisoner does not wish to speak to a solicitor either personally or on the telephone the custody officer should not ask him any further about his reasons. A note of guidance states that a prisoner does not have to give any reasons for declining legal advice and he should not be pushed into doing so.

Q: How is the right to legal advice brought to the attention of persons who do not read or understand English?
A: To make absolutely sure that all prisoners are aware of it, the code of practice demands that posters advertising it and containing translations into Welsh, the main ethnic minority languages and the principal European languages should be displayed wherever they are likely to be of use, particularly in the charging area.

Q: Can a police officer advise a prisoner that he will be much better off if he does not request the services of a solicitor?
A: No, the code of practice is quite clear in stating that police officers should not do or say anything intending to dissuade a prisoner from obtaining legal advice. If a prisoner were to be so advised by a police officer there is every likelihood that any evidence obtained after that point, would be deemed to be inadmissible.

Q: Can a person be interviewed without legal advice if he has requested it?
A: There are circumstances where a person can be interviewed without legal representation even though he has asked for it. The situations where a person is denied access to legal advice are likely to be rare and it is stressed that a decision to proceed on this basis will invariably attract a stringent examination in any subsequent proceedings.

The Code of Practice directs that a person who wants legal advice cannot be interviewed or an interview cannot be continued until that advice has been given. The provisos make exceptions to this general rule in cases where a superintendent has authorised a delay under Annex B of Code C.

Furthermore, if a superintendent or above reasonably believes that to delay the interview would cause an immediate risk of harm to persons or serious loss of, or damage, to property, or where waiting for the solicitor summoned to provide legal advice would unreasonably delay the investigation process, he may authorise the interview to commence or resume.

So far as circumstances relating to delay being caused by solicitors, the superintendent must take into account any estimate of time of arrival he has been given by the solicitor and consider this alongside other considerations including the time detention is permitted, the time of day, in particular whether a rest period is fast approaching and the requirements of any other interviews which are being conducted at the time.

It would not be regarded as appropriate to allow an interview to start or recommence if the solicitor says that he is en route to the station or will set off immediately. Taking all these matters into account, if it is still likely that the interview will commence without the solicitor being present, the solicitor should be told the period of time that the police are prepared to wait before the interview will take place so that he can make other arrangements for someone else to attend and provide legal advice in his place.

Code C adds that where the delay to legal advice is sanctioned on the basis that to delay the interview would involve a risk of harm to persons or a serious loss of or damage to property, the interview must be concluded as soon as information necessary to avert the immediate risk has been obtained and until the person has received legal advice, unless any of the other exceptions is also of application.

In addition, the interview may be held or continued if the solicitor requested or picked from a list either cannot be contacted, has given prior indication that he does not wish to be contacted or refuses to attend when his services have been requested.

In respect of all the foregoing circumstances, the alternative of the services of the duty solicitor must also have been offered and refused by the person concerned or if the duty solicitor is not available. In such cases, provided an officer of the rank of inspector or above agrees, the interview may begin or recommence immediately.

Q: What if the person in detention has second thoughts about wanting legal advice?

A: Once he has made his decision known on tape and after an inspector or above has looked into the matter and sought the person's reasons for changing his mind (and now does not wish to have legal advice), and has then authorised it, the interview can begin or recommence without any further delay.

The fact that a person has changed his mind, the reasons given, if any, and the identity of the officer authorising, should be dealt with on tape or on the record of interview at the commencement or resumption of the interview.

A note of guidance permits the inspector's authority to be given over the telephone if he is satisfied as to the circumstances.

Q: Once a person has requested legal advice and the solicitor is in a position to assist, must he be present at the interview?
A: Yes, where a solicitor is either at the police station or within easy reach when the interview is scheduled or has started, he must be permitted to be present.

The denial of access to legal advice is a serious step and must take into account circumstances pertaining to the actual solicitor nominated by the detainee or the detainee himself. If access to legal advice is wrongly denied there is a possibility that evidence subsequently obtained will be excluded under either section 76 or 78 of the Act (See *R v Samuel* (1988) and *R v Alladice* (1988)).

Q: May a police officer deny a solicitor access to a detained person if he suspects the solicitor will advise his client not to answer any questions?
A: No.

Q: What is the situation where the solicitor turns up at the police station asking to see a prisoner, perhaps having been alerted by a relative that the person is in detention?
A: Unless the delaying power is in operation, once a solicitor arrives at a police station to see a prisoner, the prisoner must be told of his presence even if he is being interviewed at the time. He should be asked whether he wants to see him.

This procedure applies notwithstanding the fact that the prisoner might already have refused legal advice or if he did request it, has subsequently consented to an interview taking place without it.

The fact that the solicitor attended at the police station and the decision taken by the prisoner must be recorded on the custody record.

Q: What is the solicitor's responsibility at the police station?
A: The duties and the manner in which a solicitor conducts himself in an interview situation are often scorned and misunderstood by police officers. In what they regard as their crusade for the truth, they often find it frustrating and sometimes annoying to find that questions posed are challenged and that advice given by solicitors to their

clients seems to be nothing more than an obstruction to justice.

A solicitor's duty is equally as demanding as the police officer's. He must place the interests of his client first and foremost above any other considerations. Not surprisingly, the solicitors' Code of Professional Conduct requires him to fight tooth and nail towards that end, no matter what.

There are those who take this duty to the very edge and there are those who occasionally go over the top. But the Code of practice is quite limiting in detailing the circumstances when a solicitor can be thrown out of an interview.

In essence, the right to exclude is only available when the conduct of the solicitor does not allow the interviewing officer to ask the suspect questions.

Q: Are the duties of a solicitor defined in the Code?
A: A qualified yes. A note of guidance advises that the solicitor's role at the police station is to act in a manner which protects and advances his client's legal rights.

The note states that there may be situations arising where the suspect may be advised to remain silent or to decline to comment on questions posed to prove the case against him.

It is pointed out that a solicitor may interrupt the proceedings to clarify the line of inquiry the officer is taking which might not be immediately clear to either himself or his client or to protest about a question which he believes to be improper. There may even be occasions where a solicitor might interject if he objects to the manner in which a question is being posed to his client.

During the interview, a solicitor may wish to provide his client with legal advice. He may ask for the interview to be suspended whilst such advice is provided.

It should always be remembered that the conduct of all parties in an interview is invariably tape recorded and may be played over in court before a judge and a jury. It goes without saying that patience and understanding are priorities which police officers cannot afford to surrender in an interview situation.

Q: Is any further advice proffered about excluding a solicitor from an interview?
A: Yes, in summary, the note of guidance states that the exclusion provision is only of application when the approach or conduct of the solicitor either directly prevents or unreasonably obstructs the interviewing officer in asking proper questions to the interviewee, or has the effect of obstructing any response he may make.

The note of guidance suggests that examples of exclusionary conduct may be answering the suspect's questions for him or giving him written answers to repeat.

A further note of guidance advises an officer who excludes a solicitor from an interview that he will need to justify his decision to a court and for that purpose he is well advised to have a look for himself at the solicitor's conduct before arriving at his decision.

Q: What procedure must take place to exclude a solicitor?

A: An investigating officer who is of the view that a solicitor should be excluded, should stop the interview and speak with the superintendent or, in his absence, an inspector who has nothing to do with the inquiry, and tell him what the situation is and the conduct objected to.

It is then at the discretion of the senior officer, who must decide whether or not the solicitor should be allowed to remain in an interview. On making a decision to exclude, the suspect must be offered the services of another solicitor before the interview recommences and that other solicitor should be allowed to be present in the interview.

Q: Will an exclusion necessarily involve the Law Society?

A: The Code of Practice makes it clear that to throw a solicitor out of an interview is a serious matter and the superintendent making such a decision should consider reporting it to the Law Society. Where the decision was made by an inspector, he must apprise his superintendent of the action he has taken and a report to the Law Society must then be considered.

If the exclusion is of the duty solicitor, any report should be copied to the Legal Aid Board.

Q: Is the term 'solicitor' defined?

A: Yes, Code C states that the term means a solicitor who holds a current practising certificate, a trainee solicitor, a duty solicitor representative or an accredited representative included on a list maintained by the Legal Aid Board.

Q: Does the Code of Practice permit a solicitor to send a clerk or legal executive to look after the interests of his client?

A: Yes. If a solicitor decides to send a non-accredited or probationary representative to represent the interests of his client and to provide him with necessary legal advice, he may do so. The person appointed should be allowed access to a police station to conduct his business unless an inspector or above decides that his presence will cause a hindrance to the investigation of crime and accordingly he effectively excludes him. The giving of proper advice to a prisoner is not to be regarded as being a hindrance. On being admitted to a police station, the provisions of the Code of Practice regarding access to legal advice, requirement to leave the interview and the removal of a solicitor from an interview apply to a legal representative in whatever form they may take.

Q: What considerations should be taken into account when an inspector is deciding the fate of a non-accredited or probationary representative?
A: He must determine whether his name and status are known; if his character is suitable bearing in mind that a person with criminal convictions apart from minor matters is hardly likely to be suitable to give legal advice; and anything else in the solicitor's letter of authorisation.

Furthermore, a note of guidance advises that if an inspector is of the view that a particular solicitor or firm of solicitors are persistently dispatching non-accredited or probationary representatives who are regarded as being unsuitable to give legal advice to prisoners and suspects, this matter should be brought to the attention of the superintendent who may decide that the Law Society should be informed.

Q: If a non-accredited or probationary representative is denied access to a police station or is excluded from an interview, does the officer need to inform the solicitor or the firm which sent him?
A: Yes, this must be done so that the solicitor can make alternative arrangements. The prisoner must also be advised as to what is happening and the custody record endorsed.

Q: There are instances which occur from time to time where a solicitor represents more than one person involved in the same offence. What is the position when there is an apparent conflict of interests?
A: A note of guidance addresses this issue advising that a solicitor may represent more than one person involved in the same inquiry. The solicitor is guided by the principles enunciated in some detail in the solicitors' code to professional conduct and any question in respect of a possible conflict of interest is for him to determine.

There is a rider to the note of guidance to the effect that if unreasonable delay to an interview is likely to be occasioned by waiting for the solicitor to give advice to another person, the interview may be commenced without further delay in accordance with section 6.6 (b) of Code C (where a superintendent reasonably believes that delay may result in an immediate risk of harm to persons or serious loss of or damage to property).

Q: What does the code of practice prescribe in respect of documentation in respect of legal advice?
A: Any request for legal advice and the action taken on it shall be recorded. If a person has asked for legal advice and an interview is commenced in the absence of a solicitor or his representative (or the solicitor or his representative has been required to leave an interview) a record shall be made in the interview record.

Q: What particular provisions are made in respect of persons arrested under the Prevention of Terrorism (Temporary Provisions) Act 1989?
A: The right to have someone notified of a person's arrest or to legal advice may be delayed in addition to those grounds already outlined if a superintendent has reasonable grounds for believing that the exercise of either right:

(a) will lead to interference with the gathering of information about the commission, preparation or instigation of acts of terrorism; or

(b) by alerting any person, will make it more difficult to prevent an act of terrorism or to secure the apprehension, prosecution or conviction of any person in connection with the commission, preparation or instigation of an act of terrorism.

These rights may be delayed only for so long as is necessary and in no case beyond 48 hours from the time of arrest. If the above grounds cease to exist within this time, the person must as soon as practicable be asked if he wishes to exercise either right, the custody record must be noted accordingly, and action must be taken in accordance with the relevant section of the code. (Section 58(13) and Annex B of Code C).

Interview

Q: When interviewing a person at what stage must a police officer administer the caution?
A: A person must be cautioned if there are grounds to suspect him of

an offence before he is asked any questions about that offence or asked any further questions where the necessary suspicion arises because of his answers to previously posed questions concerning his involvement or suspected involvement. The caution secures as evidence the answers he gives or his silence to the questions asked.

Accordingly, a caution is unnecessary where questions are asked for other purposes. A caution is not necessary if the questions are posed solely to find out who the suspect is or in relation to his ownership of a vehicle. The driver of a vehicle who may have committed an offence need not therefore be cautioned for the sole purpose of finding out who he is or asking him who the vehicle belongs to.

The Code develops this issue by stating that a person need not be cautioned in order to obtain information from him which is a statutory requirement such as the need to provide his name and address under the Road Traffic Act 1988. In addition, a caution is not needed when carrying out a proper and effective search as in circumstances where questions are being asked by an officer who has to decide whether to carry out a stop and search or to obtain the desirable co-operation when such a search is being conducted.

A caution is also unnecessary where an officer is attempting to verify a written record which is detailed in section 11.13 of Code C (written records of suspect's comments prior to formal interview).

Q: What is the position regarding suspects who are not under arrest at the time they are cautioned?

A: In such circumstances where a person is cautioned for the first time or, still not under arrest, is given a reminder that he is still under caution either before or during an interview, the officer must also tell him at that time that he is not arrested and does not have to stay with the officer if he does not wish to do so.

Q: Are the police required to caution everyone when they are arrested, without exception?

A: The general rule is that when a person is arrested he must be cautioned. However, circumstances do arise where it is not possible for the police to administer the caution. Accordingly, the Code of Practice provides exceptions in respect of persons who make the process impracticable because of their condition or because of their behaviour at the time they are arrested or a caution has already been given immediately before his arrest.

Q: In what terms must a person be cautioned?

A: The caution shall be in the following terms: 'You do not have to say anything. But it may harm your defence if you do not mention when questioned something which you later rely on in court. Anything you do say may be given in evidence.' Minor deviations do not constitute a breach of this requirement provided that the sense of the caution is preserved.

A note of guidance offers the advice that where it seems that a person does not understand what the caution means, the arresting officer should attempt to explain it to him in his own words. Having regard to the length of and the implications of the caution, the note of guidance may be regarded as a saving provision in avoiding lengthy exchanges at the scenes of crime or disturbance with suspects who even have difficulty with ordinary English without the complexities of how remaining silent might harm their defence.

While there are those who arrive in police custody well versed in procedures, there are others who are naturally obstructive or who feel isolated and frightened in the environment of a police station. Landing in the custody suite is bound to be a shock to the system of many and it is not surprising that some may react in a manner which is contrary to their own well-being.

To provide some assistance in this respect, Code C provides that where a person has been cautioned and he refuses to co-operate in such a way as to create a detrimental effect to the manner in which he is dealt with, he must be told that although he has been cautioned, there are undesirable consequences if he fails to co-operate.

If he refuses his name and address when charged, for example, he is likely to be further detained or if he refuses to comply with a statutory requirement to provide information or particulars as detailed, for example, in the Road Traffic Act 1988, he may thereby commit an offence and open up the possibility of being arrested.

Q: Once a suspect has been cautioned is any obligation placed on the interrogator to remind the suspect of his right to silence?
A: Yes, if there is a break during an interview the person must be reminded that he is still under caution. If any doubt exists, the caution must be given in full again when the interview recommences.

A note of guidance advises that in deciding whether or not to administer the caution again after a break, the interviewing officer will need to bear in mind the possibility of explaining to the satisfaction of a court the fact that his suspect understood that he was still under caution when the interview resumed.

The effect of the foregoing is to spell out in not so many words that it is prudent and wise to caution a suspect in full whenever an interview is interrupted. By doing so, any doubt as to whether the suspect understood that he was still under caution is effectively removed.

Q: What records must be made of cautions administered?

A: A record shall be made when a caution is given either in the officer's pocket book or in the interview record as appropriate.

Q: Are any special provisions made for those who are regarded as being vulnerable?

A: Yes, the code of practice provides that if a juvenile or a person who is mentally disordered or mentally handicapped is cautioned in the absence of the appropriate adult, the caution must be repeated in the adult's presence.

Q: Are there any circumstances when a caution need not be given?

A: Yes, a note of guidance advises that it is not necessary to give or repeat a caution when informing a person who is not under arrest that he may be prosecuted for an offence.

Q: Can any inferences be drawn from the failure of a person to answer questions?

A: The right to silence has been held sacrosanct in English law on the basis that a person is under no obligation to either incriminate himself or to assist the prosecution to do so. Sections 34 to 39 of the Criminal Justice and Public Order Act 1994 and the revised codes of practice made under the provisions of the Police and Criminal Evidence Act 1984 amend the law in this delicate area. Whilst it would not be correct to state that the right to silence has been abolished, the new statutory provisions have made inroads towards softening the pre-existing rules by enabling proper inferences to be drawn in respect of an accused's failure to give evidence at his trial; his refusal to answer questions put to him by the police when questioned or charged; the failure or refusal to account for objects, substances or marks; and failure to account for his presence at a particular place.

The provisions do not contain any form of punishment in respect of such a failure nor do they serve to compel an accused person to give evidence or incriminate himself. They were introduced to eliminate the 'ambush' defence which occurs when a person introduces for the first time at his trial, some sort of explanation which could have been divulged during the investigative stage.

Q: What is the extent of the Act's provisions in respect of the right to silence?

A: Section 34(1) of the Criminal Justice and Public Order Act 1994 stipulates that where, in any proceedings against a person for an offence, evidence is given that the accused-

(a) at any time before he was charged with the offence, on being questioned under caution by a constable trying to discover whether or by whom the offence had been committed, failed to mention any fact relied on in his defence in those proceedings; or

(b) on being charged with the offence or officially informed that he might be prosecuted for it, failed to mention any such fact, being a fact which in the circumstances existing at the time the accused could reasonably have been expected to mention when so questioned, charged or informed, as the case may be, the consequences detailed in section 34 (2) apply.

By virtue of section 34 (2):

(a) a magistrates' court, in deciding whether to grant an application for dismissal made by the accused under section 6 of the Magistrates' Courts Act 1980 (application for dismissal of charge in course of proceedings with a view to transfer for trial);

(b) a judge, in deciding whether to grant an application made by the accused under-
    (i) section 6 of the Criminal Justice Act 1987 (application for dismissal of charge of serious fraud in respect of which notice of transfer has been given under section 4 of that Act); or
    (ii) paragraph 5 of Schedule 6 to the Criminal Justice Act 1991 (application for dismissal of charge of violent or sexual offence involving child in respect of which notice of transfer has been given under section 53 of that Act);

(c) the court, in determining whether there is a case to answer; and

(d) the court or jury, in determining whether the accused is guilty of the offence charged, may draw such inferences from the failure as appear proper.

Subject to any directions by the court, evidence tending to establish the failure may be given before or after evidence tending to establish the fact which the accused is alleged to have failed to mention (section 34(3)).

The provision is not reserved for investigations conducted by the police but includes matters and charging procedures undertaken by bodies other than the police. Accordingly, persons being dealt with by investigators employed by government or local authority agencies are caught by the Act. Section 34(4) directs that the section applies in relation to questioning by persons (other than constables) charged with the duty of investigating offences or charging offenders as it applies in relation to questioning by constables; and in section 34 (1) the expression 'officially informed' means informed by a constable or any such person.

The effect of other legislation from which inferences may be drawn is not affected, a point made clear by section 34(5) which states that the section does not:

(a) prejudice the admissibility in evidence of the silence or other reaction of the accused in the face of anything said in his presence relating to the conduct in respect of which he is charged, in so far as evidence thereof would be admissible apart from this section; or

(b) preclude the drawing of any inference from any such silence or other reaction of the accused which could properly be drawn apart from this section.

Section 34 (6) ensures that the principles relating to retrospective legislation remain intact by stipulating that the section does not apply in relation to a failure to mention a fact if the failure occurred before the commencement of this section.

Q: What does the Act say about a person who doesn't wish to give evidence?

A: The conduct of an accused person, aged 14 years or over, at his trial is the subject of the provisions contained in section 35 of the Act. Although an accused person is not compelled to give evidence on his own behalf, his decision not to do so may lead to proper inferences being drawn if certain conditions apply.

Section 35 (l) provides that at the trial of any person who has attained the age of fourteen years for an offence, subsections (2) and (3) apply unless-

(a) the accused's guilt is not in issue; or

(b) it appears to the court that the physical or mental condition of the accused makes it undesirable for him to give evidence; but subsection (2) below does not apply if, at the conclusion of the evidence for the prosecution, his legal representative informs the court that the accused will give evidence or, where he is unrepresented, the court ascertains from him that he will give evidence.

In the circumstances where section 35 (2) applies, the court shall, at the conclusion of the evidence for the prosecution, satisfy itself (in the case of proceedings on indictment, in the presence of the jury) that the accused is aware that the stage has been reached at which evidence can be given for the defence and that he can, if he wishes, give evidence and that, if he chooses not to give evidence, or having been sworn, without good cause refuses to answer any question, it will be permissible for the court or jury to draw such inferences as appear proper from his failure to give evidence or his refusal, without good cause, to answer any question.

Where section 35(3) applies, the court or jury, in determining whether the accused is guilty of the offence charged, may draw such inferences as appear proper from the failure of the accused to give evidence or his refusal, without good cause, to answer any question.

This section does not render the accused compellable to give evidence on his own behalf, and he shall accordingly not be guilty of contempt of court by reason of a failure to do so (section 35(4)).

Section 35 (5) provides some guidance on circumstances where a refusal or failure to answer questions will not be regarded as being without just cause. The section directs that for the purposes of this section a person who, having been sworn, refuses to answer any question shall be taken to do so without good cause unless-

(a) he is entitled to refuse to answer the question by virtue of any enactment, whenever passed or made, or on the ground of privilege; or
(b) the court in the exercise of its general discretion excuses him from answering it.

Where the age of any person is material for the purposes of section 35 (1) his age shall for those purposes be taken to be that which appears to the court to be his age (section 35 (6)).

Section 35 (7) makes it clear that the Act is not retrospective by declaring that the section applies:

(a) in relation to proceedings on indictment for an offence, only if the person charged with the offence is arraigned on or after the commencement of this section;
(b) in relation to proceedings in a magistrates' court, only if the time when the court begins to receive evidence in the proceedings falls after the commencement of this section.

Q: What is the situation where an accused is found with something in his possession and refuses to say anything about it?

A: The effect of an accused's failure or refusal to account for objects, substances or marks is contained in section 36 of the Criminal Justice and Public Order Act 1994. For this section to be of application, the police must have reasonable grounds to believe that the presence of the object, mark or substance found on the accused may show him to be criminally involved. Section 36(l) provides that where:

(a) a person is arrested by a constable, and there is –
   (i) on his person; or
   (ii) in or on his clothing or footwear; or
   (iii) otherwise in his possession; or
   (iv) in any place in which he is at the time of his arrest, any object, substance or mark, or there is any mark on any such object; and
(b) that or another constable investigating the case reasonably believes that the presence of the object substance or mark may be attributable to the participation of the person arrested in the commission of an offence specified by the constable and
(c) the constable informs the person arrested that he so believes, and requests him to account for the presence of the object, substance or mark; and
(d) the person fails or refuses to do so, then if, in any proceedings against the person for the offence so specified, evidence of those matters is given, subsection (2) below applies.

By virtue of section 36(2) of the Act, where the subsection applies:

(a) a magistrates' court, in deciding whether to grant an application for dismissal made by the accused under section 6 of the Magistrates' Courts Act 1980 (application for dismissal of charge in course of proceedings with a view to transfer for trial);
(b) a judge, in deciding whether to grant an application made by the accused under-
   (i) section 6 of the Criminal Justice Act 1987 (application for dismissal of charge of serious fraud in respect of which notice of transfer has been given under section 4 of that Act); or
   (ii) paragraph 5 of Schedule 6 to the Criminal Justice Act 1991 (application for dismissal of charge of violent or sexual offence involving child in respect of which notice of transfer has been given under section 53 of the Act);
(c) the court, in determining whether there is a case to answer; and
(d) the court or jury, in determining whether the accused is guilty

of the offence charged may draw such inferences from the failure or refusal as appear proper.

Section 36 (3) of the Act declares that section 36 (1) and (2) applies to the condition of clothing or footwear as it applies to a substance or mark thereon.

By virtue of section 36 (4), section 36 (1) and (2) do not apply unless the accused was told in ordinary language by the constable when making the request mentioned in subsection (1) (c) what the effect of this section would be if he failed or refused to comply with the request.

Section 36 (5) applies the section to officers of Customs and Excise as it applies in relation to constables.

The provisions of section 36 does not prejudice the application of any other measure which enables the drawing of any inference from a failure or refusal of the accused to account for the presence of an object, substance or mark or from the condition of clothing or footwear which could properly be drawn apart from this section (section 36 (6)).

In keeping with other features of the Act, section 36 (7) states that the section does not apply in relation to a failure or refusal which occurred before the commencement of this section.

Q: What are the measures introduced by the Criminal Justice and Public Order Act 1994 to cater for persons who refuse to give an account of their presence at a particular place?

A: Where an accused fails or refuses to account for his presence at a particular place, proper inferences can be drawn provided the police reasonably believe that his presence at the place at that time may show him to be criminally involved. Section 37 of the Criminal Justice and Public Order Act 1994 provides that where:

(a) a person arrested by a constable was found by him at a place at or about the time the offence for which he was arrested is alleged to have been committed; and

(b) that or another constable investigating the offence reasonably believes that the presence of the person at that place and at that time may be attributable to his participation in the commission of the offence; and

(c) the constable informs the person that he so believes, and requests him to account for that presence; and

(d) the person fails or refuses to do so, then if, in any proceedings against the person for the offence, evidence of those matters is given, subsection (2) below applies.

Q: If the circumstances in section 37 (1) apply, what are the consequences?

A: Section 37 (2) provides that where the provision applies –

(a) a magistrates' court, in deciding whether to grant an application for dismissal made by the accused under section 6 of the Magistrates' Courts Act 1980 (application for dismissal of charge in course of proceedings with a view to transfer for trial);

(b) a judge, in deciding whether to grant an application made by the accused under,

    (i) section 6 of the Criminal Justice Act 1987 (application for dismissal of charge of serious fraud in respect of which notice of transfer has been given under section 4 of that Act), or

    (ii) paragraph 5 of Schedule 6 to the Criminal Justice Act 1991 (application for dismissal of charge of violent or sexual offence involving child in respect of which notice of transfer has been given under section 53 of that Act);

(c) the court, in determining whether there is a case to answer; and

(d) the court or jury, in determining whether the accused is guilty of the offence charged, may draw such inferences from the failure or refusal as appear proper. Section 37 (3) stipulates that section 37 (1) and (2) does not apply unless the accused was told in ordinary language by the constable when making the request mentioned in subsection (i)(c) above what the effect of this section would be if he failed or refused to comply with the request.

By virtue of section 37 (4), the section applies in relation to officers of Customs and Excise as it applies in relation to constables. The section does not preclude the drawing of any inference from a failure or refusal of the accused to account for his presence at a place which could properly be drawn apart from this section (section 37 (5)).

The question of retrospective legislation is addressed by section 37 (6) which provides that the section does not apply in relation to a failure or refusal which occurred before the commencement of this section. Transitional procedures which will apply before the abolition of committal proceedings are contained in section 37 (7).

Q: What weight can be placed on the inferences which may be drawn. Can a court convict purely on the inferences they may draw?

A: A court cannot convict on 'inference' evidence alone. Rather, inference evidence is to be regarded as being supportive to other considerations. To this end, section 38(3) provides that a person shall not have the proceedings against him transferred to the crown court for trial, nor may a court find that he has a case to answer nor convict him of an offence, solely on an inference drawn from a failure or refusal catered for in sections 34 to 37 of the Criminal Justice and Public Order Act 1994.

Q: What provisions are made in the codes of practice to reflect the special warnings which are required to be given?

A: The special warnings which are required to be given in accordance with sections 36 and 37 of the Criminal Justice and Public Order Act 1994 are contained in paragraphs 10.5A and 10.5B of Code C.

Both paragraphs provide a summary of the effect of sections 36 and 37 by outlining that if a suspect who is interviewed after being arrested either fails or refuses to provide answers to certain questions or fails or refuses to answer those questions in a satisfactory manner then, provided there has been a proper warning given, the court may draw proper inferences.

The Code of Practice details the circumstances when such proper inferences may be drawn as, firstly, when a person suspected by a police officer is arrested and in or on his clothing or his footwear, or otherwise in his possession, or in the place where he was arrested, any objects, marks or substances or marks on such objects are found and the suspect either fails or refuses to account for the objects, marks or substances found.

Secondly, proper inferences may be drawn when a person arrested by a police officer at a place at or about the time the offence for which he was arrested was allegedly committed and he fails or refuses to account for his presence at that place.

Q: Is any procedure set down in the Code of Practice to ensure that the court has the opportunity of drawing proper inferences from a suspect's failure or refusal to answer questions or to provide satisfactory answers?

A: Yes, the Code of Practice directs that for such an inference to be drawn, the officer who is conducting the interview must explain to the person in ordinary language:

    (a) the offence he is investigating;
    (b) the fact that he is requesting him to give his account for;
    (c) that he suspects that the fact he is wanting him to account for

arises because he was involved in the commission of the offence he is investigating;

(d) that if he does not answer or will not answer the question by giving his account of the fact that the officer is asking him about, a court may draw proper inferences;

(e) that the interview is being recorded and it may be given in evidence at his trial should he be prosecuted.

The wording of the paragraphs of the Code of Practice are vitally important for whilst the use of the caution is required for inferences to be drawn in respect of 'silence' under section 34 of the Act, it is not a pre-requisite in respect of the circumstances outlined in sections 36 and 37. With this in mind it is essential that police officers and others charged with the duty of investigating offences are well versed in the application of these provisions. It is prudent to mention that the nature of the warning and the manner in which it was given may well determine whether inferences may be drawn at the subsequent trial. It is suggested that the interviewing officer should take great care in telling the suspect 'in ordinary language' the matters required to be explained to him.

The fact that several of the features referred to in sections 34 to 37 of the Act may apply to a suspect should be considered with great care as the need for separate warnings in respect of each of them will invariably arise. For example, a suspect is arrested on suspicion of burglary, near to the scene and at the approximate time it is committed. He is found to have mud on his shoes similar to that near to the point of entry and wet paint from a window sill appears on the sleeve of his jacket. In the pocket of his jacket is a screwdriver and a pair of pliers. It is clear from this example that the interviewing officer will need to exercise great care in the warnings he gives in respect of each of the circumstances where proper inferences may be drawn from the suspect's failure or refusal to provide an explanation at the investigative stage. A mistake may lead to no inferences being drawn.

Q: What is there to prevent a police officer when interviewing a person utilising dubious methods or using oppression to induce a person to confess?

A: If a police officer attempts to get answers from a defendant or to obtain any form of statement from him by the use of oppression, he will be in direct breach of the Police and Criminal Evidence Act 1984 and Code C.

While Code C gives some leeway as to telling a defendant what will happen next if he refuses to answer questions or how he will be processed if he co-operates, the Code of Practice imposes a blanket ban on any action which could be mistaken for an inducement. If a person is offered some kind of unauthorised deal in return for a confession, then quite clearly any confession would be in conflict with Code C and would no doubt be ruled inadmissible.

If, however, a suspect or a defendant asks a specific question of the officer as to what will happen if he does co-operate with the investigating officer or refuses to do so in respect of either answering questions or making statements, the officer is allowed to tell him what is in store for him provided that whatever is said is proper and warranted. This provision can be readily identifiable with a prisoner raising issues such as being granted bail; his wife not being arrested for handling stolen goods etc.

The Act itself renders inadmissible a confession obtained in circumstances amounting to oppression or in circumstances which make it unreliable.

In order to obviate any interviews taking place in cars or elsewhere which may later be challenged, the code of practice directs that once a decision to arrest a suspect has been made, any interview which follows must take place in a police station or in some other place which is authorised as a place of detention. There are exceptions to the rule in circumstances where a delay which would arise would be likely:

(a) to lead to interference with or harm to evidence which exists in relation to an offence or with people being interfered with or being subjected to physical harm;

(b) to alert others who are suspects but who have not yet been detained; and

(c) to cause hindrance to the recovery of property obtained as a result of the offence.

Once the risk which raised the exception to the interview taking place at a police station etc. no longer exists or the questions which were needed to be asked to avert the risk have been asked, the interviewing must stop.

Q: What provision does Code C make in relation to those circumstances where a suspect, prior to arriving at the police station has said something to a police officer or who has remained silent in circumstances where an inference could be drawn from that silence?

A: Code C provides step by step guidance in this respect and also introduces the expression 'significant statement or silence'. Translated, a significant statement or silence is one which seems to have the capacity of being used in evidence against the person who makes or does not make it whichever is the case. The Code of Practice quotes as examples a direct admission of guilt or a failure or refusal to answer a question or a failure to answer it satisfactorily, which would invoke the drawing of proper inferences set out in the Criminal Justice and Public Order Act 1994 and Code C.

To answer the question, Code C directs that when an interview which is being conducted at a police station commences, the officer concerned, after he has administered the caution, shall ask him directly about any significant statement or silence which was said or not said prior to arriving at the police station. In particular, the officer must ask him whether he accepts it and if he wants to add anything to it.

Q: What amounts to an interview?

A: Quite simply, it is the questioning of a suspect under caution. The Code of Practice provides that it is when a person is being questioned about being involved or about his suspected involvement in a criminal offence and where the questioning needs to be conducted under caution.

The Code of Practice contains a proviso to the effect that the breathalyser procedures under section 7 of the Road Traffic Act 1988 are not interviews for the purposes of Code C.

Q: Does a suspect need to be reminded of his right to legal advice?

A: Yes, immediately before the start or resumption of an interview which is taking place at a police station or at another place which is authorised for the detention of prisoners, the person about to be interviewed or whose interview is about to recommence, must be told again about his right to have free legal advice. He must also be told that the interview will be delayed if he wishes to exercise that right. This applies on the premise that the exceptions contained in the Code do not apply. The officer conducting the interview must record the reminders given in the custody record.

Q: What does the Code of Practice say about when an interview should be brought to a halt?

A: The Code directs that as soon as a police officer inquiring into an offence believes that a prosecution should be launched against the suspect and that he has enough evidence on which a successful prosecution can be founded, he must thereupon ask the suspect if he has anything further to say. If the suspect says that he does not wish to add anything the inquiring officer must stop the interview without delay.

Because of the loose framing of this provision, difficulties are likely to emerge. Sufficient proof for one officer may not be the same for another. If two officers are conducting an interview this may lead to some conflict between them and, perhaps, an inadvertent breach of the Code.

In addition some of the evidence already obtained may later prove to be inadmissible and may have been in the officer's mind when he caused the interview to end prematurely.

There is no hard and fast rule and the Code of Practice clearly places the responsibility upon the shoulders of the officer conducting the interview. When he considers that he has enough evidence to prove his case to the satisfaction of a court, then questioning must cease - it's as simple as that.

The foregoing has no application to circumstances where officers are conducting inquiries in respect of revenue cases or are engaged in confiscation procedures under the Drug Trafficking Act or the Criminal Justice Act 1988, where suspects are asked to complete a formal question and answer record after their interview has ended.

Q: What records must be made of interviews with suspected offenders?

A: The Code of Practice lays down stringent measures to ensure that interviews and the procedures surrounding them are recorded. Specifically, the Code directs that:

(a) where an interview takes place whether at a police station or elsewhere in respect of a person who is suspected of committing an offence, an accurate record must be made of it;

(b) details of the interview including the place, time started and ended, time record made (if this is different) details of breaks and names of persons present. The record must be made on the proper form, in an official pocket book or in accordance with Code E which details the tape recording procedures; and

(c) the record is required to be made whilst the interview is being conducted. It must be a word for word account of what was said or if this is not carried out, a summarised version which is both sufficient in detail and a true record. There is an exception which applies in circumstances where an officer is of the opinion that such recording procedures are not practicable or are likely to interfere with the way the interview is being conducted.

Q: Does the exception which applies to the names of police officers being given apply in relation to interviews with terrorist offenders?

A: Yes, the Code of Practice extends protection to interview situations under the Prevention of Terrorism (Temporary Provisions) Act 1989. Warrant or other identification numbers may be used rather than names.

Q: If records are not made at the time, when must they be made?

A: As soon as practicable thereafter. The Code stresses, however, that a written interview record must be signed by the person who completes it and the time must also be stated in it.

An officer who does not record the interview whilst he is conducting it must make a note of this fact in his pocket book.

Q: Is the person interviewed asked to make any comment about the record made?

A: Yes, the Code stipulates that unless it is not practicable to do so, the interviewee must be offered the opportunity to read through the record which the officer has made of the interview and asked to sign it if he agrees that it is accurate, or to point out those parts he disagrees with. In circumstances when the interview is conducted by way of tape recording, Code E must be strictly adhered to.

Where the interviewee is unable to read or declines to read what the officer has recorded, or if he refuses to sign it, the senior police officer in attendance at the time must read it out to him and ask him to either confirm that he agrees with it by signing it or to tell him which parts are wrong according to him. The interview record should then be endorsed by the officer as to what has taken place.

Q: How does the appropriate adult or the solicitor fit into the picture in this respect?

A: If either the appropriate adult or the suspect's solicitor are in attendance at the interview, they should also be given the opportunity to read over and sign the record of the interview and, for that matter, any statement taken from the suspect in writing.

Q: Is any record required of other things which might be said which are not part of the interview?

A: Yes, written records should be made of any comments made by the suspect including any which are not directly solicited. These may have some relevance to the offence under investigation.

When this occurs, the suspect must be allowed an opportunity to acknowledge that it is correct by adding his signature or tell the officer what he believes to be wrong with it. If he declines to sign it, a record to that effect is required.

Q: Is any form of words recommended in the Code of Practice as a form of acknowledgement by the suspect who reads the interview record and agrees that what he has read over is correct?
A: Yes, an endorsement to the effect that "I agree that this is a correct record of what was said", followed by his signature will fit the bill. Where there is a disagreement with the detail recorded, a note should be made of the part which he does not agree with and he should be asked to add his signature confirming that the disagreement he has recorded is accurate. Any refusal to sign must be recorded.

Q: What protection is afforded to persons in police detention to prevent their being interviewed in unreasonable circumstances?
A: First of all, the initial decision to hand over the prisoner to the officer wishing to interview him is that of the custody officer.

Secondly there are stringent conditions laid down in the Code of Practice which strive to ensure that a suspect is not at a disadvantage during further inquiries or at an interview. The conditions cover not only those which must apply during interview but incorporate the suspect's physical and mental well-being.

So far as the latter is concerned, for example, a prisoner shall be permitted a continuous period of eight hours for rest in any period of twenty four. During that period, which should usually be during the night, there must be no questioning, travelling or interruption by police officers in connection with the matter being investigated.

An appropriate adult or his solicitor can ask that the rest period be interrupted or delayed. Other circumstances which might enable police officers to interrupt or delay the rest period are:

(a) there would thereby be a risk of harm to people or a serious loss of or damage to property;
(b) it would unnecessarily delay his release; or
(c) some prejudicial effect would be caused to the outcome of the investigation.

Q: What is the situation where a prisoner requires medical attention or when he has to be woken up in accordance with the Code of Practice at certain intervals?

A: Where the custody officer is directed elsewhere in the Code to take a certain course of action (see section 8 of Code C) or is required to act in accordance with medical advice or to attend to other matters because they are requested by either the prisoner himself, his appropriate adult or solicitor, these do not amount to interruptions and a fresh eight hour period is not thereby commenced.

Q: Presumably a prisoner is not allowed alcohol?

A: Only if it is given on medical direction.

Q: Are the police allowed to interview a person if he is unable to understand what is happening around him because he is under the influence of drink or drugs?

A: No, unless the exception regarding urgent interviews is of application under the conditions laid down in Annex C. If there is any doubt about a person's capacity the police surgeon will be able to assist.

Q: What other conditions are provided by Code C regarding the conduct of interviews with detained persons?

A: There are several and they are quite stringent. Whilst there are many restrictions, limitations and standardised procedures laid down by the Code of Practice, the process of interview is of paramount importance. It is at the interview stage where actual direct evidence might be forthcoming.

The Code of Practice provides the following conditions:

(a) So far as is practicable, police officers should conduct their interviews in properly designated interview rooms which must be satisfactorily heated, lit and ventilated.
(b) Interviewees etc must not be required to stand.
(c) Before starting the interview all police officers who are present, including the interviewing officers, must announce their identity by giving their names and ranks. (There is an exception in respect of interviews with prisoners in detention under the Prevention of Terrorism (Temporary Provisions) Act 1989 where officers must give their warrant or other identification number rather than their names.)
(d) There should be breaks in interviews at the recognised meal times. After each two hours of interview, there should be a

145

short break for refreshments. However, the interviewing officer may delay a pending break if he believes that to allow the break would expose a risk of harm to people or would involve serious loss of or damage to property, would delay the prisoner's release or prejudice the outcome of the inquiry in some other way.

(i) A note of guidance advises that a minimum of 45 minutes should be allowed for a meal and 15 minutes for a short break. In cases where a break has been delayed at the discretion of the interviewing officer, there should then be a longer break.

(ii) In addition, if a short break is to be taken and it is expected that the continued interview will itself only be a short one, the short break may be shortened further if the interviewing officer is satisfied that any of the foregoing conditions regarding harm, damage, release or prejudice are involved.

(e) If a complaint is made during an interview about compliance with the Code of Practice, the interviewing officer is required to record the complaint in the record of interview and inform the custody officer who must deal with it by making a report to an inspector in accordance with section 9 of Code C.

Q: What provisions exist to ensure that all these matters are fully documented?
A: The Code of Practice requires that:

(a) the times a prisoner is out of the custody of the custody officer must be recorded with the reason. If he has refused a request for the prisoner to be removed from his custody, this must also be recorded;

(b) details of any alcohol supplied to a prisoner must be recorded;

(c) a record must be kept of any decisions to delay a break in an interview, with reasons.

Written statements

Q: What does the Code of Practice say about written statements taken under caution at police stations?
A; They must be taken down on the forms provided in accordance with the procedure laid down for taking them under Annex D of Code C.

Q: Having regard to interviews at police stations being tape recorded or, at worst, written down contemporaneously, hasn't the need for written statements now paled into insignificance?

A: In some respects it has and this is reflected in a note of guidance which gives advice to the effect that a written statement should not ordinarily be requested. However, if a suspect asks directly, one should be taken from him. A police officer may, if he thinks fit, ask a suspect if he wishes to make a written statement.

Q: What rules must be observed in taking down a written voluntary statement?

A: Any written statement under caution must be obtained in accordance with Annex D of Code C, which stipulates the following:

(a) Statements written by the person under caution

  (i) A suspect should always be asked to write down the statement himself;

  (ii) Where a suspect wants to write out his own statement, the officer should ask him first to write out the following caution:

> 'I make this statement of my own free will. I understand that I do not have to say anything but that it may harm my defence if I do not mention when questioned something which I later rely on in court. This statement may be given in evidence.'

  (iii) Although perhaps an academic point, the words of the caution seem to conflict with the next condition which states that when a suspect writes out his own statement, the police officer must not prompt him and thus he should be allowed to complete it in his own words. The police officer can point out, however, matters which are material and he can question any ambiguity in the statement.

(b) Statements written by police officer

  (i) When a suspect asks for his statement to be written for him it should be done by a police officer who should commence by writing out a different form of caution and ask the person to sign it. It reads:

> 'I . . . wish to make a statement. I want someone to write down what I say. I understand that I do not have to say anything but that it may harm my defence if I do not mention when questioned something which I later rely on in court. This statement may be given in evidence.'

Again, it is submitted that the caution conflicts with the whole rationale of written 'voluntary' statements which are supposed to be written in a person's own words, without any prompting etc. The wording seems to suggest that a police officer should be asking questions of the suspect as he is taking the statement down. This is clearly not the objective aimed at and perhaps the following guideline exemplifies this.

(ii) When a police officer is taking down a written statement from a suspect, he must take down the exact words spoken by the person making it and he must not edit or paraphrase it. If any questions need to be asked, for example to make the statement more intelligible, they and the replies given must be recorded contemporaneously on the statement form.

(iii) After completing the statement, the officer should ask the maker to read it through and to make any corrections, alterations or additions. Once he has done that he should be asked to write out and sign the concluding caption as follows:

'I have read the above statement and I have been able to correct alter or add anything I wish. This statement is true. I have made it of my own free will.'

(iv) If he cannot read or if he refuses to write out and sign the caption at the end, the senior police officer in attendance must read it out to him and ask him if he wishes to correct alter or add anything and to sign it. This procedure must be certified on the statement by the officer.

Q: How does the Code of Practice for the Detention, Treatment and Questioning of Persons seek to offer special protection to children and young persons when being interviewed by the police?

A: Throughout the Codes of Practice, juveniles and other persons who are regarded as being at risk are provided with special provisions to ensure their protection during every stage of police procedures. This is especially so during the interview stage where vital evidence is invariably at stake.

The Code of Practice provides that a juvenile, whether he is suspected of crime or not shall not be interviewed or asked to make or sign a written statement in the absence of the appropriate adult unless the provisos relating to urgent interviews contained in Annex C of Code C apply. If the juvenile is cautioned in accordance with the code in the absence of the appropriate adult the caution must be repeated in the adult's presence.

It is worth reiterating at this stage that in respect of a juvenile, the term 'appropriate adult' means:

    (i)   his parent or guardian (or if he is in care, the care authority or voluntary organisation);

   (ii) a social worker; or

  (iii) failing either of the above, another responsible adult aged 18 or over who is not a police officer or employed by the police.

Q: Can a police officer conduct an interview at a juvenile's school?

A: It is suggested that occasions when the police would wish to conduct an interview at school will be few and far between. However such practice is permitted by the Code under strict limits.

Code C states that juveniles can be interviewed at school in exceptional circumstances and then only if the principal or his nominee gives his consent.

Both the juvenile's parents and, if appropriate, a person who has responsibility for his welfare and an appropriate adult (if different from the foregoing) should be notified by the police if at all possible that they would like to conduct an interview with the juvenile. A reasonable amount of time should be given for them to arrive. However, if waiting should cause unreasonable delay and unless the juvenile is suspected of committing an offence against the school, the principal or his nominee can act in the capacity of appropriate adult for the purpose of the interview.

Q: Is there anything in Code C concerning a juvenile being arrested at school?

A: Unless it can possibly be avoided a juvenile should not be arrested at school. If it is unavoidable, the principal or his nominee should be informed.

Q: How does the code of practice seek to protect the mentally disordered or mentally handicapped when they are interviewed or held in police detention?

A: A provision exists to protect mentally disordered or mentally handicapped persons as applies in relation to juveniles in the interview stage. The exact same conditions apply.

Q: What is the role of the 'appropriate adult'?

A: The code of practice makes the point that the appropriate adult should be informed that he is not expected to act simply as an observer. The purposes of his presence are, first, to advise the person interviewed and to observe whether or not the interview is being conducted properly and fairly; and, secondly, to facilitate communication with the person being interviewed.

Q: What special provisions exist in relation to the interviewing of foreigners?

A: The Code of Practice makes specific provisions about interviews with persons who may not be able to fully understand what is being said to them. To be more specific the Code identifies persons in this category as those who have difficulty understanding English; those who have requested an interpreter to be present; or where the interviewing officer cannot speak the person's own language.

There are two initial provisos in respect of such people. Firstly they must not be spoken to without an interpreter being present unless it is an urgent interview and Code C Annex C applies.

Secondly, once he has been arrested such a person must not be interviewed about the offence except at a police station etc. and with an interpreter unless the delay would result in a variety of consequences detailed in section 11.1 of Code C.

Q: How must an interview be conducted?

A: The officer who is conducting it must make sure that the interpreter takes a note of the interview at the time in the suspect's own language and certifies it as being accurate. This may subsequently be used if the interpreter is required to give evidence.

The interpreter must be allowed enough time to note both the questions and the answers after they have been spoken. The person must be allowed an opportunity to read the finished product or have it read to him and asked to sign it as being a correct record or to indicate any matter with which he does not agree. If the interview is tape recorded, the conditions outlined in Code E must be observed.

Q: What is the procedure when a statement is written down in a language which is not English?

A: In such circumstances the procedure is as follows:
  (a) the statement should be written down in the language in which it is made by the interpreter;
  (b) on completion the person making it should be asked to add his signature; and
  (c) a translation should be made into English.

Q: What protection does the code of practice afford to deaf persons?

A: Similar conditions apply to deaf people and interpreters as apply to people who cannot speak English and their interpreters. In particular the Code is exactly the same in relation to urgent interviews and persons being interviewed only at police stations except in certain circumstances ie where section 11.1 or Annex C of Code C apply.

Q: What about the position where a juvenile is to be interviewed and the parent or guardian acting as the appropriate adult is deaf or his hearing ability is seemingly questionable?

A: An interpreter shall be required to be present at the interview unless the urgent interview provision applies (section 11.1 and Annex A of Code 1).

Q: Is the interpreter allowed to read the interview record so he can verify its accuracy as he may be called to give evidence later?

A: Yes

Q: Does any organisation keep a list of interpreters who have appropriate knowledge and skill to interpret for the deaf?

A: Yes, the Social Services Department of Local Authorities.

Q: Does the Code of Practice provide any further guidance in relation to such persons who may be in custody at a police station?

A: Yes, every reasonable effort should be made to explain that the use of the interpreter is free.

The fact that a prisoner might have difficulty communicating with his solicitor because of hearing, speech or language difficulties has not been overlooked. Where a person has been told of his right to free legal advice and a solicitor is called and there are difficulties in this respect, an interpreter must be summoned. A rather obvious rider is added that the interpreter in respect of legal advice being obtained must not be a police officer. In any event, a police officer may only act in this capacity if the prisoner or his appropriate adult consent in writing or if the interview is tape recorded.

An interpreter is similarly required to explain to a person who is either deaf, appears to have difficulty with his hearing or his understanding of English, the charging procedures and the offence involved where the custody officer might be experiencing difficulties in this respect.

Q: What are the recording requirements in relation to interpreters?

The Code demands that action taken to call an interpreter and the consent of any relevant prisoner to be interviewed without one being present must be recorded.

Q: If then case goes to court, can the same interpreter act in that capacity there?
A: No, he will be a prosecution witness. Another person must be used as the court's interpreter.

Q: What is the extent of relaxation of the provisions of the code of practice in respect of interviews with persons who are unfit through drink or drugs; juveniles; mentally disordered or mentally handicapped persons; the deaf or foreigners?
A: Annex C of Code C deals with urgent interviews. While many of the provisions of Code C are designed to protect the vulnerable who find themselves in the hands of the police, there are circumstances which may lead to those rights being overridden. The carrying out of an urgent interview is one example of other matters taking priority over and above the prescribed rights of the vulnerable individual.

The Annex provides that where an interview is to be conducted at a police station etc. and if, and only if, an officer holding the rank of superintendent believes that any delay will:

(a) lead to interference with or harm to evidence connected with an offence or interference with or physical harm to other people; or
(b) lead to others who are suspected of the offence but not yet under arrest being alerted; or
(c) hinder the recovery of property obtained as a result of such an offence;

the following are permitted:

(i) a prisoner who is heavily under the influence of drink or drugs can be interviewed in that condition;
(ii) a juvenile or a mentally disordered or mentally handicapped person can be interviewed without an appropriate adult; or
(iii) a prisoner who has difficulties understanding English or who has hearing problems can be interviewed without an interpreter.

Q: Is an interview conducted in these circumstances restricted?
A: Yes, the questioning must cease as soon as sufficient information has been obtained to avert the risk?

Q: Do the procedures need to be recorded?
A: Yes, a record of the superintendent's decision must be recorded.

Q: Is any advice given about when urgent interviews should be conducted?
A: Yes, a note of guidance provides that all the persons in the special groups mentioned are all particularly vulnerable. The provisions of Annex C which overrides safeguards designed to protect them and to reduce the risk of unreliable evidence being produced in interviews should be used only in exceptional cases.

Q: Can a police officer question a person when in transit from one force area to another?
A: If a person arrested for an offence wishes to make a confession to a police officer wherever they are and whatever the circumstances, that confession is good evidence and in pure terms will be admissible as evidence in court.

Such a confession may be forthcoming at the place where the suspect is arrested, be it at his home or the scene of the crime, or whilst being conveyed to the police station. Similarly, a person who is sought by one police force and arrested in another may, of his own volition, decide that he wishes to make a confession.

There is nothing in the Code of Practice which outlaws evidence of this nature but there are rules as to how it must be recorded and subsequently dealt with.

There are also rules, not about a person who decides that confession is good for the soul, but in respect of questioning which is clearly outside the spirit of the Code of Practice. It may be tempting for a police officer on escort duty to strike up a conversation with a prisoner in a police vehicle en route from Gloucester to Glossop (and whose detention clock has not yet commenced because of section 41 of the Act) and to steer him towards making admissions about the offence he has been arrested for. To do so would be in direct conflict with Code C and any evidence obtained would probably not see the light of day.

Q: Can a prisoner be interviewed in hospital?
A: Only with the consent of his doctor. In addition, if he is questioned either at, or on the way to or from hospital, the detention clock will continue to run.

Fingerprinting

Section 61 of the Act specifies the circumstances when a person's fingerprints may be taken without consent.

Q: When may a person's fingerprints be taken without consent?

A: If a superintendent authorises such a course of action, or if the person has been charged etc with a recordable offence and has not had his fingerprints taken during the investigation. More precisely, section 61(3) of the Act provides that the fingerprints of a person detained at a police station may be taken without the appropriate consent:

(a) if an officer of at least the rank of superintendent authorises them to be taken; or
(b) if:
  (i) he has been charged with a recordable offence or informed that he will be reported for such an offence; and
  (ii) he has not had his fingerprints taken in the course of the investigation of the offence by the police. It will be noted that a superintendent's authority is not required in respect of the exercise of the power under section 61(3) (b).

Q: Does section 61(3) permit a superintendent to authorise fingerprints to be taken for any reason?

A: No. He can only give the authorisation required under (a) above if he has reasonable grounds:

(a) for suspecting the involvement of the person whose fingerprints are to be taken in a criminal offence; and
(b) for believing that his fingerprints will tend to confirm or disprove his involvement.

The authorisation may be given orally or in writing but if given orally it must be confirmed in writing as soon as is practicable (section 61(3) - (5)).

Q: Can a person's fingerprints be taken without consent for any other purpose?

A: Yes. A person's fingerprints may be taken without consent if he has been convicted of a recordable offence (ie an offence detailed in regulations made under section 27(4) of the Act for recording in national police records). However there is no power under that section to take fingerprints following the commission of a recordable offence in respect of which a probation order or an absolute or conditional discharge has been made — section 13 of the Powers of Criminal Courts Act 1973 refers.

If a person's fingerprints are taken at a police station whether with or without the appropriate consent:

(a) before the fingerprints are taken, an officer shall inform him that they may be the subject of a speculative search; and

(b) the fact that the person has been informed of this possibility shall be recorded as soon as is practicable after the fingerprints have been taken, (section 61(7A) and Code D section 3).

Q: What is a speculative search?

A: A speculative search in relation to a person's fingerprints or samples, means such a check against other fingerprints or samples against information derived from samples contained in records held by or on behalf of the police or held in connection with or as a result of an investigation of an offence, as is referred to in section 63A(1).

Q: Does a person have to be told the reason why his fingerprints are to be taken without consent?

A: Yes. He must be told the reason before his fingerprints are taken and the reason shall be recorded as soon as is practicable after they have been taken (section 61(7)). If the person is in police detention, the reason for taking them must be entered on the custody record (section 61(8)), a matter reiterated in the code of practice.

Whether fingerprints are to be obtained by consent or otherwise the person should also be informed that they will be destroyed if he is prosecuted and is cleared or he is not prosecuted (unless he admits the offence and is cautioned for it).

Q: If a person has been convicted of a recordable offence and dealt with at court, how may his fingerprints now be taken without consent?

A: Provisions exist under section 27 of the Act which authorised a constable at any time not later than one month after the date of the conviction to require such a person to attend a police station in order that his fingerprints may be taken.

The requirement shall give the person a period of at least seven days within which he must so attend and may require him so to attend at a specified time of day or between specified times of day.

Persons failing to appear in accordance with the requirement may be arrested.

Q: Does the Act preclude a person from giving his fingerprints voluntarily?
A: No, but if the consent is given at a time when he is at a police station the consent must be in writing (section 61(2) and code of practice).

Q: Whose consent is required in respect of the fingerprinting of juveniles?
A: It is only in certain circumstances that a person's fingerprints may be taken without 'appropriate consent'. The expression 'appropriate consent' means:

(a) in relation to a person who has attained the age of 17 years, the consent of that person;

(b) in relation to a person who has not attained that age but has attained the age of 14 years, the consent of that person and his parent or guardian; and

(c) in relation to a person who has not attained the age of 14 years, the consent of his parent or guardian (section 65).

It follows that, unless fingerprints are being taken without consent, under the authority of a superintendent or above, the consent of either parent and the juvenile is required in respect of juveniles in the 14 - 16 years inclusive category and in respect of a person who has not attained the age of 14 years the consent of his parent or guardian only.

Q: What records must be made in respect of the taking of a person's fingerprints without consent?
A: A record must be made as soon as possible of the reason for taking a person's fingerprints without consent and of their destruction. If force is used a record shall be made of the circumstances and those present.

Intimate and non-intimate samples

The Police and the Criminal Evidence Act 1984 recognises that body samples are important to police investigations and will sometimes help to prove or disprove a person's criminal liability. The Act distinguishes between 'intimate samples' and 'non-intimate samples'. Severe restrictions apply to the taking of an intimate sample from a person and consent will always be required. In respect of a 'non-intimate sample' consent is generally required but such a sample may be taken without the consent of the appropriate person in certain circumstances.

Substantial changes in relation to samples were introduced by the Criminal Justice and Public Order Act 1994. The pre-requisite of suspicion of a serious arrestable offence has been replaced by recordable offence in respect of both forms of sample. To initiate procedures to establish a national DNA database, provisions were introduced for non-intimate samples to be taken from persons convicted of recordable offences. The change to the law brings into force a process similar to that to the obtaining of fingerprints from convicted persons, with powers of arrest attached.

Intimate samples

Q: What is an 'intimate sample' and when can one be obtained?
A: An 'intimate sample' means:

  (a) a sample of blood, semen or any other tissue fluid, urine or pubic hair;
  (b) a dental impression.

An intimate sample may be taken from a person in police detention only:

  (a) if a police officer of at least the rank of superintendent authorises it to be taken; and
  (b) if the appropriate consent is given.

An officer may only give an authorisation if he has reasonable grounds:

  (a) for suspecting the involvement of the person from whom the sample is to be taken in a recordable offence; and
  (b) for believing that the sample will tend to confirm or disprove his involvement (section 62(1) and (2)).

The expression 'appropriate consent' means:

(a) in relation to a person who has attained the age of 17 years, the consent of that person;

(b) in relation to a person who has not attained that age but has attained the age of 14 years, the consent of that person and his parent or guardian; and

(c) in relation to a person who has not attained the age of 14 years, the consent of his parent or guardian (section 65).

It follows that in respect of a person specified in paragraph (b), the consent of two parties is required. The consent must be in writing (section 62(4)). A superintendent or above may give his authorisation orally or in writing but if the former must confirm it in writing as soon as practicable (section 62(3)).

Once an authorisation has been given and it is proposed that an intimate sample should be taken in pursuance of that authorisation, an officer shall inform the person from whom the sample is to be taken of the giving of the authorisation and of the grounds for giving it. In doing so, the nature of the offence in which it is suspected that the person from whom the sample is to be taken has been involved must be stated (section 62(5) and (6)).

Section 62(7A) provides that if an intimate sample is taken from a person at a police station:

(a) before the sample is taken, an officer shall inform him that it may be the subject of a speculative search; and

(b) the fact that the person has been informed of this possibility shall be recorded as soon as practicable after the sample has been taken.

An intimate sample may also be taken from a person who is not in police detention but from whom, in the course of the investigation of an offence, two or more non-intimate samples suitable for the same means of analysis have been taken which have proved insufficient:

(a) if a police officer or at least the rank of superintendent authorises it to be taken ; and

(b) if the appropriate consent is given, (section 62(1A)).

The procedure is developed in the Code of Practice which adds useful notes of guidance which advise that an insufficient sample is one which is not sufficient either in quantity or quality for the purpose of enabling information to be provided for the purpose of a particular form of analysis such as DNA analysis. An unsuitable sample is one which, by its nature, is not suitable for a particular form of analysis.

The guidance continues by advising that where hair samples are taken for the purpose of DNA analysis (rather than for other purposes such as making a visual match) the suspect should be permitted a reasonable choice as to what part of the body he wishes the hairs to be taken from. When hairs are plucked they should be plucked individually unless the suspect prefers otherwise and no more should be plucked than the person taking them reasonably considers necessary for a sufficient sample.

Where a sample is taken under section 62(1) or 62(1A), details of the authorisation, the grounds for it and the fact that consent was given must be recorded as soon as is practicable after the sample is taken. If the person is in police detention the matters must be recorded in his custody record (section 62(7) and (8)). All the foregoing procedural provisions are repeated in the relevant code of practice.

Q: Who may take an intimate sample?
A: An intimate sample, other than a sample of urine or saliva, may only be taken from a person by a registered medical or dental practitioner as appropriate (section 62(9) and code of practice).

Q: As consent is essential to the taking of an intimate sample, are the provisions of section 62 of the Act toothless and unnecessary?
A: No. While consent is pre-requisite to the taking of a sample a court may draw inferences from a refusal to give such a sample. The Act specifies that where the appropriate consent to the taking of an intimate sample from a person was refused without good cause, in any proceedings against that person for an offence:

  (a) the court, in determining: (i) whether to grant an application for dismissal made by that person under section 6 of the Magistrates' Courts Act 1980 (application for dismissal of charge in course of proceedings with a view to transfer for trial); or (ii) whether there is a case to answer; and
  (b) the court or jury, in determining whether that person is guilty of the offence charged;

may draw such inferences from the refusal as appear proper (section 62(10)). The code of practice stipulates that before a person is asked to provide an intimate sample he must be warned that a refusal may be treated, in any proceedings against him, as corroborating relevant prosecution evidence. He must also be reminded of his entitlement to have free legal advice and the reminder must be noted in the custody record.

Q: Must the warning as to the consequences of refusing to give an intimate sample be in a special form?

A: Before a person is asked to provide an intimate sample, he must be warned that if he refuses without good cause, his refusal may harm his case if it comes to trial. The code of practice gives guidance on the point and suggests the following form of words may be utilised:

'You do not have to (provide this sample) (allow this swab or impression to be taken), but I must warn you that if you refuse without good cause, your refusal may harm your case if it comes to trial.'

A record must be made of the giving of a warning and the fact that a person has been informed that samples may be the subject of a speculative search. If he is in police detention and not legally represented, he must also be reminded of his entitlement to have free legal advice and the reminder must be noted in the custody record. In the case of a person who is not in police detention and who is attending a police station voluntary on the basis that he has provided two unsuitable non-intimate samples and has consented to the taking of an intimate sample, the officer shall explain to him his entitlement to free legal advice.

Q: What effect have the provisions of section 62 on the taking of samples in respect of the drinking and driving legislation?

A: None. The section does not affect sections 4-11 of the Road Traffic Act 1988.

Q: Will a person's willing and true consent to give an intimate sample negate the necessity for adherence to section 62 of the Act?

A: No. In respect of other powers detailed in the Act a person may volunteer to do certain things, such as submit himself to search, or open a bag in circumstances which fall short of those which would justify the use of the relevant coercive power.

In respect of 'intimate samples' being required from a person in police detention, or from a person who is not in police detention but from whom two or more non-intimate samples have been taken section 62(1) and 62(1A) of the Act make it abundantly clear that such a sample may only be taken if authorised by an officer of at least the rank of superintendent and this may only be given if the specified grounds exist. If the person is not in police detention then he could volunteer to give an intimate sample. Section 62 of the Act has thus no application to victims of crime who consent to giving such samples.

Non-intimate samples

Q: What does the expression 'non-intimate' sample mean?
A: 'Non-intimate sample' means:

(a) a sample of hair other than pubic hair;
(b) a sample taken from a nail or from under a nail;
(c) a swab taken from any part of a person's body including the mouth but not any other body orifice;
(d) saliva;
(e) a footprint or a similar impression of any part of a person's body other than a part of his hand (section 65).

Q: In what circumstances may a 'non-intimate' sample be obtained?
A: With certain exceptions, a non-intimate sample cannot be taken without the written consent of the person from whom it is taken.

A non-intimate sample may be taken from a person without the appropriate consent (and by force if necessary) if:

(a) he is in police detention or is being held in custody by the police on the authority of a court; and
(b) an officer of at least the rank of superintendent authorises it to be taken without the appropriate consent.

Such an officer may only give his authorisation if he has reasonable grounds:

(a) for suspecting the involvement of the person from whom the sample is to be taken in a recordable offence; and
(b) for believing that the sample will tend to confirm or disprove his involvement.

The officer's authorisation may be given orally or in writing but if given orally the officer must confirm it in writing as soon as is practicable (section 63(1) - (4)). The foregoing matters are all reiterated, simplified and clarified in the code of practice.

The power has been extended by section 63, subsections (3A) and (3B) of the Police and Criminal Evidence Act 1984 which authorises non-intimate samples to be taken from persons charged with or reported for recordable offences and those convicted of a recordable offence.

Section 63(3A) provides a non-intimate sample may be taken from a person (whether or not he falls within subsection (3)(a)) without the appropriate consent if:

(a) he has been charged with a recordable offence or informed that he will be reported for such an offence; and

(b) either he has not had a non-intimate sample taken from him in the course of the investigation of the offence by the police or he has had a non-intimate sample taken from him but either it was not suitable for the same means of analysis or, though so suitable, the sample proved insufficient.

By virtue or section 63 (3B) a non-intimate sample may be taken from a person without the appropriate consent if he has been convicted of a recordable offence. (This provision does not apply to person convicted before the date on which section 63(3B) came into force).

Q: What rights has a person got in respect of a non-intimate sample being taken under an authorisation, without his consent?
A: Where an authorisation has been given and it is proposed that a non-intimate sample shall be taken in pursuance of the authorisation, an officer shall inform the person from whom the sample is to be taken: (i) of the giving of the authorisation; and (ii) of the grounds for giving it including the nature of the suspected offence and that the sample will be destroyed if he is subsequently prosecuted and is cleared or he is not prosecuted (unless he admits the offence and is cautioned).

In fulfilling this duty an officer must state the nature of the offence in which it is suspected that the person from whom the sample is to be taken has been involved (section 63(6) and (7) and code of practice).

In the case where, by virtue of section 63 (3A) or (3B), a sample is taken from a person without the appropriate consent:

(a) he shall be told the reason before the sample is taken; and

(b) the reason shall be recorded as soon as practicable after the sample is taken (section 63(8A)).

In addition, if a non-intimate sample is taken from a person at a police station, whether with or without appropriate consent:

(a) before the sample is taken, an officer shall inform him that it may be the subject of a speculative search (ie it may be checked against other samples or against information derived from other samples as referred to in section 63A(1) and

(b) the fact that a person has been informed of this possibility shall be recorded as soon as practicable after the sample has been taken (section 63 (8B)).

Q: What records must be made in respect of the taking of a non-intimate sample?

A: If a non-intimate sample is taken without the consent of the person details of the authorisation by virtue of which it was taken and the grounds for giving it shall be recorded as soon as practicable after the sample is taken. In the event of the sample being taken from a person detained at a police station the record shall be recorded in the person's custody record (section 63(8) and (9)).

The code of practice also dictates that a record must be made as soon as practicable of the reason for taking a sample or a body impression and of its destruction. If force is used a record shall be made of the circumstances and those present. If written consent is given to the taking of a sample or impression the fact must be recorded in writing.

Q: Does the Act affect the taking of intimate and non-intimate samples from the victims of crime?

A: Only insofar as it underlines the fact that the consent of such persons will always be necessary. In a note of guidance to Code D, it is pointed out that nothing in the Code prevents intimate samples being taken for elimination purposes with the consent of the person concerned but the provisions of paragraph 1.11 relating to the role of the appropriate adult should be applied.

Q: In taking intimate or non-intimate samples from a person what provisions exist to preserve the modesty of the individual?

A: Where clothing needs to be removed in circumstances likely to cause embarrassment to the person, no person of the opposite sex, who is not a medical practitioner or nurse, shall be present (unless in the case of a juvenile or a mentally disordered or mentally handicapped person that person specifically requests the presence of a particular adult of the opposite sex who is readily available), nor shall anyone whose presence is unnecessary. However, in the case of a juvenile this is subject to the overriding provision that such a removal of clothing may take place in the absence of the appropriate adult only if the juvenile signifies in the presence of the appropriate adult that he prefers the search to be done in his absence and the appropriate adult agrees.

Fingerprints and samples –
further statutory provisions

Q: What directions does the Act give about the use of samples obtained?

A: Section 63A has been added to the Police and Criminal Evidence Act 1984 by section 56 of the Criminal Justice and Public Order Act 1994. The section clarifies this point by directing that fingerprints or samples or the information derived from samples taken under any power conferred by this Part of this Act from a person who has been arrested on suspicion of being involved in a recordable offence may be checked against other fingerprints or samples or the information derived from other samples contained in records held by or on behalf of the police or held in connection with or as a result of an investigation of an offence.

Q: What guidance is given regarding the actual taking of samples?

A: Section 63A (2) provides that where a sample of hair other than pubic hair is to be taken the sample may be taken either by cutting hairs or by plucking hairs with their roots so long as no more are plucked than the person taking the sample reasonably considers to be necessary for a sufficient sample.

Q: What about the person who might be in prison, can a sample be obtained from him?

A: Yes, section 63A (3) states that where any power to take a sample is exercisable in relation to a person the sample may be taken in a prison or other institution to which the Prison Act 1952 applies.

Q: Where a person is not in police detention, what procedures apply to the obtaining of a sample from him?

A: In such circumstances, the Police and Criminal Evidence Act 1984 has been radically amended. By virtue of section 63A (4), any constable may, within the allowed period, require a person who is neither in police detention nor held in custody by the police on the authority of a court to attend a police station in order to have a sample taken where:

   (a) the person has been charged with a recordable offence or informed that he will be reported for such an offence and either he has not had a sample taken from him in the course of the investigation of the offence by the police or he has had a sample so taken from him but either it was not suitable for the same means of analysis or, though so suitable, the sample proved insufficient; or

(b) the person has been convicted of a recordable offence and either he has not had a sample taken from him since the conviction or he has had a sample taken from him (before or after his conviction) but either it was not suitable for the same means of analysis or, though so suitable, the sample proved insufficient.

Q: What is the allowed period?

A: The period allowed for requiring a person to attend a police station for the purpose specified in section 63A(4) is:

(a) in the case of a person falling within paragraph (a), one month beginning with the date of the charge or one month beginning with the date on which the appropriate officer is informed of the fact that the sample is not suitable for the same means of analysis or has proved insufficient, as the case may be;

(b) in the case of a person falling within paragraph (b), one month beginning with the date of the conviction or one month beginning with the date on which the appropriate officer is informed of the fact that the sample is not suitable for the same means of analysis or has proved insufficient, as the case may be.

Q: Does the section stipulate a time period during which a person must attend a police station?

A:Yes, a person must be given at least 7 days within which he must so attend; and he may be directed to attend at a specified time of day or between specified times of day.

Q: Is any sanction attached to a failure to comply with such a requirement?

A:Yes. Any constable may arrest without a warrant a person who has failed to comply with a requirement under subsection (4).

Q: Who is the appropriate officer?

A:In this section 'the appropriate officer' is:

(a) in the case of a person falling within subsection (4)(a), the officer investigating the offence with which that person has been charged or as to which he was informed that he would be reported;

(b) in the case of a person falling within subsection (4)(b), the officer in charge of the police station from which the investigation of the offence of which he was convicted was conducted.

Q: What is meant in relation to samples being sufficient or insufficient?
A: The expressions are developed in section 65 of the Act which explains that "sufficient" and "insufficient" in relation to a sample, means sufficient or insufficient (in point of quantity or quality) for the purpose of enabling information to be produced by the means of analysis used or to be used in relation to the sample.

Destruction of fingerprints and samples

Q: The Act allows fingerprints or samples to be taken from a person in connection with an offence. What must happen to them if the person is cleared of the offence or no proceedings are instituted against him?
A: They must be destroyed as soon as is practicable after the conclusion of the proceedings. If:

(a) fingerprints or samples are taken from a person in connection with such an investigation; and

(b) (i) he is cleared of the offence, or (ii) it is decided that he shall not be prosecuted for the offence and he has not admitted it and been dealt with by way of being cautioned by a constable, they must except as provided in section 64(3A) be destroyed as soon as is practicable after that decision is taken (section 64(1) and (2) and code of practice).

In addition when fingerprints are destroyed, access to relevant computer data shall be made impossible as soon as it is practicable to do so.

Q: Can the police retain the fingerprints of a person taken in connection with the investigation of an offence which the person subsequently admitted and was cautioned for?
A: Yes.

Q: Does the Act make any provision in respect of elimination fingerprints taken from the occupier of a burgled house or samples taken from a victim of crime?
A: Yes.

If: (a) fingerprints or samples are taken from a person in connection with the investigation of an offence; and (b) that person is not suspected of having committed the offence, they must except as provided in section 64(3A) be destroyed as soon as they have fulfilled the purpose for which they were taken.

Q: What is the exception referred to in section 64 (3A)?

A: The section provides that samples which are required to be destroyed under section 64(1) (2) or (3) need not be destroyed if they are taken for the purpose of the same investigation of an offence of which a person from whom one was taken has been convicted, but the information derived from the sample of any person entitled (apart from this subsection) to its destruction under section 64 (1) (2) or (3) shall not be used:

(a) in evidence against the person so entitled; or
(b) for the purposes of any investigation of an offence.

Section 64 (3B) further provides that where samples are required to be destroyed under section 64 (1) (2) or (3) and section 64 (3A) does not apply, information derived from the sample of any person entitled to its destruction under section 64 (1) (2) or (3) shall not be used.

(a) in evidence against the person so entitled; or
(b) for the purpose of any investigation of an offence.

These seemingly complicated provisions are summed up much more simply in Code D where it is stated that samples need not be destroyed if they were taken for the purpose of an investigation into an offence for which someone has been convicted, and from whom a sample was also taken. An accompanying note of guidance explains that provisions for the retention of samples allow for all samples in a case to be available for any subsequent miscarriage of justice investigation. But such samples – and the information derived from them – may not be used in the investigation of any offence or in evidence against the person who would otherwise be entitled to their destruction.

Q: What is there to prevent the police keeping copies of fingerprints and only destroying the original set?

A: If fingerprints are destroyed:-

(a) any copies of the fingerprints shall also be destroyed; and
(b) any chief officer of police controlling access to computer data relating to the fingerprints shall make access to the data

impossible as soon as it is practicable to do so. (Provision exists for a person to be supplied with a certificate within 3 months of a request made by him that this has been done) (Section 64(5) and 64(6A)).

Q: How can a person be assured that the police have destroyed his fingerprints?
A: A person who asks to be allowed to witness the destruction of his fingerprints or copies of them shall have a right to witness it. He must be told when they are taken that he may witness their destruction if he asks to do so within five days of being cleared or informed that he will not be prosecuted.

Charging of detained persons

Q: What action must be taken when a detained person is charged?
A: A: The Code of Practice gives directions which effectively continue procedures from the time when an officer is required to terminate an interview. The Code places responsibility upon the officer to determine not only when he believes that he has sufficient information to launch a prosecution but when he considers that a prosecution will succeed. In such cases and provided that the interviewee has said all that he wants to say about the offence, the officer must present him to the custody officer. The responsibility for deciding whether or not he should be charged thereupon shifts to the custody officer.

There is a proviso. If a prisoner is in detention for other matters as well, his presentation before the custody officer can be delayed until the foregoing is satisfied in respect of those other matters as well. (The provisions of section 11.4 of Code C – which relate to confiscation inquiries – may also override this provision.)

Any action which follows must be carried out in the presence of the appropriate adult when the prisoner is a juvenile or is a mentally disordered or mentally handicapped person.

Q: Has the formal caution before charge altered?
A: Yes, it reads:

> 'You do not have to say anything. But it may harm your defence if you do not mention now something which you later rely on in court. Anything you do say may be given in evidence.'

Q: Is there a requirement to give the person a copy of the caution and charge form?

A; Yes, the Code of Practice instructs that when a person is charged he must be handed a notice in writing which sets out the offence charged and gives the name of the officer in charge of the case. There is an exception in cases charged under the Prevention of Terrorism (Temporary Provisions) Act 1989 when a warrant or other identification may be given instead of an officer's name. Details of the officer's station and the case reference number must also be contained in the notice.

So far as possible the charge should be in simple terms but, at the same time, shall indicate the precise offence he is charged with. Where the prisoner is a juvenile, or is a mentally disordered or mentally handicapped person, the caution and charge form should be handed to the appropriate adult.

Q: What action must a police officer take if at any time after a person has been charged with or informed he may be prosecuted for an offence, a police officer wishes to bring to the notice of that person any written statement made by another or the content of an interview with another person?

A: He must hand him a true copy of the written statement made by the other person or tell him about what has been stated in the interview record. The officer must neither say nor do anything at that stage which invites a response except to tell him that he does not have to say anything but that anything he does say may be given in evidence. Effectively therefore, yet another caution is added to the list. The person must also be reminded that he is entitled to free legal advice.

If the prisoner is unable to read, the officer may read it to him and if he is a juvenile, or is a mentally disordered or mentally handicapped person the copy of the statement or the content of the interview record must also be brought to his attention.

Q: In what circumstances may a person be interviewed in connection with an offence with which he has been charged or informed he may be prosecuted for?

A: Whether a person who has been charged (or told that he may be prosecuted) with an offence can be further questioned about that offence has been a difficulty for many years. Whilst the rigid rules of old have disappeared, there are still quite restrictive measures in the Code of Practice which must be considered with care. Officers should not lose sight of the fact that even though the prevailing conditions may seem to allow a further interview at the time, there is likely to be a legal challenge in subsequent court proceedings. A decision in this respect should therefore be made with some circumspection.

The Code of Practice provides that further questioning is not allowed except where there is a need for them to be asked for the purpose of preventing or minimising harm or loss to another person or to the public or to clear up an ambiguity in a previous answer or statement made by him.

There is a further relaxation of the restriction which applies where it is considered necessary in the interests of justice that the person should have put to him and have an opportunity to comment on information which has been revealed since he was charged (or told that he may be prosecuted).

Before the process commences the person must be warned that he does not have to say anything but that anything he does say may be given in evidence. He must also be reminded of his entitlement to legal advice.

It is stressed that the interests of justice proviso will only apply in relation to information which has come to light after he has been charged etc. It does not therefore include matters which have arisen during the interview or information which was previously overlooked.

Q: Does the Notice of Intended Prosecution fit into this restrictive provision?

A: No, where a road traffic offender is served with a Notice of Intended Prosecution in accordance with sections 1 and 2 of the Road Traffic Offenders Act 1988, he may still be questioned about the offence. A note of guidance states that this procedure does not amount to informing a person that he may be prosecuted.

Q: Does the Code of Practice require these matters to be recorded?

A: Yes, including what is said by the person when he is charged.

In addition, if a person is questioned after he has been charged etc., both the questions and answers must be recorded in full and contemporaneously. The recording must be on the form designed for the purpose of contemporaneous interviews. On conclusion, the person should sign the record. If he refuses the officer conducting the interview and any other party present should sign them.

Where the further interview is tape recorded, Code E must be complied with.

Q: What provisions does Code C make about a juvenile' s aftercare once he has been charged?
A: There are detailed requirements outlined in section 38(6) of the Police and Criminal Evidence Act 1984 which has been amended by the Criminal Justice Act 1991 and the Criminal Justice and Public Order Act 1994. They are summarised in the Code of Practice.

The section directs that where a custody officer authorises an arrested juvenile, who has been charged with an offence, to be kept in police detention under section 38(1) of the Act, the custody officer shall secure that the arrested juvenile is moved to local authority accommodation – unless he certifies:

(a) that by reason of such circumstances as are specified in the certificate, it is impracticable to do so; or,

(b) in the case of an arrested juvenile who has attained the age of 12 years that no secure accommodation is available and that keeping him in other local authority accommodation would not be adequate to protect the public from serious harm from him.

Section 38(6A) develops the terminology used in section 38(6) and adds to it. The section defines 'local authority accommodation' 'secure accommodation' 'sexual offence' and 'violent offence' and adds that any reference in relation to an arrested juvenile charged with a violent or sexual offence, to protecting the public from serious harm from him shall be construed as a reference to protecting members of the public from death or serious personal injury, whether physical or psychological, occasioned by further such offences committed by him.

A comprehensive note of guidance is provided by Code C which advises that unless the provisions of section 38(6) apply, the custody officer cannot use the juvenile's behaviour or the circumstances of the offence he is charged with as grounds amounting to impracticability in seeking to make arrangements to transfer him to local authority accommodation.

The fact that there is secure accommodation available is only a consideration the custody officer must have in mind in relation to a juvenile aged 12 years or over when the local authority accommodation which is available is inadequate to protect the public from serious harm from him.

The responsibility placed upon the custody officer in this respect applies just as much to a juvenile who is charged during the day as well as to one charged during the night providing of course that the provisions of section 46 of the Act are complied with (provisions relating to detention after charge).

Q: What kind of certification is required if arrangements cannot be made to transfer the juvenile into local authority care?
A: The custody officer must record the reasons and prepare a certificate for production at court with the juvenile.

CHAPTER 6

CODES OF PRACTICE

Section 66 of the Police and Criminal Evidence Act 1984 imposes upon the Secretary of State a duty to issue codes of practice in connection with: powers of stop and search which may be exercised without first arresting a person; the detention, treatment and questioning and identification of persons by police officers; searches of premises by police officers; and the seizure of property found by police officers on persons or premises. Save for the code of practice concerning identification, which lends itself to being dealt with separately, the provisions of the other codes have been blended into the text. The duty of the Secretary of State to issue a code of practice in connection with the tape recording of interviews is contained in section 60(1)(a) of the Act.

Q: When did the latest edition of the codes come into effect?
A: 10th April 1995

Q: What particular changes do the new codes incorporate?
A: Revisions to the codes were made to implement recommendations of the Royal Commission on Criminal Justice which reported in 1993; to implement changes in the law brought about by the Criminal Justice and Public Order Act 1994; and to meet comments on the previous editions of the codes made by the courts, police, legal practitioners and members of the public. Significant changes to the codes include:

    (a) new provisions on stop and search in Code A reflecting section 60 (searches in anticipation of violence) and section 81 (searches for prevention of terrorism) of the Criminal Justice and Public Order Act 1994;

(b) a revised caution and related matters in Codes C and E reflecting the provisions on inferences from an accused's silence in sections 34-39 of the Criminal Justice and Public Order Act 1994;

(c) new provisions on the taking of body samples in Code D reflecting section 54-59 of the Criminal Justice and Public Order Act 1994:

(d) a new Annex E to Code D dealing with group identifications.

Q: Will failure on the part of a police officer or other persons charged with the duty of investigating offences to comply with any provision of such a code of practice render such person liable to any criminal or civil proceedings?

A: No, but in all criminal and civil proceedings any code of practice shall be admissible in evidence and if any provision of such a code appears to the court or tribunal conducting the proceedings to be relevant to any question arising in the proceedings it shall be taken into account in determining that question (section 67(10) and (11)).

Q: How may members of the public acquaint themselves with the provisions of the various codes?

A: The codes of practice must be readily available at all police stations for consultation by police officers, detained persons and members of the public.

CHAPTER 7

EVIDENCE

> The Police and Criminal Evidence Act 1984 makes amendment to the law relating to the principles governing the admissibility of evidence. The rules relating to the admissibility of convictions and acquittals is brought up to date. A new criterion is introduced in respect of confession evidence and a statutory rule to replace rules at common law regarding the exclusion of unfairly obtained evidence is introduced. The common law rules relating to the competency and compellability of the accused's spouse have been overturned and effectively replaced by the Act's provisions.

Q: In some cases it will be necessary to prove either a person's conviction or acquittal. Does the Act make any provision in respect of these matters?

A: Yes. The Act consolidates a number of archaic provisions previously found in various statutes. The means of proving convictions is described in section 73 of the Act.

Where in any proceedings the fact that a person has in the United Kingdom been convicted or acquitted of an offence, otherwise than by a Service court is admissible in evidence, it may be proved by producing a certificate of conviction or, as the case may be, of acquittal relating to that offence, and proving that the person named in the certificate as having been convicted or acquitted of the offence is the person whose conviction or acquittal of the offence is to be proved (section 73(1)).

The Act stipulates that a certificate of conviction or acquittal:

(a) shall, as regards a conviction or acquittal on indictment, consist of a certificate, signed by the clerk of the court where the conviction or acquittal took place, giving the substance and effect (omitting the formal parts) of the indictment and of the conviction or acquittal; and

(b) shall, as regards a conviction or acquittal on a summary trial, consist of a copy of the conviction or of the dismissal of the information, signed by the clerk of the court where the conviction or acquittal took place or by the clerk of the court, if any, to which a memorandum of the conviction or acquittal was sent; and a document purporting to be a duly signed certificate of conviction or acquittal under this section shall be taken to be such a certificate unless the contrary is proved (section 73(2)).

The provisions of section 73 of the Act are in addition to and not to the exclusion of any authorised manner of proving a conviction or acquittal (section 73(4)).

In other words section 73 does not prejudice existing provisions whereby convictions may be proved by fingerprints or by personal identification.

Q: To what extent will a person's conviction be admitted as evidence of the commission of an offence?

A: Although the necessity will arise infrequently the Act provides that in any proceedings the fact that a person other than the accused has been convicted of an offence by or before any court in the United Kingdom or by a Service court outside the United Kingdom shall be admissible in evidence for the purpose of proving, where to do so is relevant to any issue in those proceedings, that that person committed that offence, whether or not any other evidence of his having committed that offence is given (section 74(1)).

The provision can be identified with admissibility of a thief's convictions in proceedings against the handler; the admissibility of a principal offender's conviction in proceedings against an aider and abettor, etc.

In any proceedings in which by virtue of section 74(1) a person other than the accused is proved to have been convicted of an offence by or before any court in the United Kingdom or by a Service court outside the United Kingdom, he shall be taken to have committed that offence unless the contrary is proved (section 74(2)). In effect section 74(1) dictates that the evidence will be admissible and section 74(2) describes the cogency of that evidence in respect of the conviction of a person other than the accused.

The accused person is catered for by section 74(3) of the Act which dictates that in any proceedings where evidence is admissible of the fact that the accused has committed an offence, insofar as that evidence is relevant to any matter in issue in the proceedings for a reason other than a tendency to show in the accused a disposition to commit the kind of offence with which he is charged, if the accused is proved to have been convicted of the offence:

(a) by or before any court in the United Kingdom; or
(b) by a Service court outside the United Kingdom, he shall be taken to have committed that offence unless the contrary is proved.

Where proof of the accused's previous convictions is allowed by the court, eg in cases where special evidence is admitted to prove guilty knowledge in handling cases, the conviction is conclusive proof that the accused committed that previous offence unless he proves otherwise on a balance of probabilities. The provision cannot be used merely to prove evidence of similar facts, ie that the accused had a propensity to commit the type of offence charged.

Section 75 of the Act contains supplementary provisions concerning the admissibility of documentary evidence to prove the convictions and the authentication of those documents.

Q: Does the Act provide any safeguards for an accused person in respect of any confession made by him?
A: The Act brings together law previously found in various sources, ie statute, common law and the former Judges' Rules. It provides that in any proceedings a confession made by an accused person may be given in evidence against him insofar as it is relevant to any matter in issue in the proceedings and is not excluded by the court in pursuance of this section (section 76(1)).

A 'confession' includes any statement wholly or partly adverse to the person who made it, whether made to a person in authority or not and whether made in words or otherwise (section 82(1)).

A confession may be excluded on the grounds that it was or may have been obtained by oppression or in consequence of something said or done which makes the confession unreliable. More precisely, section 76(2) of the Act declares that if in any proceedings where the prosecution proposes to give in evidence a confession made by an accused person, it is represented to the court that the confession was or may have been obtained:

(a) by oppression of the person who made it; or
(b) in consequence of anything said or done which was likely, in the circumstances existing at the time, to render unreliable any confession which might be made by him in consequence thereof, the court shall not allow the confession to be given in evidence against him except insofar as the prosecution proves to

the court beyond reasonable doubt that the confession (notwithstanding that it may be true) was not obtained as aforesaid.

Effectively section 76(2) ensures that confessions obtained by oppression will be excluded as will those induced by other means which render the confession unreliable. The section thus gives statutory effect, with some modification, to the rules of voluntariness and reliability hitherto found in a multiplicity of decided cases.

The expression 'oppression' includes torture, inhuman or degrading treatment and the use or threat of violence (whether or not amounting to torture) (section 76(8)).

It is submitted that the term 'threat of violence' will include a veiled threat.

In any proceedings where the prosecution proposes to give in evidence a confession made by an accused person, the court may of its own motion require the prosecution, as a condition of allowing it to do so, to prove that the confession was not obtained as mentioned in section 76(2) (section 76(3)).

Q: If a confession is excluded by reason of it being, or possibly having been obtained by oppression or in consequence of things said or done which make it unreliable, will this affect the admissibility of matters discovered as a result of the confession?
A: No. The fact that a confession is wholly or partly excluded shall not affect the admissibility in evidence:

(a) of any facts discovered as a result of the confession; or
(b) where the confession is relevant as showing that the accused speaks, writes or expresses himself in a particular way, of so much of the confession as is necessary to show that he does so (section 76(4)).

It follows that if a person's confession of stealing and subsequently secreting cartons of cigarettes and spirits in his home were rendered inadmissible, the prosecution would nonetheless be able to tender in evidence their discovery of the stolen goods in that person's home and, evidence of his fingerprints being on them if that were the case.

But, in such circumstances it remains the prerogative of the defence to reveal that the facts were discovered as a result of a statement made by the accused (section 76(5)).

There is thus no scope for the prosecution making mention of a confession or part of a confession which has been rendered inadmissible when they introduce evidence of matters discovered in consequence of it. Similarly, despite the fact that a person's confession may have been excluded, the prosecution will be able to depend on the person's verbal confession to show that he speaks with, say, a particular regional accent or with a lisp or other impediment. Likewise his written confession may be used to indicate his style of writing or mode of expression.

Q: Do any special provisions exist in respect of the confessions made by mentally handicapped persons?

A: Yes. The Act demands that a confession made by such a person be treated with particular caution in the event of it being made otherwise than in the presence of an independent person. More precisely, the Act declares that without prejudice to the general duty of the court at a trial on indictment to direct the jury on any matter on which it appears to the court appropriate to do so, where at such a trial:

(a) the case against the accused depends wholly or substantially on a confession by him; and
(b) the court is satisfied:
   (i) that he is mentally handicapped; and
   (ii) that the confession was not made in the presence of an independent person, the court shall warn the jury that there is special need for caution before convicting the accused in reliance on the confession, and shall explain that the need arises because of the circumstances mentioned in paragraphs (a) and (b) above (section 77(1)).

Section 77(2) of the Act imposes on magistrates' courts a duty to treat such cases as demanding the need for special caution before convicting the accused on his confession.

'Independent person' does not include a police officer or a person employed for, or engaged on, police purposes; and 'mentally handicapped', in relation to a person, means that he is in a state of arrested or incomplete development of mind which includes significant impairment of intelligence and social functions (section 76(3)).

It will be noted that the provisions of the section do not apply to all confessions made by mentally handicapped persons. Three criteria must be satisfied before the section becomes operative:

(a) the case against the accused depends wholly or substantially on the confession;
(b) the maker is mentally handicapped; and,

(c) the confession was not made in the presence of an independent person.

Q: Will evidence obtained unfairly by the police automatically be excluded?

A: Evidence of confession obtained by oppression will always be inadmissible. The court must also always exclude evidence of confession or part of such a confession which was or may have been obtained in consequence of anything said or done which was likely to render the confession unreliable. In all other cases the truth may be admitted in evidence even though it might have been obtained unfairly or unlawfully. Courts will, however, be able to exercise discretion as to whether to admit or disallow evidence obtained in such circumstances.

Section 78(1) of the Act stipulates that in any proceedings the court may refuse to allow evidence on which the prosecution proposes to rely to be given if it appears to the court that, having regard to all the circumstances, including the circumstances in which the evidence was obtained, the admission of the evidence would have such an adverse effect on the fairness of the proceedings that the court ought not to admit it.

Q: Will evidence obtained contrary to the procedural requirements of the various codes of practice be automatically excluded?

A: No. The Act recognises that it would be contrary to the interests of justice to discipline the police by excluding relevant evidence in the criminal courts. The Act preserves a trial judge's discretion in determining the admissibility of evidence. The fact that evidence obtained in breach of the codes of practice or unlawfully may be allowed in evidence, does not, of course, prevent the launching of disciplinary or civil proceedings as the case may be.

Q: To what extent does the Act amend the law relating to the competency and compellability of an accused person's spouse?

A: In any proceedings the wife or husband of the accused shall be competent to give evidence:

(a) for the prosecution; and
(b) on behalf of the accused or any person jointly charged with the accused (section 80(1)).

In any proceedings the wife or husband of the accused shall be compellable to give evidence on behalf of the accused (section 80(2)).

Instances where the spouse will be compellable on behalf of the prosecution are detailed in section 80(3) of the Act which dictates that in any proceedings the wife or husband of the accused shall be compellable to give evidence for the prosecution or on behalf of any person jointly charged with the accused if and only if:

(a) the offence charged involves an assault on, or injury or a threat of injury to, the wife or husband of the accused or a person who was at the material time under the age of sixteen; or

(b) the offence charged is a sexual offence alleged to have been committed in respect of a person who was at the material time under that age; or

(c) the offence charged consists of attempting or conspiring to commit, or of aiding, abetting, counselling, procuring or inciting the commission of, an offence falling within paragraph (a) or (b) above.

All the foregoing rules of competency and compellability are subject to the exception that where a husband and wife are jointly charged with an offence neither spouse shall at the trial be competent or compellable by virtue of subsection (1)(a), (2) or (3) above to give evidence in respect of that offence unless that spouse is not, or is no longer, liable to be convicted of that offence at the trial as a result of pleading guilty or for any other reason (section 80(4)). Effectively this protects an accused spouse from self-incrimination whilst still in jeopardy of conviction.

In any proceedings a person who has been but is no longer married to the accused shall be competent and compellable to give evidence as if that person and the accused had never been married (section 80(5)).

The term 'sexual offence' in section 80(3) (b) above means an offence under the Sexual Offences Act 1956, the Indecency with Children Act 1960, the Sexual Offences Act 1967, section 54 of the Criminal Law Act 1977 or the Protection of Children Act 1978 (section 80(7)).

The failure of the wife or husband of the accused to give evidence shall not be made the subject of any comment by the prosecution (section 80(8)).

Those who are euphemistically described as 'common law husband' or 'common law wife' enjoy no legal recognition in respect of competency and compellability and thus in all cases a 'common law' spouse will always be both competent and compellable to give evidence against his or her partner.

CHAPTER 8

A MISCELLANY

Police complaints and discipline

The main criticism of the police complaints and discipline procedures for many years has been that because the police investigate complaints against police officers they are, in effect, the judge of their own cause. Prior to Part IX of the Police and Criminal Evidence Act 1984 coming into force, although the Director of Public Prosecutions and the Police Complaints Board supplied the independent element so far as decision-making was concerned, there was no independent element in the actual investigative process. In establishing the Police Complaints Authority the Act rectifies the shortcomings of the previous legislation and takes one more step towards what some may regard as the inevitable fully independent complaints investigation body.

Q: What effect does the Act have on the police complaints procedure?
A: The Act creates the Police Complaints Authority whose duty is to oversee the decision-making process in respect of all complaints and to supervise the investigation of certain serious complaints against the police. A standard procedure is established to deal with all complaints and those complaints which must be referred to the authority are stipulated. Chief officers of police have power to refer non-complaint matters and the authority may call in any others which are not in the mandatory class.

Part IX of the Act requires the authority to issue a statement of satisfaction in respect of the investigation of mandatory complaints which is necessary before any decision may be made by the chief officer of police as to criminal or disciplinary charges. Although the

Director of Public Prosecutions is still involved to some extent with criminal offences arising from complaints, more responsibility is placed upon chief officers of police in the decision-making process, which is subsequently subject to review by the Police Complaints Authority. In addition a new informal resolution procedure is created to cater for those complaints which, even if proved, would not result in criminal or disciplinary charges being referred.

Q: Are police officers allowed to be represented by a barrister or a solicitor in disciplinary proceedings?
A: A police officer cannot be dismissed, required to resign or be reduced in rank unless he is given the opportunity to be legally represented at the hearing (section 102).

Community consultation

Q: The police are charged with the responsibility of enforcing law and preserving order. In attaining these objectives to what extent must the police have regard to the community?
A: The Act recognises the recommendation of the Scarman Report that the views of the community on policing should be sought. In particular it provides that arrangements shall be made in each police area for obtaining the views of people in that area about matters concerning the policing of the area and for obtaining their co-operation with the police in preventing crime in the area (section 106(1)).

Acting ranks

Q: The Act entrusts specific powers to police officers of the rank of superintendent, or above, and officers of the rank of inspector or above. May such powers be delegated to officers holding lower ranks?
A: Yes. For the purpose of any provisions of this Act or any other Act under which a power in respect of the investigation of offences or the treatment of persons in police custody is exercisable only by or with the authority of a police officer of at least the rank of superintendent, an officer of the rank of chief inspector shall be treated as holding the rank of superintendent if:

(a) he has been authorised by an officer holding a rank above the rank of superintendent to exercise the power or, as the case may be, to give his authority for its exercise, or

(b) he is acting during the absence of an officer holding the rank of superintendent who has authorised him, for the duration of that absence, to exercise the power or, as the case may be, to give his authority for its exercise (section 107(1)).

In respect of the powers conferred on inspectors, or above – for the purpose of any provision of this Act or any other Act under which such a power is exercisable only by or with the authority of an officer of at least the rank of inspector, an officer of the rank of sergeant shall be treated as holding the rank of inspector if he has been authorised by an officer of at least the rank of chief superintendent to exercise the power or as the case may be, to give his authority for its exercise (section 107(2)).

The spirit of the legislation is to cater for officers entrusted to perform duties in a higher rank in consequence of absences due to sickness, annual leave or courses. It is submitted that it would be an abuse of the provision to utilise the provision as part of a 'responsibility sharing exercise' whereby the superintendent's responsibilities were assumed after specified times on certain days of the week.

It will be noted that there is no scope for an inspector who is an 'acting chief inspector' being further invested with the powers accompanying the rank of superintendent. Similarly a constable who is 'acting sergeant' cannot be further authorised to assume the powers conferred upon an inspector. Neither hold the rank of chief inspector or sergeant, as the case may be.

Use of force

Q: The Act confers on police officers a number of powers. To what extent may force be used in the exercise of them?

A: Where any provision of the Act:

(a) confers a power on a constable; and

(b) does not provide that the power may only be exercised with the consent of some person, other than a police officer, the officer may use reasonable force, if necessary, in the exercise of the power (section 117).

The amount of force used must not be disproportionate to the resistance to be overcome. What constitutes 'reasonable force' is a question of fact to be determined by the circumstances of the particular case. No more positive guidelines can be provided.

CHAPTER 9

CODE OF PRACTICE FOR THE IDENTIFICATION OF PERSONS BY POLICE OFFICERS

> This code of practice details the procedural considerations to be taken account of in respect of the identification of suspected offenders and, in doing so, makes specific provision for identification parades, group identifications, video identifications, confrontations, identification by photographs as well as reiterating some of the Act's provisions regarding identification by body samples, swabs and impressions.

Q: How does the code of practice protect the mentally handicapped, the mentally disordered, juveniles and persons suffering from some other form of handicap?
A: In similar fashion to the Code of Practice for the Detention, Treatment and Questioning of Persons by Police Officers, the Code of Practice for the Identification of Persons by Police Officers makes special provision for those who are regarded as most at risk.

If a police officer suspects or receives information offered in good faith that a person may be mentally disordered or mentally handicapped he must treat him as a mentally disordered or mentally handicapped person within the provisions of the Code of Practice. The same principle applies to a person who does not have the mental ability of appreciating the significance of questions put to him or his answers to such questions.

A note of guidance advises that the generic term 'mental disorder' is used throughout the Code. 'Mental disorder' is defined in section 1(2) of the Mental Health Act 1983 as 'mental illness, arrested or incomplete development of mind, psychopathic disorder and any other disorder or disability of mind'. It should be noted that 'mental disorder' is different from 'mental handicap' although the two are dealt with similarly throughout the code. Where the custody officer has any doubt as to the mental state or capacity of a person detained, an appropriate adult should be called.

If anyone appears to be under the age of 17 then he shall be treated as a juvenile for the purposes of this code in the absence of clear evidence to show that he is older.

Additionally the Code of Practice provides that unless there is compelling evidence to the contrary, where a person apparently is blind or seriously visually handicapped, deaf, cannot read or speak or by reason of a speech impediment has difficulty in communicating orally, he should be treated as such.

Where a suspect's consent is a pre-requisite to any procedure, the agreement of a person who is mentally disordered or mentally handicapped will only be regarded as a proper consent if given when the appropriate adult is present. In the case of a juvenile, his parent or guardian's consent is also required unless he is under 14 in which case the consent of the parent or guardian is sufficient in itself. Where a juvenile is in the care of the local authority or a voluntary organisation, the consent required of a parent or guardian may be given by the local authority or organisation.

In the Code of Practice, the term appropriate adult is the same as that provided in Code C. It is reiterated that a number of persons are excluded from acting as appropriate adults. These include a parent or guardian who is suspected of involvement in the offence, is a witness to or victim of the alleged offence, is somehow involved in the inquiries and investigation into the alleged offence or before assuming the role, has received admissions from the suspect. Where a juvenile expressly objects, a parent from whom he is estranged should not be invited to act as the appropriate adult.

In the cause of fairness, where a juvenile makes an admission either to a social worker or in his presence when he is not acting as appropriate adult, another social worker should act.

The interests of a person who is mentally disordered or mentally handicapped and all concerned may be better served if the appropriate adult is a person who has special experience or training in the care of such persons as opposed to a relative who has none. However, if the suspect prefers a relative to act as the appropriate adult instead of the better qualified person or if he objects to a person acting as the appropriate adult, then wherever practicable his wishes should take precedence.

A procedure which demands information to be imparted to or obtained from a suspect must be conducted in the presence of the appropriate adult if the suspect is a vulnerable person ie mentally disordered or mentally handicapped or a juvenile. If such information is first imparted to or required from the suspect in the absence of the appropriate adult, the procedure must be repeated upon the arrival of the appropriate adult.

Where the suspect is apparently deaf or there is uncertainty about his ability to hear or speak or his ability to understand English and the police officer cannot effectively communicate with him, the services of an interpreter must be utilised.

Where a person who is mentally disordered or mentally handicapped or a juvenile is required to actively participate in a procedure, irrespective of whether he is a suspect or witness, such participation must take place in the presence of the appropriate adult but such person must be prevented from prompting an identification by a witness.

Further protection for the blind, seriously visually handicapped and those unable to read is provided for by the requirement that the custody officer must ensure the availability of such a person's solicitor, relative or appropriate adult, or some other person likely to take an interest in his welfare and who is not involved in the investigation, to help in checking documentation. The person who is assisting may, in respect of anything which requires written consent or signification, be asked to sign on behalf of the suspect if the suspect so wishes. The notion of a representative signing on behalf of a blind or visually handicapped person or one who is unable to read, seeks to protect both the individual and the police.

Precluded from acting as appropriate adult are solicitors and lay visitors who are present at a police station in that capacity.

Q: Are any procedures under other statutes affected by the provisions of the code of practice?

A: No. In introducing the general aspects of the Code of Practice for the Identification of Persons by Police Officers it is provided that nothing in the code affects any procedure under:

(i) sections 4 to 11 of the Road Traffic Act 1988 or sections 15 and 16 of the Road Traffic Offenders Act 1988;

(ii) paragraph 18 of Schedule 2 to the Immigration Act 1971; or

(iii) the Prevention of Terrorism (Temporary Provisions) Act 1989: section 15(9), paragraph 8(5) of Schedule 2, and paragraph 7(5) of Schedule 5.

However, the provisions of part 3 of the code on the taking of fingerprints and of part 5 on the taking of body samples, do apply to persons detained under section 14 of, or paragraph 6 of Schedule 5 to, the Prevention of Terrorism (Temporary Provisions) Act 1989. So far as fingerprints are concerned, section 61 of the Police and Criminal Evidence Act 1984 is amended by the provisions of the Prevention of Terrorism (Temporary Provisions) Act 1989 (section 15(10) and Schedule 5). Similarly, sections 62 and 63 of the Police and Criminal Evidence Act 1984 are amended by section 15(11) of the 1989 Act. The modifications effectively permit fingerprints and samples to be taken in terrorist cases to help establish whether the suspect is or has been involved in terrorism as well as those cases where there are reasonable grounds to suspect that a person was involved in a specific offence.

There is, no statutory requirement (and, consequently, no requirement under paragraph 3.4 of the code) to destroy fingerprints or body samples taken in terrorist cases. Similarly, requirements to tell the person from whom these were taken, that they will be destroyed, and to offer such persons an opportunity to witness the destruction of their fingerprints do not apply to terrorist cases.

Q: Does the Code of Practice make reference to what may be regarded as a photograph?

A: Yes. In Code D any reference to photographs, negatives and copies also refer to images stored or reproduced through any medium.

Q: In the identification process what requirement does Code D impose in relation to the initial steps to be taken by the police?

A: A record must be made of the description of the suspect as first offered by a witness or potential witness. The record must be made before the witness or potential witness takes part in a parade, group identification, video film, confrontation or where photographs are to be shown. The Code does not specify in what form the record should be made or kept. It may be kept or made in any form provided the first description as offered by the witness can be subsequently provided in written form to be supplied to the suspect or his legal adviser in accordance with the Code's provisions.

Before any of the various identification procedures are conducted, a copy of the record of the first description must be provided to the suspect or his solicitor.

A note of guidance adds that where it is intended to conduct a photographic identification, it is the responsibility of the officer in charge of the investigation to confirm to the officer who supervises and directs the showing of photographs that the first description supplied by the witness has been recorded. Where a first description has not been recorded, the photographic identification procedure must be postponed.

This provision is of the utmost significance and may have far-reaching consequences in all forms of the identification process as the record of the potential witness' first description of the suspect must be provided to the suspect or his solicitor before any of the identification procedures commences.

It is vital that the record made of the description first given is accurate. From a practical viewpoint, witnesses should not be pressed into making calculated guesses merely to provide investigating officers with a more complete picture of the suspect. There is every likelihood that the first description will become a central evidential issue in any case contested on the grounds of identification.

Q: What does the code of practice demand in respect of the identification of a suspect who is at a police station?

A: Firstly, a decision as to which method of identification is to be used. In a case involving disputed identification evidence and where the suspect's identity is known to the police and he is available, the options available are a parade, a group identification, a video film or a confrontation.

Accompanying notes of guidance develop the issues of whether a person is available or deemed to be 'known'. So far as the former is concerned, 'being available' means immediate availability or availability within a reasonably short time to take part in the relevant procedure. A suspect will be deemed to be 'known' if the police are in possession of sufficient information to justify the arrest of a person on suspicion of complicity in the offence.

The code dictates that whenever a suspect disputes an identification, an identification parade shall be held if the suspect consents unless the conditions outlined in paragraphs 2.4, 2.7 or 2.10 of Code D apply. A parade may also be held if the officer in charge of the investigation considers that it would be useful and the suspect consents.

An officer not below the rank of inspector who is not involved in the investigation shall be responsible for making the arrangements for and conducting the identification procedures, irrespective of which of the four methods is used. Such a person is referred to as the identification officer. All officers involved in the investigation of the case are precluded from taking part in any identification procedure.

Once a decision has been made as to which method of identification is to be used, unless confrontation has been decided upon, before any identification procedure is arranged, the suspect must be informed orally and in writing – by notice – of the decision and matters explained to him.

The suspect must be informed by the identification officer of the following: the object of the identification parade, group identification or video identification, as the case may be; of his right to free legal advice; the procedures including his right to have a solicitor or friend present; if he is a juvenile or mentally disordered or mentally handicapped, the special arrangements which exist for such persons; he cannot be compelled to take part in a parade or to co-operate in a group identification or the filming of a video recording, (if it is proposed to conduct a group identification or hold a video identification) of his right to opt for an identification parade if it is practicable to arrange one; his refusal to participate in a parade or non-co-operation in a group identification or the making of a video recording, such refusal or non-co-operation would not prevent the police from proceeding covertly without his knowledge and consent and nor would such refusal or non co-operation preclude the police from making other arrangements to establish whether a witness identifies him.

Additionally, the identification officer must explain to the suspect: that if, between the taking of his photograph on the occasion of his arrest or after being charged, and the time of any attempt to conduct an identification procedure, he should significantly change his appearance, evidence of this fact may be given if the case were to proceed to trial and other methods of identification may be considered; on the occasion of an identification parade, a group identification or a video identification, a photograph or a video recording may be taken or made of him, as the case may be; whether before his identity became known and during investigations the witness had been shown any photograph, photo-fit, identi-kit or similar picture (note, it is the duty of the investigating officer to inform the identification officer of this, if such action has taken place); that if he changes his appearance prior to a parade being held it might not be possible to arrange one on the day in question or later and by reason of him changing his appearance, alternative methods of identification may be considered; the provision to him or his solicitor of details of the 'first description' given by any witness who is to attend the identification line-up, group identification, video identification or any confrontation which might be arranged.

The suspect must be given all the foregoing information in a written notice. After being given a reasonable opportunity, by the identification officer to read it, the suspect must be asked to sign a second copy of the written notice and asked to indicate whether or not he is agreeable to participating in an identification parade, group identification or co-operate in the making of a video recording of him. The identification officer should keep the signed second copy of the notice.

Q: What does the Code of Practice generally prescribe in respect of identification parades?

A: Subject to the consent of the suspect, whenever such person disputes an identification, an identification parade must be held. To this general rule there are exceptions. A parade need not be held if the identification officer decides that it would not be practicable to get together sufficient people who resemble the suspect to make a parade fair. The identification officer may so decide because of the unusual appearance of the suspect or any other reason. Similarly an identification parade need not be held where either the prescribed group identification or video film identification methods are to be used.

Subject to the consent of the suspect an identification parade may be held if the officer in charge of the investigation considers it would be useful. Where an identification parade is conducted it must satisfy the conditions and requirements which are set out in the following paragraphs.

The suspect must be afforded a reasonable opportunity to have a solicitor or friend present and should be asked by the identification officer to signify, on a second copy of the notice, his wishes in this respect. The venue of the parade must be in a normal room or in a room furnished with a screen which permits witnesses to view members of the parade out of the sight of those forming the parade. Irrespective of whether the parade takes place in a room or one equipped with a screen, the procedures for the composition and conduct of the identification parade are identical.

However, where a screen is used, a parade may only take place where either the suspect's solicitor, friend or appropriate adult is present or the identification procedure is video recorded. Additionally, everything said to or by a witness at the venue of the parade must be said in the presence of the suspect's solicitor, friend or appropriate adult or be video recorded.

Prior to the parade being held, details of the first description of the suspect given by any witnesses to be used on the parade must be given to the suspect or his solicitor. Provided it is practicable to do so and no unreasonable delay to the investigation is likely, the suspect or his solicitor should also be permitted to examine any material released to the media by the police with a view to the suspect being recognised or traced.

Subject to there being no security problems consequential upon him leaving his place of detention, where a prison inmate is required for identification such person may be asked to take part in a parade or a video identification. A parade conducted in a prison or other Prison Department establishment must, as far as practicable, be conducted in accordance with normal parade rules. The parade shall be made up from members of the public unless there are serious security or control objections to the admission to the establishment of persons assisting. In such circumstances or if a group or video identification is conducted within the prison or establishment, prison inmates may take part.

If a prison inmate is the suspect he must not be required to wear prison uniform for the parade. An exception to this rule is where the other persons taking part are inmates in uniform or members of the public who are willing to wear prison uniform for the parade. In conducting the parade, immediately prior to its commencement, the suspect must be reminded by the identification officer of the procedures and caution him in the manner prescribed by Code C. Only authorised persons may be present in the place where the parade is conducted. Once the parade is in position, everything thereafter concerning it must occur in the presence and hearing of any interpreter, friend or appropriate adult who is present, subject to the qualification that where a screen identification parade is being held everything said to or by a witness must be in both the presence and hearing of the suspect's solicitor, friend or appropriate adult or, alternatively, is video recorded.

The parade shall be made up of not less than eight persons (in addition to the suspect). The persons making up the parade shall so far as possible resemble the suspect's characteristics in respect of age, height, general appearance and position or status in life. A parade shall include only one suspect except where there are two suspects of roughly the same appearance. In such circumstances the two suspects may be paraded together with not less than 12 other persons. A parade shall never include more than two suspects. Where separate parades are conducted they must be made up of different persons.

Separate parades shall be conducted for each member of the group, where all members of a similar group are possible suspects. However, if there are two suspects of similar appearance, they may appear on the same parade with not less than 12 members of the same group who are not suspects. In an identification parade made up of police officers in uniform, numerals or other badges of identification must be concealed.

Upon his arrival at the venue of the parade, the identification officer must ask the suspect whether he has any objection to the arrangements for the parade or the persons participating in it. Before the parade commences the suspect may obtain advice from his solicitor or friend. Where grounds of objection are lodged, where practicable, steps shall be taken to remove those grounds. In the event of this not being practicable the identification officer must explain to the suspect why his objections cannot be satisfied.

The suspect has the right to select his position in the line. In cases where there is more than a single witness, after each witness has left the room, the officer conducting the parade must inform the suspect that he can change his position in the line if he so wishes.

By means of a number laid on the floor in front of each person on the parade, or by any other means, each position must be clearly numbered. To secure the integrity of the parade the identification officer is responsible for ensuring that prior to attending the parade itself, witnesses are unable to communicate with each other, overhear a witness who has seen the parade, or see any member of the line-up. The identification officer must also ensure that on the occasion of the parade witnesses do not see or are reminded of any photographs or the suspect's description or are given any indication of his identity. In conducting a witness to the line-up the officer must not discuss the line-up's composition and must not reveal whether an identification has been made by a previous witness.

Witnesses must be brought into the parade individually and immediately prior to inspecting the parade they must be told by the identification officer that the person they saw may or may not be in the line-up. A witness must also be told that if he cannot make a positive identification he should say so but should not make any decision before looking at each person on the line-up at least twice. A witness should then be asked by the identification officer to look at each and every member of the line-up at least twice. He should be further advised to take as much care and time as he wishes. Once satisfied that the witness has properly looked at each member of the line-up, the identification officer shall ask him whether the person he saw on an earlier relevant occasion is in the line-up.

Identification should be made by the witness indicating the number of the person he identifies. In the event of an identification being made by the witness after the parade has ended, the suspect shall be informed. If still present, his solicitor, interpreter or friend must also be apprised of the identification. When such eventuality takes place, allowing the witness a second opportunity to identify the suspect should be considered.

In the event of a witness wanting to hear any member of the line-up speak, see him move or take up any particular posture or stance, the witness must first be asked by the identification officer whether he is able to identify any person on the line-up by appearance only. When a witness asks to listen to members of the line-up speak, the identification officer must remind the witness that the persons on the line-up have been chosen on the basis of their physical appearance only. Once these procedural points have been satisfied, the identification officer may then request the members of the parade to either speak, move, or take up any particular posture or stance.

In cases where the investigators have released video films or photographs to the media with a view to the suspect being identified or traced, the investigating officer must ask each witness whether he has seen any broadcast or film or photographs which have been published relating to the offence. The witness's response must be recorded.

At the conclusion of the parade and once the last witness has left the appointed room, the suspect should be asked whether he wishes to offer any comments on the way the parade has been conducted. A record of the identification parade shall be made by either a colour photograph or a video recording, a copy of which must be supplied to the suspect or his solicitor within a reasonable time. At the conclusion of the proceedings, the colour photograph or video recording must be destroyed or wiped clean, as the case may be, unless the suspect is convicted of the offence or admits it and is cautioned for it. Where a person is requested by the identification officer to leave a line-up by reason of him interfering with the conduct of the parade, the circumstances must be recorded. Also to be recorded are:

(a) details of all persons present whose names are known to the police;
(b) the circumstances of any parade comprised of prison inmates; and
(c) (on the forms provided) a record of the parade being conducted.

Q: What action can be taken if a suspect refuses to attend an identification parade or, having agreed to attend one he fails to turn up or if it is impracticable to hold or organise a parade?
A: If practicable, arrangements should be made for the witness to see the suspect in a group identification, a video identification or a confrontation.

Q: What is a group identification?
A: This method of identification is where the witness seeks to identify a suspect amongst an informal group of people.

A group identification can take place either with or without the suspect's consent and co-operation. A covert group identification may be relied upon where the suspect has refused or failed to attend an identification parade or a group identification.

This method can also be utilised if the investigating officer is of the opinion that in the circumstances a group identification is to be preferred, by reason of fear on the part of the witness or for some other reason.

Q: Is the suspect's consent a pre-requisite to a group identification being conducted?
A: No, the suspect's consent must be first sought and he must be given the required notice of rights both verbally and in writing. In the event of the suspect not giving his consent, the discretion rests with the identification officer to carry out a group identification if it is practicable to do so.

Q: What are the procedural requirements for a group identification?
A: The requirements are contained in the paragraphs which follow.

First of all, they are designed to ensure that a group identification follows the principles and procedures for an identification parade, so far as is possible, in order that there is fairness to the suspect in respect of the manner in which the witness's ability to identify a suspect is tested.

It is the prerogative of the identification officer to determine the venue for the group identification. In doing so he may have regard to representations made by the suspect, his solicitor, friend or appropriate adult.While the identification officer may choose the location, it must be a place where there are passers-by or persons waiting around informally in groups such that the suspect is able to join them in circumstances where both he and the other persons in the group can be seen at the same time by the witness. Places where people are to be found in the circumstances envisaged by the Code of Practice would include a factory exit, an escalator or even a thoroughfare in a busy shopping mall or pedestrian precinct, public transport stations or interchanges, cinema queues or other similar locations where people are sitting or standing. If a group identification is being conducted without the co-operation and consent of the suspect, the choice of locations will be restricted to those places which the suspect frequents where other people are present at the same time. Public places which the suspect frequents, such as clubs, dance-halls, betting shops and public transport facilities or routes which are known to be frequently used by him are potentially sound locations.

In arranging and organising a group identification, the identification officer has no control or direction in respect of the number, gender, race, general description and fashion styles of other persons who will be present at the chosen location. Nonetheless, in determining the venue, the identification officer must consider the general appearance and numbers of persons likely to be there. If the identification officer believes that by reason of the unusual appearance of the suspect, none of the locations meet the criteria necessary to ensure an identification which is fair to the suspect, a group identification need not be held. A colour photograph should be taken or a video recording made of the general scene immediately following the group identification procedures if this is practicable so as to provide a general impression of the scene and the persons present. This must be done irrespective of whether the procedure was conducted with consent or covertly. Alternatively, if feasible, a video recording may be made of the group identification itself.

In those circumstances where it is impracticable to take a colour photograph or make a video recording in accordance with the above, the scene should be photographed or a film made of it subsequently at a time decided upon by the identification officer, if he considers that it is practicable to do so.

Q: Is the integrity of a group identification prejudiced if at the time of being seen by a witness the suspect was on his own as opposed to forming part of a group of persons?
A: No, provided the identification procedures satisfy the Code's provisions.

Q: Must the identification officer be in uniform when supervising a group identification?
A: No

Q: What procedures must be complied with prior to a group identification being conducted?
A: Details of the 'first description' of the suspect provided by any witness or witnesses who are to be used on the group identification should be provided to the suspect or his solicitor. Additionally, if it is practicable to do so and no unreasonable delay would be caused to the investigation, before the group identification takes place the suspect or his solicitor should be permitted to examine any material released to the media by the police for the purpose of the suspect being recognised or traced.

Q: In the case of an identification parade, the identification officer is obliged, in cases where photographs or video films have been released to the media by the police with the objective of the suspect being recognised or traced, to ask each witness whether he has seen any broadcast or published films or photographs relating to the offence. Is this also a procedural requirement of a group identification?

A: Yes, and as with a parade, the witness's response should be recorded.

Q: What specific procedures must be followed where a suspect agrees to participating in a group identification?

A: The suspect must be afforded a reasonable opportunity of having a solicitor or friend present and he should be invited by the identification officer to indicate on a copy of the notice of rights form whether or not he wishes such persons to be present.

At or near the place where the group identification is being held, the identification officer and the witness and, if present, the solicitor, friend or appropriate adult of the suspect may be concealed from the view of the group under observation if the identification officer is of the opinion that such action would facilitate the conduct of the identification process.

When taking a witness to a group identification, the accompanying officer must not talk to the witness about the forthcoming group identification nor must he reveal whether an identification has been made by a previous witness.

Any verbal communication made to or by the witness during the identification procedure about the identification should be said within both the presence and hearing of the identification officer and, if present, the solicitor, friend. appropriate adult or interpreter acting on behalf of the suspect.

Before a witness attends a group identification, the identification officer must take steps to ensure that the witnesses are unable to communicate with each other or overhear a witness who has been given the opportunity of seeing the suspect in the group, or see the suspect before being formally conducted to the group; or likewise on that occasion, do not see or are reminded of any photographs or descriptions of the suspect or be given any other indication of the identity of the suspect.

The observation process of the group must be effected by witnesses being taken one at a time to the place where they are to observe. The witness must be told by the identification officer, immediately prior to being requested to look at the group, that the person he saw may or may not be in the group. The witness must also be advised that if he cannot make a positive identification he should say so. Once these formalities have been carried out, the witness should be asked to observe the group in which the suspect is to appear. Obviously, the mode of observation will be determined by whether the group is still or moving.

Q: If, for instance, the group in which the suspect is to appear is leaving a cinema or sports stadium or is moving down an escalator ie a moving group, does the Code of Practice prescribe any special conditions or procedures?
A: Yes. If more than one suspect agrees to a group identification, a separate identification procedure should be conducted for each suspect. These separate identification procedures may be carried out following on from each other on the same occasion.

The witness should be told by the identification officer to look at the group and point out any person he thinks he saw on an earlier relevant occasion. Once this procedural step has been complied with the suspect should be permitted to take up a position himself in the group wherever he wishes. In the event of the witness giving such an intimation of identification, if practicable, the identification officer shall arrange for the witness to take a closer look at the person he has pointed out and ask him if he can make a positive identification. In the event of this not being practicable, the witness should be asked by the identification officer how sure he is that the person he pointed out is the relevant person.

In the case of a moving group, even though a positive identification may have been made, the witness should be required to continue to observe the group. This should be for such time as the identification officer reasonably believes to be necessary in the circumstances for the witness to make comparisons between the suspect and other persons who are of similar appearance by reason of age, sex, race, general description, type of clothing worn etc.

Q: What are the Code's dictates in respect of a group identification conducted where the persons forming the group are not moving?
A: In the event of there being two or more suspects who consent to a group identification, separate identification procedures should be carried out for each suspect unless the suspects are of broadly similar appearance, in which case, they may appear in the same group.

A stationary group identification thus has a little more leeway than a moving one. When separate group identifications are conducted, the group must be composed of different persons.

The suspect's rights entitle him to choose any position in the group. In cases where there are two or more witnesses, the suspect must be informed by the identification officer of his right to change his position in the group. This information must be conveyed out of the witness' sight and hearing.

When conducting a group identification with the stationary group, the witness must be asked by the identification officer to pass amongst or along the group. The witness should also be requested to look at each person in the group on at least two occasions and he must be advised to take as much care and time as the circumstances permit before making an identification.

Once the witness has fulfilled these requirements, the witness must be asked by the identification officer whether the person he saw on an earlier relevant occasion is in the group. If he says that he did, the officer must ask him to indicate the person in a manner considered appropriate in the circumstances by the identification officer. If such means are not practicable, the witness should be asked to point out the person he identifies. After the witness has made an identification the identification officer shall, if practicable, arrange for him to look at that person more closely and enquire as to how certain he is that the person he has identified is the person he saw on the earlier relevant occasion.

Q: Are there additional general conditions which apply to all forms of group identifications?

A: Yes, these are contained in the following paragraphs. The identification officer may treat as a refusal to co-operate in a group identification actions on the part of the suspect whereby he unreasonably delays joining the group, or having joined it, conceals himself from the witness' view. In the event of a person other than the suspect being identified by a witness, an officer should inform him what has occurred and ask him if he is prepared to provide his name and address. There is no statutory obligation on the person concerned to give this information.

Neither is there any obligation to make a record of any of the persons in the group or at the place where the procedure is carried out. Upon completion of the group identification the suspect should be asked by the identification officer whether he wishes to make any comment on the way the group identification has been conducted. The suspect should be told by the identification officer of any identification made by a witness if the suspect has not been previously apprised of this.

Q: Does the Code of Practice detail any provision in respect of covert group identifications?

A: Yes, the Code stipulates that a group identification held covertly without the consent of the suspect should follow the rules for a group identification conducted with the consent of the suspect as far as is practicable.

Since a covert group identification will be conducted without the knowledge and consent of the suspect, the suspect has no right to have a solicitor, friend, appropriate adult etc. present.

In a group identification effected without the suspect's consent, more than one suspect may be identified on that occasion.

Q: Is there anything to preclude a group identification being conducted in a police station?

A: The Code of Practice is restrictive in this respect and only allows them to be conducted in a police station for safety and security reasons or if it is impracticable for one to be conducted somewhere else.

In the event of a group identification being held in a police station it may take place in a location considered appropriate by the identification officer or in a room equipped with a screen which allows a witness to see members of the group without being seen himself.

Additionally, if the identification officer considers it practicable to do so, the additional safeguards concerning identification parades should be applied.

Q: Can a group identification be used in respect of a prison inmate?

A: Yes but only in a prison establishment or at a police station. The arrangements to be followed are the same as those prescribed in respect of conducting a group identification in a police station. When conducted within a prison, other inmates may take part. Where an inmate of the prison is a suspect he should not be required to wear prison uniform unless the same uniform is being worn by other people participating in the group identification.

Q: Reference has been made earlier to a colour photograph or a video recording being made of the general scene of the venue of a group identification where this is practicable. To what purpose can this documentary evidence be put and what records must be kept of a group identification?

A: Obviously, it might be used by the prosecution with a view to establishing that the group identification was conducted within the requirements of the Code of Practice.

In these cases where a colour photograph was taken or a video recording made, the suspect or his solicitor can request a copy of the photograph or video recording. The request must be acceded to within a reasonable time.

In the event of the suspect being shown in the photograph or video, the document should be retained until proceedings have been concluded when it should be destroyed or wiped clean, as the case may be, unless the suspect has been convicted of the offence or admits it and is cautioned for it. In such cases, the photograph or video may be retained.

In respect of general documentation, a record must be made, on the proper forms, of the conduct of any group identification. The record must include any comment made by either the suspect or the witness in respect of any identification made or the conduct of the group identification. The record must also detail the reasons why the identification officer decided it was not practicable to satisfy any of the Code's requirements concerning group identifications.

Q: Mention has been made of video identification. What procedures must be followed in such cases?

A: A video recording of a suspect may be shown to a witness by the identification officer, if the identification officer is of the opinion that this would be the most satisfactory course of action whether because of the suspect's refusal to participate in an identification parade or group identification or any other reason.

The consent of the suspect must be sought. The suspect should also be advised in accordance with the requirements of the Code of Practice in respect of matters being explained to him and a confirmatory 'Notice to Suspect' should be served on him. The suspect's refusal to co-operate in the making of a video recording does not preclude the identification officer, in exercising his discretion provided by the Code, from proceeding with a video identification if it is practicable to do so.

The Code of Practice stipulates, in Annex B, that a video identification must be conducted in the form detailed in the following paragraphs.

The identification officer or identification officers who are not concerned with the investigation of the offence under investigation have the responsibility of arranging, supervising and directing the making and showing of a video recording. The suspect, with not less than eight other persons of similar age, height, general appearance and position or status in life must be depicted in the film. Unless there are two suspects of roughly the same description and appearance, the film should show only one suspect. In the event of two suspects being shown in the film, the video recording of the suspects should be shown with not less than 12 others. The suspects and other people shown in the video recording must be filmed in the same position or undertaking the same actions and under identical circumstances so far as is possible.

The video recording must facilitate each person depicted in the film to be identified by a number. When the video recording is made up of police officers, their service numbers or other badges of identification must be concealed. Whether appearing as a suspect or otherwise, if a prison inmate appears on a video recording, either all or none of the other participants should appear in prison uniform.

Prior to the film being shown to any witness, the suspect and his solicitor, friend or appropriate adult must be given a reasonable opportunity to view the completed recording. Where practicable, any reasonable objection to the content of the recording or the persons taking part in it, should be removed. Where taking such action is not practicable the suspect and/or his representative should be informed why the objection cannot be satisfied. Details of the objection and the reason why it cannot be met must be recorded.

When practicable, the suspect's solicitor or, if he is not represented, the suspect himself, must be given reasonable notice of the time and venue of a video identification which is intended to be carried out so as to allow him to be represented by a friend, an appropriate adult or someone else. The suspect is prohibited from attending a video identification during such time as the video recording is being played over to witnesses. Where the suspect is unrepresented when the film is being shown, the viewing itself shall be video recorded. During the conducting of a video identification, no unauthorised persons may attend. The 'first description' given by a witness to be called to the video identification shall be given to the suspect or his solicitor prior to the video identification being conducted. They should also be allowed sight of any material released to the media with the object of the suspect being recognised or traced subject to it being practicable to do this and the investigation not being delayed unreasonably.

Q: How does the Code of Practice regulate the actual conducting of a video identification?
A: As well as prescribing general procedural requirements detailed above, Annex B to the Code prescribes a number of procedures which must be rigidly adhered to. In similar fashion to the Annexes pertaining to identification parades and group identifications, the

Code of Practice makes provision for action to be taken before, during and after the showing of the film.

An onus is placed on the identification officer to ensure that prior to viewing the film, witnesses are prevented from communicating with one another about the case. Witnesses must also be prevented from overhearing a witness who has viewed the recording. Under no circumstances must the identification officer talk to a witness about the composition of the video recording or reveal whether an identification has been made by a previous witness.

The video recording must only be viewed by one witness at a time. The identification officer must inform the witness immediately before the identification procedure commences that the person he saw on an earlier relevant occasion may or may not be on the film about to be shown.

The witness has the right to view any particular part of the film again. Similarly, he has the right to ask for a particular shot to be frozen for him to study. The witnesses must be informed of these rights by the identification officer who should also advise the witness that he can view the film in its entirety or any part of it as many times as he wishes. The witness should be requested not to make a positive identification or indicate that he is unable to identify anyone until he has viewed the entire video recording not less than twice.

Having viewed the whole recording not less than twice and having intimated that he does not wish to see the film or any particular element of it further, the witness should be asked by the identification officer whether the individual he saw in person on an earlier occasion was shown on the video recording. If he says that he has made an identification the witness should be asked the number of the person he has picked out. To confirm the identification, the video recording of the person identified must again be shown to the witness by the identification officer.

Special care must be taken by the officer conducting the procedure not to direct the attention of the witness to any particular person shown on the recording. Nor should the identification officer give any indication of the identity of the suspect. A witness should not be reminded of any description of a suspect nor of any photograph, photo-fit, identi-kit, or other similar pictures from which he has previously made an identification, once the suspect is available for identification by other methods under the Code's provisions.

In cases where the police have issued video films or photographs to the media with the object of establishing the suspect's identity, or tracing him, each witness must be asked by the identification officer whether he has seen any broadcast or published video recordings or photographs in connection with the offence. A record must be made of the witness' response.

Q: What provision is made by the Code of Practice in respect of preserving the integrity of the video tape and the ultimate destruction of it?
A: All relevant video tapes must be kept securely and any movement of them properly accounted for. It is the responsibility of the identification officer to ensure compliance with these matters. Prior to the film being shown to witnesses, no officer involved in the investigation must be allowed to see it.

In the event of the suspect being prosecuted for the offence and acquitted of it, or no proceedings being instituted against him, (unless he admits it and is cautioned for it), all copies of the video recording in the possession of the police must be destroyed.

The suspect must be afforded the opportunity of witnessing the destruction of the film(s) if he asks to do so within five days of being acquitted or informed that no proceedings are to be instituted against him.

Q: In what form must the holding of a video identification be recorded?
A: A record, on the proper form of the conduct of the use of this method of identification must be made. It must include details of all those who took part in the film and those who saw it whose names are known to the police.

Q: Confronting the suspect with a witness is permissible if an identification parade or a group identification or a video identification is not practicable. What other conditions must be satisfied in relation to a confrontation?
A: This method of identification does not demand the consent of the suspect and can be utilised when none of the other methods of identification are practicable.

The procedural requirements are contained in Annex C of Code D and these are detailed in the paragraphs which follow.

Prior to arranging for the witness to confront the suspect, the witness must be told by the identification officer, who is responsible for the conduct of any confrontation, that the individual he saw on a previous relevant occasion may not be the person he is about to confront. The witness must also be told that he should say if he is unable to make a positive identification.

Details of the 'first description' provided by the witness who is to attend the confrontation must be provided to the suspect or his solicitor before the suspect is confronted. The suspect or his solicitor must also be permitted to see any material released to the media by the police with a view to recognising or tracing the suspect, subject to it being practicable to do so and the investigation not being unreasonably delayed by such action.

Confrontation should take place by each witness independently confronting the suspect and being asked by the identification officer: 'Is this the person?' Unless unreasonable delay would be caused, the suspect must be confronted in the presence of his solicitor, interpreter, or friend where he has one. A confrontation effected within the Code of Practice must take place in a normal room or one fitted with a screen which allows the witness to see the suspect without being seen, within a police station. Irrespective of which type of room is used, the procedures are the same, subject to the restriction that a 'screened' room may only be used if the suspect's solicitor, friend or appropriate adult is present or a video recording is made of each confrontation.

As with other methods of identification, where the police have previously released video films or photographs to the media with the object of the suspect being recognised or traced, after the identification procedure, each witness must be asked by the identification officer whether he has seen any broadcast or published films or photographs about the offence. The witness' reply must be recorded.

Q: What action may be taken under the Code of Practice to trace and establish the identity of a suspect who is not known?

A: With a view to tracing and identifying a person whose identity is not known, a witness may be taken to a particular neighbourhood, area or place by a police officer. Prior to such course of action taking place, the officer should make a record of any description of the suspect given by the witness where this is practicable. The officer should be careful not to draw or direct the attention of the witness to any particular person.

When the identity of a suspect is known to the police and the suspect is available to attend an identification parade, a witness must not be shown any photograph, identi-kit, photo-fit or similar picture of the suspect.

The showing of photographs etc. to a witness is permissible if the suspect's identity is not known but this must be done following the procedures prescribed in Annex D to the Code of Practice.

If a suspect is subsequently arrested and any of the three principal methods of identification are contemplated, the suspect must be told of this fact by the identification officer before any of the procedures are utilised and the information detailed in the written notice must be served on the suspect.

Q: What are the procedures prescribed in Annex D in respect of the showing of photographs or other pictures to a witness?
A: Whereas all the previously mentioned methods of identification must be conducted by an identification officer ie an officer in uniform (except for a group identification) who must not be below the rank of inspector, an officer of the rank of sergeant or above must be responsible for supervising and directing the showing of photographs. The sergeant's role may be a supervisory one only; a constable or civilian employee may undertake the actual showing of the photographs to a potential witness.

Prior to the showing of photographs to a witness, the responsible officer, ie the officer of the rank of sergeant or above, must confirm that a record of the 'first description' given by the witness has been recorded. If he is unable to establish that a record has been made of the 'first description' then the showing of the photographs must be postponed.

The witness must look at the photographs without any other witnesses being present. He should be given as much privacy as is practicable and must be prevented from communicating with other witnesses in the case. Not less than 12 photographs should be shown to a witness at a time and, as far as possible, the photographs should all be of a similar type.

Upon the photographs being shown to the potential witness, he must be told that the photograph of the person he saw on the previous relevant occasion may or may not be amongst them. There must be no prompting of the witness, not should he be guided in any way and he must be allowed to make any selection without assistance.

Once a positive identification has been made photographs should not be shown to other witnesses unless the person identified is otherwise eliminated from the inquiry.

Unless identification of the suspect is not in dispute, all witnesses, including the one who has made the positive identification must be asked to attend an identification parade or take part in a group identification or video identification if practicable.

In cases where identi-kit, photo-fit or similar picture, such as an artist's impression has resulted in a suspect being available who could be requested to attend an identification parade or take part in a group identification or video identification, other possible witnesses should not be shown the identi-kit etc.

An onus is placed on the officer in charge of an investigation to inform the identification officer that a witness attending a parade has previously had sight of photographs, an identi-kit, photo-fit or similar picture. Prior to the parade taking place both the suspect and his solicitor must be informed that the witness has seen photographs etc.

Irrespective of whether an identification is made, the photographs used in the identification must be preserved as they may be required for court. Each photograph must be numbered and the frame or part of the photograph album from which the witness made the identification should itself be photographed so that the frame or part can be rebuilt if this is necessary.

In accordance with the documentation procedures running through the Codes of Practice a record must be kept of the showing of the photographs and any comments made by the witness. This must be done irrespective of whether an identification was made.

Q: In respect of all the various methods of identification provided for by the Code of Practice, the Code demands that certain matters be recorded. Are there any general instructions relating to the keeping of records?

A: The preamble to the Code of Practice specifies that where a record is made of an action which requires the authority of a person of a specified rank, the record must include that person's rank and name. Excepted from this general rule are investigations into offences connected with terrorism. In such cases the officer's rank and warrant or other identification number shall be recorded instead.

Records must be timed and signed by the person making them, except in cases under the Prevention of Terrorism (Temporary Provisions) Act 1989 in which case the person need not sign but record his warrant or other identification number instead.

Apart from those cases which demand a record to be made on a form specially provided for the purpose, the records to be made must be made on the individual's custody record if he is in custody at the time.

Q: In recent years there has been a growing tendency for the media to be utilised by the police for the showing of videos or photographs of an incident with a view to suspects being identified or traced. Does the Code of Practice make any provision for such action?

A: The Code specifies that such action is permissible, whether the material is shown nationally, locally or to police officers for the purpose described. The Code goes on to stipulate that when such video films or photographs are shown to potential witnesses with a view to identifying the suspect, so as to prevent any possibility of collusion, the material must be shown to each potential witness separately. So far as possible the procedures and principles governing photographic identification and video identification should be adhered to. The foregoing, as with all other provisions of the Code, with the exception of that pertaining to photographs being shown under the supervision of a sergeant, is applicable to police officers who are potential witnesses as well as civilian witnesses.

Where national or local media utilise the material released to them by the police with a view to the suspect being recognised or traced, a copy of the material released to the media must be preserved. Before any identification procedure is conducted, the suspect or his solicitor should be permitted to see the material, subject to it being practicable to do so and no unreasonable delay being caused to the investigation. After a witness has taken part in an identification procedure, the investigating officer must ask him whether he has seen any broadcast or films or photographs which have been published. The Code requires his reply to be recorded.

Q: Are the police empowered to take the photograph of a person held in custody without his consent?

A: Not in every case. The photograph of any person who has been arrested may be taken at a police station with his written consent. In some circumstances, a prisoner's photograph may be taken without his consent but irrespective of whether his photograph is taken with or without consent he must be informed why it is being taken. He must also be told that in the event of him either being prosecuted for the offence and acquitted or, (unless he admits the offence and is cautioned for it) no prosecution is launched in respect of it, the photograph, negatives and all copies of it will be destroyed. The person need not be informed of this nor need any destruction of photographs, copies or negatives take place if he has a previous conviction for a recordable offence.

In addition to the foregoing, the person must be informed of his right to witness the destruction or to be provided with a certificate confirming destruction. He must apply within five days of being cleared or told that he will not be prosecuted. The police must record the destruction of the photographs etc. The destruction procedures do not, of course, extend to copies of photographs appearing in the Police Gazette.

It is pointed out in a note of guidance that the admissibility and the weight of evidence of identification may be prejudiced by a potential witness in an identification procedure seeing a photograph of a suspect otherwise than in the terms prescribed by the Code of Practice.

Upon the photograph being taken, the arrested person must be advised that should he significantly alter his appearance in the time between the photograph being taken and arrangements being made to conduct an identification procedure, this fact may be given in evidence against him if the case proceeds to prosecution.

Q: In what circumstances may the photograph of an arrested person be taken without his consent?

A: The Code of Practice describes four sets of circumstances where such action is permissible but in doing so the Code prescribes that force may not be used.

The first situation described by the Code of Practice concerns the arrest of a number of people at the same time or where there is a likelihood that other people will be arrested in addition to the prisoner. Where officers are carrying out arrests, lodging prisoners and resuming their task immediately, for example where a raid is taking place on a rave party, at a large scale public order incident, at a football match or at a dog fight, it is permissible for a photograph of the prisoner to be taken without his consent in order that it may be established who was arrested, at what time and at what place. From a practical viewpoint, the arresting officer's identity in such circumstances will also be useful if the photograph of the prisoner is taken with the arresting officer.

The consent of the prisoner is not necessary where he has been charged with or reported for a recordable offence and has not been released or taken before a court.

Similarly, where the photograph of a person has not been taken under the provisions outlined in the above two paragraphs, it may be taken without his consent upon his conviction for a recordable offence. No power of arrest exists to enable a photograph to be taken and the provision may only be utilised where the person is in custody by virtue of some other authority, for example where he has been arrested under section 27 of the Act for his fingerprints to be taken.

The final instance where a person's photograph may be taken without consent is where authority is given by a police officer of or above the rank of superintendent, based on reasonable grounds for suspecting that he has been involved in a criminal offence in respect of which there is identification evidence available.

Where the photograph of a person is taken without his consent, a record of the reason must be made as soon as possible.

CHAPTER 10

CODE OF PRACTICE ON TAPE RECORDING

This code of practice details the procedural considerations in respect of the tape recording by the police of their interviews at police stations with suspected persons.

The code of practice is made under the authority of section 60(1) (a) of the Police and Criminal Evidence Act 1984. The Act's principles relating to the effect of non-compliance with the provisions of a code of practice are of equal application to the code of practice now under review. As with the other four codes of practice, accompanying 'Notes of Guidance' do not form part of the code itself and non-adherence to guidance offered will not attract the risk of disciplinary proceedings or evidence being rendered inadmissible.

As with the other codes of practice, that on tape recording should be readily available for consultation by police officers, detained persons and members of the public at every police station.

Q: Can interviews with suspects in police stations be covertly tape recorded?
A: No, in order to instill confidence in a tape recording's reliability as an impartial and accurate record of an interview, the tape recording of an interview must be conducted openly.

An accompanying note of guidance to Code E advises that while police officers will wish to ensure, as far as possible, that arrangements for tape recording an interview are unobtrusive, the fact that no opportunity exists for the tapes or the tape recording equipment to be interfered with must be obvious to the interviewee.

Q: What provisions exist to ensure the integrity of the tape?

A: An interview will be recorded by means of a twin-decked machine which, as the description implies, utilises two tapes, or a single-deck machine, using only one tape. In the case of a twin-decked machine, one of the two tapes used in the machine will be regarded as the master tape whilst the second tape will be a working copy. In a single-decked machine, a copy made of the single master tape will be the working copy.

Irrespective of which type of machine is used, the master tape must be sealed before it leaves the presence of the suspect.

Q: What is the object of sealing the master tape before it leaves the suspect's presence?

A: To secure the interviewee's confidence that the integrity of the tape recording is preserved. The note of guidance addressing this consideration advises that where a single-decked machine is used, the working copy must be made from the master tape in the presence of the interviewee and without the master tape having left his sight. Where further working copies are required, such copies should be made from the working copy. A further point raised in the note of guidance is that the recording equipment should have a time coding or other security device. Perhaps rather obviously the note adds that any reference in the Code to tapes includes a reference to a tape where a single-decked machine is used to record the interview.

Q: Which interviews need to be tape recorded?

A: The Code of Practice details three types of interview at a police station which must be tape recorded, the first of which is an interview carried out under caution (within the terms of Code C, paragraph 10) with a person who is suspected of committing an indictable offence (including those triable either way).

Where a police officer puts further questions to a suspect about such an offence after he has been charged with or informed that he may be prosecuted for it, the interview must be tape recorded.

Any interview in which a police officer wishes to bring to the notice of a person after he has been charged with or informed that he may be prosecuted for an offence which is indictable (including one triable either way) any written statement made by another person or the content of an interview with another person, must also be tape recorded. In respect of such cases, paragraph 16.4 of Code C details the exact procedures to be followed in drawing to the attention of a person charged the things said by another. A note of guidance also points out that one method of making a person aware of the content of an interview with another person may be the playing over of a tape recording of that interview.

Q: Are there any exceptions to the generality of the foregoing answer?

A: Yes, exceptions are provided by the Code itself and a note of guidance contained within it.

By the Code itself, the interview of a person arrested under section 14(1)(a) or Schedule 5 of the Prevention of Terrorism (Temporary Provisions) Act 1989 need not be tape recorded. Neither need an interview be tape recorded where the interviewee is being questioned about an offence where there are reasonable grounds for suspecting that it is connected to terrorism or committed in furtherance of an organisation engaged in terrorism.

However, the exceptions described in this paragraph are only applicable to terrorism in connection with matters concerning Northern Ireland or is terrorism of any other type except that connected with the affairs of the whole or part of the United Kingdom, excluding Northern Ireland.

For the purposes of the Code, the expression 'terrorism' has the same meaning as that provided by section 20(1) of the Prevention of Terrorism (Temporary Provisions) Act 1989, ie the use of violence for political ends and includes any use of violence or putting the public or any section of the public in fear.

The Code of Practice also prescribes that the interview of a person suspected on reasonable grounds of contravening the provisions of section 1 of the Official Secrets Act 1911 need not be tape recorded.

Applicable to both of the exceptions is a note of guidance which advises that in respect of an interview which is being tape recorded, only when it becomes clear that the suspect may have committed an offence connected with terrorism (as defined and within the Code's provisions) or an offence of espionage within section 1 of the Official Secrets Act 1911 should the tape recorder be switched off by the officer conducting the interview.

The Code of Practice dictates which interview must be recorded. A note of guidance spells out that the Code's provisions in this regard are not intended to prevent the police, at their discretion, tape recording interviews with persons suspected of offences outside the Code's purview, or responses made by persons after they have been charged with or informed they may be prosecuted for an offence. The exercise of such discretion is, however, conditional upon the Code of Practice being complied with.

Q: Are there any other circumstances when an interview need not be tape recorded?

A: Yes. The custody officer may give the investigating officer authority not to tape record an interview where it is not reasonably practicable to do so because of:

(a) equipment failure;
(b) non-availability of a suitable room;
(c) non-availability of a tape recorder;

and he, the custody officer, is of the opinion, based on reasonable grounds, that the interview should not be delayed until the problems itemised at (a) to (c) have been remedied.

In respect of the non-availability of either room or recorder, a note of guidance offers the advice that interviews with persons suspected of more serious offences should be given priority, where practicable.

The custody officer may also give authority to the interviewing officer not to tape record the interview where, from the outset it is clear that no prosecution will ensue.

In cases where the custody officer gives the investigating officer authority for an interview to be conducted without being tape recorded, the interview must be conducted and recorded within the terms and conditions prescribed by Code C, paragraph 11. The Code also demands that the specific reasons for not tape recording an interview must be recorded and, in this regard, an accompanying note of guidance offers the reminder that the authorising officer should be prepared to justify his decision which may be subject to comment in any subsequent judicial proceedings.

Q: What provision is made by the Code of Practice in respect of the tape recording of an interview with a person who has voluntarily attended a police station for interview?

A: If he is a suspect from the outset, any interview with him concerning the offence should be tape recorded, unless the custody officer gives authority for the interview not to be tape recorded. Where a person is attending a police station voluntarily and an interview is taking place as soon as the interviewing officer has grounds to believe that the person has become a suspect, the continuation of the interview must be tape recorded unless authority is given to the interviewing officer by the custody officer, within the terms of his authority to do so, that the continuation of the interview need not be recorded.

Q: On some occasions, when interviewing a suspect, some time may be devoted to questioning which provides non-incriminating material or to indicating to the suspect the weight of evidence against him. Need all the interview be recorded or can the machine be switched on once it becomes apparent that the suspect may be about to make incriminating replies?

A: An interview must be recorded in its entirety. This includes the taking and reading back of any statement.

Q: Are there any special procedures to be followed at the commencement of a tape recorded interview?

A: A number of formalities must be rigidly adhered to.

Without delay, once the suspect arrives in the interview room, in the sight of the suspect, the interviewing officer must load the tape recorder with previously unused (ie clean) tapes, having first unwrapped them or otherwise opened them in the suspect's presence. (In this regard the Code of Practice offers a helpful reminder that the interviewing officer should try and estimate the duration of the interview and ensure that there are sufficient unused tapes and identification labels to seal the master tapes available in the room where the interview is being conducted).

Once the initial mechanics of unwrapping and loading are complete, the Code spells out the obvious command that the machine must be set to record.

The suspect must be formally told by the interviewing officer about the tape recording. He must say that the interview is being tape recorded, state his name and rank and the name and rank of any other officer present. He must give the name of the suspect and the name of any other persons present e.g. a solicitor or appropriate adult. The date, time and place of the interview must be announced and it must be stated that the suspect will be given a written notice about what will happen to the tape. With an obvious view to ROTI' s and transcripts, the interviewing officer should also ask the person being interviewed and each person present to identify themselves for voice identification purposes.

Having completed the introductory formalities, the Code dictates that the suspect must then be cautioned by the interviewing officer in the following terms:

> 'You do not have to say anything. But it may harm your defence if you do not mention when questioned something which you later rely on in court. Anything you say may be given in evidence.'

The Code stipulates that provided the general gist of the caution is preserved, minor deviations do not amount to the requirement being breached. A note of guidance echoes the contents of Code C in respect of the Treatment and Questioning of Suspects stating that if it is apparent that the interviewee does not understand the significance of the caution, the interviewing officer should explain it in his own words.

Once the interviewee has been cautioned, he must be reminded by the interviewing officer of his right to free and independent legal advice and that he can, in accordance with the provisions of Code C, speak to a solicitor on the telephone.

Q: How does the Code of Practice deal with conversations which have taken place before the tape recorded interview?

A: The Code specifies that after the suspect has been reminded of his right to legal advice, the interviewing officer must put to the suspect any significant statement which was made before the commencement of the tape recorded interview. Similarly, the suspect's silence, that is, any failure or refusal to answer a question or to answer it satisfactorily must be put to the interviewee. The suspect should then be asked by the interviewing officer whether he confirms or denies that earlier significant statement or silence or whether he wishes to add anything.

Q: What will be deemed to be a significant statement or silence?

A: A statement or silence on the part of the suspect which appears to be admissible in evidence against him. The Code of Practice further provides that, in particular, a direct admission of guilt on the part of the suspect, or his refusal or failure to answer a question or answer a question satisfactorily, which might give rise to an inference under Part 111 of the Criminal Justice and Public Order Act 1994 will be within the scope of a 'significant statement or silence'.

Q: In certain circumstances special warnings must be given to a suspect. How do such warnings feature in the Code of Practice relating to tape recording?

A: Code E usefully outlines the circumstances when proper inferences may be drawn from the conduct of the suspect. The Code offers the reminder that if an interviewee after arrest fails or refuses to answer certain questions or to answer them satisfactorily, after due warning, a court or jury may draw a proper inference from the suspect's silence under sections 36 and 37 of the Criminal Justice and Public Order Act 1994 (see Chapter 5).

It is worth re-iterating at this stage that in order for a court or jury

The Police and Criminal Evidence Act 1984

to draw an inference from the refusal or failure on the part of the suspect to answer a question about one of the matters specified or to answer a question satisfactorily, the suspect must be told, in ordinary language, by the interviewing officer of the offence under investigation. It must also be explained to him in ordinary language what fact he is being asked to account for and that the interviewing officer believes that the fact in question may be attributable to the suspect having taken part in the commission of the offence. The interviewing officer must also tell the suspect that a court or jury may draw a proper inference from his silence if he fails or refuses to account for the fact about which he is being questioned. In addition he must be reminded by the interviewing officer that a record of interview is being made which may be admissible in evidence if proceedings are instituted against him.

Q: A person may refuse to co-operate with the police despite the fact that such conduct may be detrimental to his position. Does the Code of Practice cater for such an eventuality?

A: Yes. It is reiterated that the suspect should be informed notwithstanding being cautioned that his immediate treatment may be influenced by his refusal or failure to co-operate. The Code further directs that the person should be advised of any relevant consequences and that they are unaffected by the administering of the caution. In exemplifying this element of the Code of Practice, reference may be made to the likelihood of detention being continued in respect of a person who declines to give details of his name and address when he is charged. Another example is where a person might be inclined to refuse to conform to a statutory obligation, for instance under the provisions of the Road Traffic Act 1988 which would thereupon constitute an offence and render him liable to arrest.

Q: Are there any provisions to cater for those who may be hard of hearing?

A: Yes. If there is any uncertainty about the interviewee's hearing ability or he is deaf, the interviewing officer shall make a contemporaneous note of the interview. Such notes should be taken in accordance with Code C. As well as contemporaneously recording the interview in written form, the interview should also be tape recorded in accordance with the terms of Code E.

Q: What is the rationale of tape recording an interview with a deaf person?

A: A note of guidance explains that the reason for the requirement is to give deaf persons equal rights of first hand access to the full record of interview enjoyed by other suspects.

A further note points out that the provisions of Code C regarding interpreters for the deaf or for interviews with suspects who have difficulty in understanding English, will be of application. The note also points out that in an interview which is being tape recorded the interviewing police officer is under no duty to ensure that a note of the interview is also made by the interpreter, a requirement under Code C paragraph 13 which is of application to interviews in foreign languages.

Q: Some suspects might take an exception to an interview being tape recorded. What can be done in respect of a suspect who puts forward such an objection?

A: If at the commencement of or during the interview or during a break in it, the interviewee registers his objection to the interview being tape recorded, the interviewing officer must explain to the suspect that the interview is being tape recorded. The police officer must also explain to the suspect that the provisions of the Code of Practice demand that the objections by the interviewee must be recorded on tape.

The interviewing officer may only switch off the tape recorder when the suspect's objections have been recorded on tape or when he has refused to allow his objections to be recorded. In such circumstances, the interviewing officer must state that he is switching off the machine, give his reasons for doing so and switch the machine off. A written record of the interview, following the requirements of Code C, paragraph 11 must then be made by the interviewing officer. However, if the interviewing officer reasonably considers that he may continue the interview with the suspect with the tape recorder switched on, he may do so. In this regard, a cautionary word is offered by a note of guidance to the effect that interviewing officers should note that to continue to record the interview contrary to the wishes of the suspect may attract comment in any subsequent judicial proceedings.

Q: What action should be taken in the event of a suspect or his legal representative, or anyone else acting on his behalf, complaining about the conduct of the interview?

A: The interviewing officer must record that fact and inform the custody officer ie he must act in accordance with the requirements of paragraph 12.8 of Code C.

An accompanying note of guidance advises that in circumstances where the custody officer is immediately summoned to attend to the complaint, wherever possible the machine should be kept running until the custody officer has attended the interview and spoken to the suspect. The interviewing officer has a discretion to continue or terminate the interview pending the initiation of any action by an inspector as contemplated by paragraph 9.1 of Code C.

A further note of guidance addresses the possibility of the suspect, his solicitor or someone acting on his behalf registering a complaint during the tape recorded interview concerning an issue unconnected with Codes C and E. In such circumstances the interviewing officer has the discretion to decide whether to continue with the interview. In the event of the interviewing officer deciding to continue the interview with the suspect, the suspect must be informed that the custody officer will be informed of his complaint once the interview is concluded. Upon the conclusion of the interview, the custody officer must be told of the existence of the complaint and the nature of it by the interviewing officer.

Q: From time to time suspects may be willing to give information provided it is not recorded. What should be done when this occurs?

A: The Code of Practice contemplates the possibility of the suspect wanting to inform the interviewing officer about something which is not directly connected with the offence for which he is under suspicion and in respect of which he is unwilling to be tape recorded. In such an eventuality, the Code of Practice stipulates that the opportunity should be provided for the interviewee to inform the interviewing officer about these issues once the formal interview has been concluded.

Q: What action should be taken when the tape is running out?

A: When the tape machine indicates, whether by bleep, buzz, or otherwise, that the tape(s) are almost full, the suspect must be told by the interviewing officer that the tapes are coming to an end and he must round off that part of the interview. If the interviewing officer does not have another set of tapes immediately available, he should obtain one. Whilst this is being done, the suspect must not be left alone in the interview room.

In respect of the actual changing of the tapes, the Code stipulates that the interviewing officer will be responsible for the removal of the tapes from the machine and the insertion of new ones. The Code reiterates that the new tapes must be unwrapped or otherwise opened in the presence of the suspect and goes on to state that once the tapes have been changed the tape recorder should then be set to record.

So as to prevent and avoid confusion between tapes, the Code sensibly advocates that care must be exercised particularly when a number of tapes have been used. In this connection the Code commends as good practice the marking of tapes with an identification number immediately after removal from the machine.

Q: What provision does the Code of Practice make in respect of breaks during an interview?

A: The action to be taken is determined by whether the interview room is to be vacated during the break.

When the interview room is to be vacated by the suspect when a break is taken during an interview, the fact that a break is to be taken, the reason for it and the time must be tape recorded. The tapes must be taken out of the machine and the prescribed procedures for concluding an interview adhered to.

Where both the interviewing officer and the suspect are to remain in the interview room and the break is to be a short one, the Code again dictates that the fact that a break is being taken, the reason for it and the time must be tape recorded. In these circumstances however, the machine may be turned off but it is unnecessary to remove the tapes and the same tapes can be used once tape recording recommences when the interview is resumed. The time of the resumption must be recorded on the tape.

On the occasion of a break in an interview with a person under caution, the police officer conducting the interview must ensure that the interviewee is aware that he is under caution and of his entitlement to legal advice. In cases where there is any uncertainty, upon the interview being resumed, the caution must be given in full.

Developing on the issue of considering the necessity or otherwise to administer a caution after a break, a note of guidance points out that an interviewing officer should be mindful of the fact that he may have to convince a court that the suspect was aware that he was still under caution when the interview recommenced.

Interviewing officers will sometimes be called upon to account for what transpired between the suspect and himself during a break in an interview or between interviews. In particular he may be called upon to show to the court that nothing untoward occurred during a break which might have influenced the suspect's account or explanation. In this regard, a further note of guidance advises that following a break in an interview or at the commencement of a subsequent interview, the interviewing officer should consider summarising on the tape recording the reason for the break and seeking the suspect's confirmation of this.

Q: What about technical hitches?

A: The Code of Practice makes separate provision for an equipment failure which can be quickly remedied and those of a kind which prevent a prompt resumption of a tape recorded interview. So far as the former is concerned, such as where the problem is resolved by placing new tapes in the machine, the prescribed procedures for changing tapes should be applied. In addition, upon the recorded interview being resumed, the interviewing officer must explain what has occurred and state the time of the resumed interview.

Where the equipment has failed to the extent that that particular machine cannot continue to be used for recording and a replacement recorder or a recorder in another interview room is not readily available, the interview may proceed without being recorded. The continuation of the interview in such circumstances is, however, dependent upon the custody officer's authority and the previously described procedures in this regard must be adhered to.

A note of guidance also addresses the issue of technical hitches arising from one of the tapes breaking whilst the interview is in progress. In such circumstances, the note of guidance advises that in the presence of the interviewee, the broken tape should be sealed as a master tape and the interview recommenced at the point it left off. The note continues by advising that the unbroken tape should be copied and, in the presence of the interviewee, the original sealed as a master tape. It is envisaged in the note that such action may sometimes take place after the interview is over.

In recognising that equipment for copying the unbroken tape might not be readily accessible, the note of guidance advises that in such circumstances both the defective tape and that containing the recorded interview should be sealed in the presence of the suspect and the interview started again from the beginning. Cases where a single decked machine is being used and the tape breaks are also referred to. Where a copy of the broken tape cannot be made on available equipment, the broken tape must be sealed as a master tape in the presence of the suspect and the interview started afresh.

Q: Once tapes have been removed from the machine, how should they be dealt with?

A: The Code of Practice dictates that they should be retained and dealt with in accordance with the prescribed procedures. However, prior to these administrative procedures being followed, at the conclusion of the interview the interviewing officer must offer the suspect the opportunity to clarify anything he has said or to add anything further.

Once this formality has been attended to at the end of the interview, including the recording and reading back of any written statement, the interviewing officer must state the time and switch the machine off. Once sealed with a master tape label, the master tape must then be dealt with in the manner prescribed by the Force Standing Orders etc. as an exhibit.

The suspect and his solicitor and any other party present should be invited to sign the master tape label by the interviewing officer who should sign the label himself. In the event of the suspect or a third party present refusing to sign the master tape label, an officer not below the rank of inspector or, if such an officer is unavailable, the custody officer, must be summoned to the interview room and asked to sign the label. It will be sufficient in a case linked to terrorism investigations for a police officer who signs the label to use his warrant or other identification number.

A notice which details the use which will be made of the tape recording and arrangements for access to it must be handed to the suspect. The notice also explains that a copy of the recorded interview will be supplied as soon as practicable if the suspect is charged or informed that he will be prosecuted for the offence.

Q: What records have to be made in respect of a tape recorded interview?

A: The interviewing officer must make a record in his notebook of the fact that the tape recorded interview has taken place, its time, duration and the master tape's identification number. So far as written transcription of the tape recorded interview is concerned, a note of guidance records that any written record of an interview which has been recorded must be in accordance with National Guidelines approved by the Home Secretary.

Q: In the event of there being no proceedings instituted against a suspect who has been the subject of a tape recorded interview, can the tapes be destroyed immediately?

A: No, they must be kept securely in accordance with the Code's provisions concerning tape security.

Q: What directions does the Code stipulate in respect of preserving the security and integrity of the tapes?

A: At each police station where tape recorded interviews with suspects are conducted, the officer in charge of the station must make arrangements for master tapes to be kept securely. He must also arrange for the movements of the tapes to be properly accounted for in the same manner as any other item which may be used for evidential purposes, in accordance with his Force instructions.

A note of guidance explains that the foregoing provision of the Code is addressing the security of the sealed master tape. The note goes on to advise that working copies should be taken care of on the ground that the loss or destruction of such tapes may unnecessarily lead to the need for access to master tapes.

Q: There are bound to be instances of the working copy being damaged, defective or lost. In such circumstances is it permissible for a police officer to use the master copy?

A: The Code of Practice imposes very stringent conditions in this regard. Suffice it to say at the outset that the Code specifies that a police officer has no authority to break the seal on a master tape which is required for criminal proceedings. In circumstances where access to the master tape is necessary, the following procedures must be followed:

(a) arrangements must be made by the police officer for the presence of a member of the Crown Prosecution Service when the master tape seal is broken;

(b) the accused person or his solicitor must be informed and allowed a reasonable opportunity to be in attendance;

(c) in the event of either the accused or his solicitor exercising their right to be present, he must be asked to re-seal and sign the label of the master tape;

(d) in the event of the accused or his solicitor either not exercising the right to be present or refusing to sign, the CPS representative must re-seal and sign the master tape.

These procedural matters are supplemented by two notes of guidance, the first of which addresses the possibility of committal proceedings having taken place and the tape having been transferred to the custody of the Crown Court. In such circumstances, an application for the release of the tape must be made to the chief clerk of the Crown Court by the Crown Prosecutor for unsealing by him.

The second note advises that any reference in Code E to either the CPS or the Crown Prosecutor shall be construed as including any other body or service with statutory responsibility for the institution of proceedings for whom any tape recorded interviews are conducted by the police.

Q: At some stage, where no criminal proceedings have been instituted it will be necessary to break the seals of tapes and dispose of them. What provisions exist in this respect?
A: When this becomes necessary, it is the responsibility of the Chief Constable to make the necessary arrangements.

INDEX